DISABILITY SPORT: A VEHICLE FOR SOCIAL CHANGE?

IAN BRITTAIN, EDITOR

DISABILITY SPORT: A VEHICLE FOR SOCIAL CHANGE?

IAN BRITTAIN, EDITOR

First published in 2013 in Champaign, Illinois, USA
by Common Ground Publishing LLC
as part of the Sport and Society Book Series

Library of Congress Cataloging-in-Publication Data

Disability sport : a vehicle for social change? / Ian Brittain, editor.
    pages cm.
  ISBN 978-1-61229-214-4 (pbk : alk. paper) -- ISBN 978-1-61229-215-1 (pdf)
  1. Sports for people with disabilities. I. Brittain, Ian.

GV709.3.D585 2013
796.087--dc23

                          2013018220

Cover photo kindly provided by Isabel deVugt, CEO and founder of Sport 4 Socialisation

Table of Contents

Chapter 1: Introduction

Ian Brittain (Coventry University, UK)

The Basis for this Volume

This book contains a selection of papers presented at the "Disability Sport: A vehicle for Social Change?" conference hosted by the Centre for Peace and Reconciliation Studies (CPRS) at Coventry University from 23rd – 25th August 2012. The brainchild of conference organiser Dr. Ian Brittain, who is a Research Fellow in Sport and Peace in CPRS and Project Manager for their 'Peace, Olympics, Paralympics' programme' the conference brought together around forty academics and practitioners in the field of sport for people with disabilities from around the world. They came from all corners of the globe including Afghanistan, Australia, Canada, Germany, Ghana, Japan, The Netherlands, Norway, Spain, Sri Lanka, Switzerland, United Arab Emirates, United Kingdom, United States and Zimbabwe. They spent their time discussing the wide variety of ways in which sport can help change and enhance the lives of people with disabilities ranging from grass roots to the elite level and in a variety of situations including post-conflict zones and areas devastated by natural disasters such as earthquakes. They also discussed sport's potential impact upon soldiers disabled in combat and individuals either born with impairments or disabled as a result of an accident. The conference participants were made up of an interesting mixture of academics (staff and PhD students) and practitioners from a variety of NGOs and other organisations that use sport as a tool in order to try and improve the lives of people with disabilities in a wide variety of situations around the world. This mixture of academics and practitioners from around the world form the basis for this book. A main aim of the conference was to get academics and practitioners talking and working more closely together and by presenting perspectives from both sides this book attempts to provide a varied and interesting perspective on the field that highlights topics and issues rarely publicised in the usual academic outputs. In addition the conference has been successful in forming new networks of practitioners and academics aimed at creating new knowledge and improving programmes that use sport as a tool to enhance the lives of people with disabilities.

Why is Disability an Issue?

The presence of a disability may have a huge psychological and social impact upon the lives of any individual as their identification as a person with a disability by the rest of society may lead to this becoming their dominant identity. This may, in turn, bring with it a variety of possible impacts, some of which are outlined below:

Social Exclusion and Discrimination

The Department for International Development (DFID) in the United Kingdom (UK) broadly defines social exclusion as a process by which certain groups are systematically disadvantaged because they are discriminated against on the basis of their ethnicity, race, religion, sexual orientation, caste, descent, gender, age, disability, HIV status, migrant status or where they live (2005: p.3). Discrimination occurs in public institutions, such as the legal system or education and health services, as well as social institutions like the household. Devine (1997) claims that society has a prescribed set of standards by which we are all measured and when someone's biological make-up or function fails to meet these standards they are 'assumed to be inferior and are subject to a decrease in inclusion in society' (Devine, 1997; p. 4). For many of the non-disabled population the prefix 'Dis' brings with it connotations of less able, less important and less worthy (Brittain, 2004). The idea that people with disabilities are incapable of doing things for themselves clashes with the need of human beings to feel a sense of independence within their own lives. Therefore, those individuals with disabilities who do require help to perform certain tasks within their daily lives can be made to feel a burden by the actions (conscious or unconscious) of family, friends and carers. This, combined with the loss of any feeling of independency or control over their lives, can lead many of these individuals to feel that they have become a burden upon society.

DFID 2005

The Economic and Social Position of People with Disabilities

In the UK, statistics from the Office for Disability Issues within the Department for Work and Pensions show that disabled people are far less likely to be in employment. They cite the Labour Force Survey (2010) which showed that that the employment rates of disabled people in the UK are around 48 per cent, compared with around 78 per cent of non-disabled people. In addition to this Oliver (1996; p.115) points out that 60% of people with disabilities in both Britain and the USA currently live below the poverty line. Crawford (2004; p.12) points out that in Kenya roughly 81 percent of the parents or guardians of people with disabilities come from groups that subsist well below the poverty line. This, of course, means that for many disabled people around the world just having enough money to feed and clothe themselves is often difficult, let alone havin enough time, money and energy to become involved in sport.

Oliver (1993) claims that work is central to industrial societies due to the fact that it not only produces the goods to support life, but also helps to create some of the social relationships necessary for a satisfactory life. French (1994) claims that there is considerable evidence to show that people with disabilities can be just as productive and efficient as their non-disabled counterparts, as well as being far less likely to have accidents at, or be absent from, work. However, she goes on to state that this information is generally not known or ignored and that it is usually presumed that people with disabilities will be unable to cope, may deter or upset clients and are more likely to have accidents.

Accessibility of the Built Environment

Because the built environment in which we all have to live our lives is, on the whole, designed, built, paid for and operated by those within the non-disabled majority it is, more often than not built only with their needs in mind. This often leads to a great deal of accessibility issues for people with a wide variety of impairments. However, when accessibility is taken into account and adaptations such as ramps are added to buildings it is not just people with disabilities that may benefit. In the case of ramps these make access for parents with small children in pushchairs and the elderly who may struggle with steps far easier and more dignified, thus aiding the inclusion process for a wide variety of individuals.

Self-Confidence and Self-Image

When constantly confronted with negative perceptions about their abilities to carry out tasks that most people take for granted, and also bombarded with images of 'physical perfection' that most of the general public could not live up to, it is little wonder that many people with disabilities suffer from low self-esteem (Hargreaves, 2000). Seymour (1989) sums this up when she states:

> The body in which I live is visible to others. It is the object of social attention. I learn about my body from the impressions I see my body make on other people. These interactions with others provide critical visual data for my self-knowledge (Seymour, 1989 cited in Hargreaves, 2000; p. 185)

This socially imposed feeling of worthlessness and low self-esteem brought on by the reaction of others to obvious physical difference can have very strong and long-term effects on people with disabilities.

These are just a few examples of the impacts that disability may have upon an individual and may explain some of the reasons why sport has taken on such an important role in attempting to ameliorate some of these impacts upon their lives. Without the financial wherewithal to take part in various activities and compounded by a hostile built environment and unwelcoming reactions by many within the non-disabled population it is easy to see how inclusion within the wider society is an extremely difficult proposition for many people with disabilities.

The Benefits of Participation in Sport and Physical Activity

Sir Ludwig Guttmann (1976; pp. 12-13), the universally accepted initiator of the Paralympic Games and leading proponent of the use of sport to enhance the lives of people with disabilities highlighted three main areas in which participation in sport could be of benefit:

1. Sport as a Curative Factor

According to Guttmann, sport represents the most natural form of remedial exercise and can be used to successfully complement other forms of remedial exercise. Sport can be invaluable in restoring the overall fitness, including strength, speed, co-ordination and endurance, of someone receiving a disabling injury. Tasiemski *et al.* (1998) point out how sport can be of particular benefit to individuals with certain disabilities. Following a pilot study on individuals recovering from a spinal cord lesion, they state:

> Systematically practised physical activity and sports allows the disabled person to keep the high level of physical fitness that was obtained during rehabilitation. It also helps to maintain compensatory processes and prevent complications caused by inactivity. Physical activity and sports are amongst the most important factors that determine the effectiveness and final outcomes of physical rehabilitation. (Tasiemski *et al.*, 1998; unpublished)

They also found that the annual frequency of hospital readmissions following discharge was three times less in athletes than it was in non-athletes, adding weight to their claim that those involved in activities away from the home, especially physical ones such as sport, are physically fitter, more independent and have fewer avoidable complications. Similar claims have been made by Groff, Lundberg and Zabriskie (2009) who state:

> Several studies have suggested that participation in sport may impact elements of quality of life such as one's overall enjoyment with life, sense of well-being, and ability to complete daily life activities. Researchers have concluded that athletes with disabilities exhibit higher levels of positive mood, increased wheelchair mobility skills, lower levels of tension and depression and have better perceived health and well-being (Greenwood, Dzewaltowski and French,1990; Campbell and Jones, 1994). (Groff, Lundberg and Zabriskie, 2009; p. 319)

2. The Recreational and Psychological Value of Sport

Guttmann claims that the big advantage of sport for the disabled over other remedial exercises lies within its recreational value in that it restores 'that passion for playful activity and the desire to experience joy and pleasure in life, so deeply inherent in any human being' (1976; p. 12). Guttmann also points out that much of the restorative power of sport is lost if the person with the disability does not enjoy their participation in it. As long as enjoyment is derived from the activity, then sport can help develop an active mind, self-confidence, self-dignity, self-discipline, competitive spirit and camaraderie, all of which are essential, especially in helping to overcome the all-consuming depression that may occur with sudden traumatic disability.

3. Sport as a Means of Social Re-integration

There are certain sports where people with disabilities are capable of competing alongside their non-disabled peers e.g. archery, bowls, table tennis, as Neroli Fairhall of New Zealand proved when she competed from a wheelchair in archery at the 1984 Olympic Games in Los Angeles (Associated Press, 2006). This helps create a better understanding between people with disabilities and their non-disabled peers and aids in their social re-integration through the medium of sport. Since Fairhall led the way a further five Paralympians, have competed at an Olympic Games. In Atlanta 1996 Paola Fantato (ITA) who had polio competed in archery. In Sydney 2000 visually impaired Marla Runyan (USA) competed in the 1500m. In Beijing 2008 leg amputee Natalie Du Toit (RSA) competed in swimming and Natalie Partyka (POL) who was born without a right hand or forearm competed in table tennis and in London 2012 Natalya Partyka once again participated in table tennis and Oscar Pistrious, a double leg amputee from South Africa, competed in the 400m. This was kind of opportunity was the main reason Guttman selected archery as the sport for the first Stoke Mandeville Games in 1948. Guttmann (1952) claims that archery was 'of immense value in strengthening, in a very natural way, just those muscles of the upper limbs, shoulders and trunk, on which the paraplegic's well-balanced, upright position depends.' However, it was far more than just that. It was one of very few sports that, once proficient, paraplegics could compete on equal terms with their non-disabled counterparts. This led to visits of teams from Stoke Mandeville to a number of non-disabled archery clubs in later years, which were very helpful in breaking down the barriers between the public and the paraplegics. It also meant that once discharged from hospital the paraplegic had an access to society through their local archery club.

The papers that follow, therefore, highlight the above mentioned issues in a wide variety of contexts from both an academic and a practitioners perspective and show the multi-faceted ways in which sport is and has been used to try and enhance and improve the lives of people with disabilities around the world, whilst at the same time attempting to change in a positive manner the perceptions of people with disabilities amongst the non-disabled members of society.

Chapter Anthology

In chapter 2 entitled, "Transformational Learning through Disability Sport Experiences", Jo Hardman & Andy Pitchford highlight the impact volunteering at disability sports events can have upon undergraduate sports students at a UK university. By putting the students in situations that are both 'demanding and thought provoking' they are forced to interrogate their own inhibitions, as well as their own perceptions regarding what people with disabilities are capable of through the medium of sport. Underpinned by service-learning theory the chapter takes you on a journey with the students as they prepare for and then participate as volunteers at a disability sports festival hosted at their university and highlights how feedback from the student's individual journeys enabled the authors to add to and improve the training programme for the following year's cohort.

In chapter three Douglas Cripps and Kerri Staples take a slightly different perspective in their paper entitled, 'Canadian Initiatives in Disability Sport and Recreation: An Overview of the Moving to Inclusion and Changing Minds, Changing Lives programs', in which they provide an overview of two Canadian initiatives designed to increase opportunities for Canadians with a disability to participate in sport, physical activity, and recreational pursuits. The first programme, Moving to Inclusion, promoted by Active Living Alliance for Canadians with a Disability is a resource designed to help physical activity leaders plan and lead a variety of inclusive physical activity programmes. Now available as an online resource and aimed at a wide range of potential providers from teachers to coaches to community leaders the programme aims to give greater access to sport and leisure activities to Canadians with disabilities by giving providers of these services access to information and resources designed to make their programmes more accessible and inclusive. The second programme, Changing Minds, Changing Lives, promoted by the Canadian Paralympic Committee is designed to try and ensure that every Canadian with a physical disability is given the opportunity to benefit from the empowerment and confidence that comes from participating in sport.

In chapter four Jackie Lauff, CEO and Founder of her own NGO – Sport Matters, discusses the relevance of disability, sport and development to the millennium development goals. In a paper entitled, "Disability, Sport and the Millennium Development Goals (MDGs): Disability in the Context of Development in the Asia-Pacific Region", she explores a number of disability-inclusive sport for development initiatives in the Pacific and Asia. Providing interesting practical insights into the potential for these programmes to impact upon the lives of people with disabilities in the region and the difficulties inherent in such attempts she provides the reader with much to think about in a paper that crosses the boundaries between disability, disability sport and the rapidly emerging field of sport for peace and development.

Continuing the practitioner perspective in chapter 5, Steve Harknett highlights some of the work carried out by Handicap International and how their inclusive sport and leisure projects have developed based upon past and current experiences in Bangladesh, Sri Lanka, Mozambique, Tunisia and Mali. In a paper entitled, "Sports for All: Handicap International's Experiences Promoting Social Inclusion in Developing Countries through Inclusive Sport, Leisure and Cultural Activities", Harknett highlights some of the numerous difficulties that can occur when trying to implement programmes aimed at people with disabilities in countries where there is a lack of and/ or a low awareness of disability policies, where segregation may still be the norm and where sports clubs are under-resourced, focussed on competitive sport and have little or no social development focus within their mandates. Harknett highlights Handicap International's role in providing community level social development oriented programmes that can link up to the performance level programmes in order provide a development pathway for those who desire to progress beyond community level sport whilst maximising the impact on social inclusion, in terms of opportunity and awareness, for the 'most vulnerable children and youth with disabilities'.

In chapter 6 Isabel de Vugt, another CEO and founder of her own small NGO called Sport 4 Socialisation, describes in detail the work of the social inclusion programme she designed to help over 500 children with disabilities and their families in Mutare, Zimbabwe. Entitled "Sport as a Tool for Rehabilitation and Social Inclusion of Children with Disabilities in Developing Countries" de Vugt describes how the social inclusion programme works in practice, using sport and physical activity as a key component, whilst providing a whole range of services designed to improve the lives of the children and their families. De Vugt also highlights the lessons that have been leant as the programme has been developed as well as highlighting some of the issues and challenges the programme still faces. Overall the paper provides an interesting introduction to the day to day practical problems faced by small NGOs working in challenging environments on limited budgets.

Chapter 7 is a second paper by Jackie Lauff from Sport Matters entitled "Tackling Stigma towards Disability: Using Sport to Break Down Barriers in Developing Countries" in which she uses two case studies from South Africa and Fiji to highlight how 'sport can play a unique and powerful role in changing attitudes, breaking down barriers experienced by people with disabilities and promoting social inclusion'. The case studies highlight a 'train the trainer basketball programme' in South Africa headed by RESPO International, an international NGO, and an Australian Sports Outreach Programme, headed by the Australian Sports Commission. Sport Matters was involved in the implementation of both projects. Highlighting two very different partnership approaches to the implementation of their programmes Lauff clearly depicts in practical terms the flexibility required by practitioners necessary to work with different partners and in different environments, particularly those in which the stigma attached to being disabled is deeply entrenched within that society.

In chapter 8 Albert Marti, Alexandra Rauch, Michael Baumberger and Carwyn Hill continue the theme of the previous chapter in a paper entitled "Fighting the Stigma of Persons with Disabilities in Haiti" that describes the impact of the devastating earthquake that killed around 220,000 people in Haiti in 2010 and left hundreds of thousands of others with an acquired disability. Marti et al highlight the impact of 'The Dream' project implemented by an English NGO – Haiti Hospital Appeal – and dedicated to supporting a team of disabled Haitian athletes seeking to qualify for the Paralympic Games in London 2012. The aim of the project is to help change the perceptions of non-disabled Haitians regarding people with disabilities following a discrimination survey in northern Haiti that highlighted both discrimination and even abuse of Haitians with disabilities. The paper highlights the case of Leon Gaesli, who sustained a spinal cord injury in the earthquake as well as losing his wife and 8 children. It shows how involvement in sport slowly allowed him to re-build his life and how his qualification for London 2012 as a handcycling athlete has had many positive impacts in the way people with disabilities are viewed in Haiti.

In chapter 9, Sarah Green, a final year PhD student investigates a growing and highly under-researched area of disability sport. In a paper entitled "Identity of the Warrior and the Impact of Spirituality through Disability Sport for Traumatically Injured British Service Personnel" Green draws upon her PhD research to highlight the role of sport in the rehabilitation process for traumatically injured British service personnel. She is particularly interested in the role sport plays in the identity adaptation process for an individual that has gone from non-disabled combat soldier to an individual with a disability and the disparity between injury and illness and the requirements of a combat soldier enshrined within current 'military mentality' that can exacerbate the psychological impact upon the individual with a newly acquired disability. Green also looks at the impact of spirituality in this process. However, she uses spirituality in a non-religious context of the perceived purpose, meaning and direction of an individual's life and uses this to look at how sport might assist traumatically injured veterans to redefine the purpose, meaning and direction of their own lives following injury.

Chapters 10 and 11 take a look at another barometer and mediator of societal attitudes to disability, namely the media. In chapter 10 Jill LeClair in a paper entitled "Print Media Inclusions and Omissions in Sport and Disability: Disability and Gender in the 2011 International Sport Press Survey (Canada)" presents the Canadian results of an international sport press survey that took place in twenty countries between 15th April and 2nd July 2011. The results she presents from Canada relate specifically to the areas of disability and gender, highlighting the almost total lack of articles appearing in the selected Canadian newspapers during this period. With respect to disability this appears to underline the fact that coverage of disability sport beyond that of the Paralympic Games is yet to be seen as a priority for the majority of the media. LeClair concludes by suggesting strategies to support and raise awareness of these issues going forward.

Continuing the media theme in chapter 11 Josep Solves Almela, in a paper entitled "Spanish Media Coverage of the Beijing Paralympic Games", investigated the levels and quality of reporting of the Beijing 2008 Paralympic Games in a variety of Spanish media including general and sports press, radio and state and regional television. Overall the findings were mixed with coverage in the general press very minimal and wide variations in coverage between the state and regional sports press, with the regional sports press providing far more in-depth coverage. The evening sports magazine type broadcasts on the radio was found to provide the greatest and most in-depth of the radio coverage, whilst only one television station was found to provide any kind of detailed coverage. Almela did find that the media strategy of the Spanish Paralympic Committee in paying the expenses of special correspondents from the press and inserting advertising in six selected newspapers did positively impact upon the level and quality of the coverage received.

Over the last decade China has come to dominate the medal table at the Paralympic Games. In chapter 12 Joshua Pate in his chapter entitled "A Great Leap: The Evolution of China's Involvement in the Paralympic Games" uses the three stages of the Paralympic Games identified by Prystupa et al (2006) to explain and chart the development of China's participation in, and rise to dominance of, the summer Paralympic Games.

Based upon a series of semi-structured interviews with current and former Paralympians, active and retired disability sport administrators, social researchers of disability and disability sport, as well as disability rights advocates chapter 13 by David Purdue entitled "Legacy or Fallacy?: Paralympic Stakeholders' Hopes for the London 2012 Paralympic Games' Legacy" looks at the nature and perceived sustainability of aspects of the anticipated legacy in the lead up to the London 2012 Paralympic Games. Purdue critically analyses the two broad categories of hope for Paralympic Games legacies, namely a sporting legacy and secondly desires for a legacy which would create wider social change. He also raises the important question of who (which organisations/ individuals) should be the key driving forces responsible for taking any legacy plans forward post-London 2012.

In chapter 14 entitled "Paralympism and Diplomacy: Re-Assessing Interest Representation" Aaron Beacom investigates the links between the Paralympic movement and international diplomacy and how these links have grown as the Paralympic movement has aligned itself more closely with the Olympic movement and the Olympic Games, which have long been a site of diplomatic tension. A central theme of the paper is the link between disability rights and the mainstreaming of disability sport whereby Beacom claims that as disability rights have become more prominent within domestic and international political discourse it has acted as a catalyst for the mainstreaming of disability sport. This in turn has given certain disability sports organisations (IPC, NPCs) varying degrees of agency in promoting wider political changes.

In chapter 15 Josh Pate and Robin Hardin investigate "Athletes' and Coaches' Perceptions of Service Quality at a U.S. Paralympic Training Site". Lakeshore Foundation in Birmingham, Ala., was designated as the first U.S. Paralympic Training Site in 2003 and is the training location for three U.S. Paralympic teams: men's wheelchair rugby, women's wheelchair basketball, and women's goalball. Focussing on the functional and environmental attributes of service quality and taking a qualitative case study approach to the investigation the authors found that U.S. Paralympic teams were satisfied with their training experience at Lakeshore due to the service quality provided by Lakeshore employees through their personal attention to detail. Additionally, the teams cited Lakeshore's accessible facilities as contributing to the overall positive training experience.

Although a relatively brief paper, chapter 16 entitled "The Influence of Team Composition on Paralympic Success" by Jennifer Wong, Joeri Verellen and Yves Vandlandewijck highlights some of the financial impacts of participation in the Paralympic Games for different countries and how those financial constraints might impact upon how big a team a country might enter and even what kind of sports they might enter. Based upon the premise that as participation and competition increase in Paralympic sport, countries are seeking strategies and scientific evidence to support financial investment and resource allocation to increase their chances of success and using data from the 2008 Paralympic Games, the authors categorized participating countries by population and wealth to highlight trends in team size, number of sports/team sports and type of sports of medal winning and non-medal winning nations. The overall aim of the paper is to provide a useful starting point for strategic Paralympic development and lead to further research at the policy level, consequently increasing the empirical

_ce available to countries seeking strategic investment to improve their :ipation and success at future Paralympic Games.

Chapter 17 is based upon Knut Magne Aanestad's PhD research "Climbing and Impairment" that is still in progress. The paper provides some reflections upon a group of disabled climbers in Norway (RettOpp!/ Straight Up!). After introducing the theme of climbing and disability the paper focusses upon the 'unexpected gains' experienced by the members of the climbing group in connection with their climbing activities. These gains concern physiological as well as psychological aspects for the individual, and are also interconnected to issues of collectivity and the politics of identity. The 'unexpected gains' are presented in relation to the fact that climbing is in itself an activity regarded by some as being off-limits to persons with disabilities.

The final paper in this collection is very different to all the others, but interesting nonetheless. In chapter 18, entitled "A Paralympian Alpine Skier in a Wind-Tunnel: A Case Study" Nelson Vinagre, Andreas Dillmann, Thais Russomano and Andree Niklas present the results of a series of wind-tunnel tests upon a Paralympian alpine skier in order to ascertain the impact of athlete position and posture upon performance. The results lead the authors to believe that there is a direct relationship between posture, equipment used and the manner of its use and aerodynamic performance. They conclude that the drag force generated by the body area and volume as a function of air resistance on the Paralympic alpine skier may represent a significant difference to an event outcome – information that may be of considerable use to winter sport athletes, coaches and officials trying to improve their chances of medal success in events where victory is often measured in hundredths if not thousandths of a second.

References

Associated Press. 2006. Neroli Fairhall, Champion Archer, Dies at 61 in The New York Times online. Available at http://www.nytimes.com/2006/06/13/sports/13fairhall.html (Accessed 28th April 2013)

Brittain, I. 2004. "Perceptions of Disability and Their Impact Upon Involvement in Sport for People with Disabilities at All Levels". Journal of Sport and Social Issues, 28(4); 429-452.

Campbell, E. & Jones, G. 1994. "Psychological well-being and wheelchair users". Adapted Physical Activity Quarterly, 11; 404-415.

Crawford, J. 2004. "Constraints of Elite Athletes with Disabilities in Kenya". Unpublished Masters Thesis, University of Illinois at Urbana-Champaign, USA.

Devine, M.A. 1997. "Inclusive Leisure Services and Research: A Consideration of the Use of Social Construction Theory". Journal of Leisurability, 24(2); 3 – 11.

DFID. 2005. Reducing poverty by tackling social exclusion, London: Department for International Development.

French, S. 1994. Disabled health and welfare professionals, in French, S. (ed.) 1994. On equal terms: working with disabled people, Oxford; Butterworth-Heinnemann Ltd; 220-237.

Greenwood, C. M., Dzewaltowski, D. A. & French, R. 1990. "Self-efficacy and psychological well-being of wheelchair tennis and wheelchair non-tennis participants". Adapted Physical Activity Quarterly, 7; 12-21.

Groff, G., D., Lundberg, N., R., and Zabriskie, R. B. 2009. "Influence of adapted sport on quality of life: Perceptions of athletes with cerebral palsy", Journal of Disability and Rehabilitation, 31(4): 318-326.

Guttmann, L. 1976. Textbook of Sport for the Disabled, Oxford; Alden Press.

Guttmann. L. 1952. "On the Way to an International Sports Movement for the Paralysed". The Cord, 5 (3); 7 – 23.

Hargreaves, J. 2000. Heroines of Sport: The Politics of Difference and Identity, London: Routledge.

Office for Disability Issues. 2011. Disability facts and figures: Employment. Available at http://odi.dwp.gov.uk/disability-statistics-and-research/disability-facts-and-figures.php#im (Accessed 28th April 2013)

Oliver, M. 1996. Understanding Disability: From Theory to Practice, London; MacMillan Press Ltd.

Oliver, M. 1993 Disability and dependency: a creation of industrial societies? in Swain, J., Finkelstein, V., French, S. and Oliver, M., (eds.), Disabling Barriers – Enabling Environments, Milton Keynes; Open University, 49-60.

Prystupa, E., Prystupa, T., & Bolach, E. 2006. Development trends in sports for the disabled: The case of summer Paralympics. Human Movement, 7(1); 77-83.

Seymour, W. 1989. Body Alterations, London: Unwin Hyman.

Tasiemski, T., Bergstrom, E., Savic, G. & Gardner, B. P. 1998. Sports, Recreation and Employment Following Spinal Cord Injury – a Pilot Study, (Unpublished).

Chapter 2: Transformational Learning through Disability Sport Experiences

Joanna Hardman and Andrew Pitchford (University of Gloucestershire, UK)

Service-learning programmes provide participants with the opportunity to think creatively and to deal with situations that are demanding and thought provoking. Participants are encouraged to think about *what* they are doing, *why* they are doing it and *how* they are doing it, forming a connection between learning in the classroom and what is happening in the real world. *How* they deal with these situations will contribute to their greater self-knowledge and personal growth. This paper explores how a group of students responded to the opportunity to engage in this type of learning. The specific focus is to investigate the experiences and perceptions of Thirty Two undergraduate sport students, who participated in a second year 'Adapted Physical Activity' (APA) module, and Twelve PGCE Physical Education students who coordinated and delivered a disability sports festival. Underpinned by Service- Learning Theory this paper relates the stories of these students and illustrates how volunteering at disability sport events provides opportunities for transformational learning for sports students.

The specific aim of this chapter is to explore how volunteering in a disability sport environment helps to develop key characteristics of an authentic service-learning programme, as identified by Eyler and Giles (1999) and the National Service-Learning Commission, more specifically:

- Whether volunteering at disability sport events impacts the students understanding of theoretical concepts related to disability and disability sport provision? Did practical experience lead to a deeper learning?
- Whether volunteering in a practical environment and getting "hands on" experience led to a "shift" in their thoughts and feelings towards the notion of disability?

- Whether the experience was relevant and meaningful to the student from a personal perspective? What particular questions or issues did the experience raise for the students?

What is Service-Learning Theory?

Service-learning is a teaching and learning strategy that integrates meaningful community service with instruction and reflection to enrich the learning experience, teach civic responsibility, and strengthen communities (Learn and Serve, n.d.)

In essence the process of service-learning in a pedagogical environment requires learners to engage in an actual service in the community, which provides opportunities for reflection (before, during and after) and links hands on experience to theoretical concepts underpinning the subject being studied. Eyler and Giles (1999) suggest that the following characteristics are pivotal to an authentic service-learning programme:

- Opportunities for learning should be positive, meaningful and real to the participants.
- Skills associated with teamwork, community involvement and citizenship are developed and promoted.
- Learners should be provided with the opportunity to tackle complex problems in intricate settings that make them "think outside the box" and challenge pre-conceived ideas.
- There should be opportunities to engage in problem-solving activities, which encourage learners to think critically and raise questions about issues that have impacted their learning journey.
- Learners are encouraged to think deeply and reflect about their experiences. They are not just reading case studies in a book – they are actively engaging in the process.
- "Authentic and meaningful" experience should lead to a learning process that encourages and develops the all-round learning domains of an individual – performance, cognitive understanding and affective development.

(Adapted from Eyler and Giles, 1999)

Service-Learning Theory in a Higher Education Setting

As students enter the increasingly competitive and consumerist higher education market place, there will be a need for academics to find ways of teaching that support good scholarship, employability and the development of global citizenship. According to Carson (2008) and Miller & Nendel (2011) Service-Learning Theory has been recognised as a pedagogical tool that has the potential to embrace these concepts. Service-learning is underpinned by Dewey's notion of experiential learning (1963). In a changing educational climate where

Universities are encouraged to provide opportunities for students to develop key skills linked to employability universities across the country are developing placement modules that provide opportunities for learners to connect theory to practice, start to think about their role in the society and their social responsibility beyond the classroom.

Applying Service-Learning in the School of Sport and Exercise Science

Students in the School of Sport and Exercise Science take a module entitled 'Adapted Physical Activity' (APA). The module is designed to simulate critical awareness and understanding of physical activity and sport as it relates to disabled participants in the United Kingdom. Lectures, seminars and assessment tasks are crafted to promote analyses of current theories, strategies and programmes in the local community. Students are encouraged to make "direct contact" with issues that substantiate theoretical concepts (such as adaptation theory, empowerment, humanism, normalization, self-determination and personal meaning etc) through the completion of a placement. This connection of theory and practice enhances their learning continuum by encouraging them to take part in experiential learning that is relevant, meaningful and connected to the field of study. Students can sit in a classroom and learn about the various disabilities that exist in today's society but to be effective and knowledgeable instructors or coaches, students need to be able to reflect on real life experiences. The premise is that such a learning experience invites students to move beyond thinking about disability issues in sport as "abstract encounters" (Eads, 1994:35) and to "see theory through reality" (Conville and Weintraub, 2001:7).

In this particular case study students extend their placement experience by volunteering at a community sports event that is organised for ten local special schools. One hundred young people with various disabilities attended the event, called the Hexathlon Sports Festival, where they participated in five different activities (Boccia, Seated Volleyball, Table Top Games, Athletics and Street Dance). A group of trainee teachers on a PGCE PE programme organised, planned and delivered the event, whilst the APA students acted as coaches, working one-on-one with the young people from the local schools. Students attended a training day where they were provided with ideas about how to deliver the various activites. This session was delivered by a disability sports coach, who had competed and coached Boccia at the elite level.

Data Collection and Analysis

A social constructivist research approach was adopted, since the focal point of this research was to draw on the critical experiences of the trainee teachers and APA students who were directly involved in the design and delivery of the Hexathlon event. The aim of this paper is to provide a reflective commentary on the development of an experiential learning event that embraces the notion of Service-Learning Theory. This reflective commentary focuses on analysing (a)

Critical moments from the event that may have challenged or reinforced the attitudes adopted by the students involved (b) The views and responses of students to critical incidents and how this experience may have impacted their learning process and (c) Key themes raised from existing literature on Service-Learning Theory and how they relate to the data collected in this study.

Data was collected in the form module evaluations, open ended survey, focus groups and one-to-one interviews. Underpinned by the concept of Thematic Coding (Flick 2009:319) significant categories, themes and views related to Service-Learning Theory were identified in the text, so that an understanding of key issues related to the student's constructed views of the impact of "real life", "hands on" experiences could be formed and analysed in relationship to transformational learning.

Results

All of the students involved in the Hexathlon event commented that it had been an extremely positive experience because it had provided them with the opportunity to:

> "work with a variety of disabilities and try something new in a real life environment"

> "apply what they had been taught in lectures by planning and designing activities for actual people"

> "experiment by differentiating and adapting activities to meet the needs of all individuals"

> "receive immediate feedback from experienced practitioners"

> "learn about new activities and sports that we could use in our teaching and coaching"

A number of specific themes emerged from the data and these will be discussed in more depth.

Feelings and Attitudes

When asked to reflect on how they felt immediately before the event the following adjectives were used by the students:

"Nervous"   "Unsure"   "Apprehensive"

"Overwhelmed"   "Worried"   "Anxious"

Students responded that they felt like this because they:

> "...lacked of awareness of various disabilities ... I was worried I might say or do the wrong thing"

> " ... worried about their opinion of me – I wanted them to have a good day but I was worried that they wouldn't because of me and my lack of knowledge"

"... worried about pitching it at the right level so they could all do it and get something out of it"

A number of students commented, however, "that once the young people arrived any negative feelings I had disappeared".

Avramidis and Norwich (2002) conclude that the attitudes of teachers can have a significant impact on the learning environment, suggesting that attitudes can play a major role in the development of inclusive sport and physical activity programmes. Other researchers (Meegan and MacPhail, 2006, Tsangaridou, 2008) have also highlighted the critical role that teachers' beliefs can play in delivery and planning.

In a Review of Literature 1995 – 2005 by Block and Obrusnikova (2007) it was concluded that teachers had negative attitudes towards the inclusion of disabled pupils in PE. This particular investigation, however, substantiates findings by Martin and Kudlacek (2010) in that although the students in this study were *"nervous"* about including disabled pupils in a sports event to start with, these feelings of *"unease"* disappeared once they actually got to meet the young people. The students in this study were nervous because they felt they were unprepared and they focused on their own insecurities in terms of providing a safe, welcoming and stimulating learning environment for all individuals. These comments and responses align with previous research completed by Vickerman and Coates (2009:137) who concluded that trainee teachers, on the whole, lacked a *"perceived readiness"* when it came to including disabled pupils in physical education. Lieberman and Houston-Wilson (2002) and Smith and Green (2004) also suggest that teachers feel uneasy and out of their depth when asked to include when it comes to inclusive practice.

Providing Meaningful Learning Experiences

When reflecting on what they had gained from the placement and taking part in the Hexathlon Sports event students responded that the opportunity to participate in *"real life experiences was amazing"* as it gave them *"hands on experience"*. A number of students commented that the experience allowed them to *"connect theory to practice"*. Specifically students responded that the experience had:

"Confirmed what we have learnt in lectures"

"... allowed for the application of the theory to happen"

Students also reflected that through the Hexathlon event the community became part of the classroom and provided the students with critical moments that they were able to reflect on afterwards:

"Reading up on the theories allowed me to reflect on how they were implemented throughout the day"

As Conville and Weintraub, (2001:7) suggest students need to *"see theory through reality"*. Eads (1994:35) concludes that this is a key feature of service-learning theory and one of the reasons why this type of pedagogy works – because it directly involves individuals in the learning process by allowing them to make *"direct contact"* with issues that substantiate theoretical concepts rather than just thinking about *an "abstract encounter"*

Personal Development

A dominant theme that emerged through the data analysis was the fact that the students felt that by engaging in a service-learning programme certain personal skills developed. The specific themes that emerged from the interviews related to the development of personal skills included; an increased level of responsibility, increased confidence, the ability to think creatively, improved communication and social skills, opportunities to lead and deliver, dealing with challenging situations, being able to think on their feet, opportunities to work in a diverse environment and increased knowledge of subject area.

One of the key goals of service-learning is that participants are required to work in environments that they might sometimes find challenging and which take them out of their comfort zone. One particular student described in an interview how they found working with a young person with autism very challenging during the Hexathlon event but that with the help and advice of a teaching assistant they learnt how to respond to the young persons' demands and how to use various communication techniques to encourage the young person to participate in the days activities. Hazelbaker (2011:53) suggests that *"because students are challenged and overcome certain adversity in their service-learning projects, they develop an awareness of self and observe gains in other personal education skills"*.

Gray et al. (2000) suggested that when individuals participate in a service-learning programme, they often feel a greater sense of social responsibility and connection to the programme they had been working with. In this particular case a number of the students reflected that they felt they had a high level of responsibility to ensure that the young people who turned up on the day participated fully in the activities, enjoyed themselves and developed their social and physical skills. The students had to think carefully about how they could adapt activities to ensure that everyone could participate. One student commented how they had taken some of the lecture content from the APA module, where they had been introduced to adaptation theory and various strategies to change and adapt activities to meet the needs of all individuals. They commented that they realised during the session *"how easy it can be to get everyone involved with some thought"*. During a seated volleyball session they realised that one of the young people, with a visual impairment was struggling to see the volleyball so they swapped the ball for a bright pink training volleyball. Another group of young people were having issues keeping the ball up in the air so the students swapped the ball for a balloon and then progressed to a beach ball. When asked by one of the PGCE students why they had done this, one of the undergraduate students responded *"because it is my duty to ensure that all of these young people have a fantastic day and are able to part in the activities"*. A number of students also commented that they felt their leadership skills developed during the day, supporting the findings of Astin et al. (2000).

Working with Partners in the Local Community

As previously mentioned service-learning programmes connect theory to practice by providing authentic and meaningful opportunities for students to learn in the community. One of the key benefits of utilizing the community as a classroom is that learners get to work with experienced practitioners – in this case community coaches, teachers and teaching assistants. The students commented that they *"learnt a lot from the teachers and they were very supportive"*. It was also interesting to note that the students also felt that they learnt from each other on the day – *"Working with the PGCE students was really interesting as I want to be a teacher when I graduate"*. This reciprocal learning process is central in the development of service-learning theory because as Kolb and Kolb (2005:207) emphasise *"Human beings naturally make meaning from their experiences through conversation"*. There were numerous opportunities during the training day and the actual Hexathlon sports day for the students to engage in conversation with each other and practitioners from the local community. An example of a particular significant incident where this occurred will be discussed in more detail under the disability awareness section.

One student reflected that they "felt like I had done something for the local community and the young people. A lot of the time on this course it's just about ticking a box". This illustrates that not only can a service-learning programme provide real-life learning experiences but they can also develop and strengthen links between Higher Education Institutions and the local community. It should also be recognised that the experiences are not just beneficial for the students in terms of their personal development; they are twofold in that, as McAleavey (1996) points out the local community also benefits from the programme in that over one hundred young people from local schools get to participate in a range of sports and physical activities, meet new people and receive one-to-one coaching in excellent facilities.

Increased Disability Awareness

During the theory lectures of the APA module students are introduced to Lieberman and Houston-Wilson's (2002) levels of disability awareness: (1) Exposure, (2) Experience and (3) Advocacy. The students in this study were exposed to different disabilities during the Hexathlon event and they also experienced working in a disability sport environment. During the training day, prior to the actual event, a level six student, who is an elite level Boccia player and coach delivered a Boccia session, where members of the local Boccia club taught the students how to play the game. The students reflected that being taught Boccia by someone who actually played the game at an elite level was really meaningful and that being able to ask specific questions about the game and disability issues had a major impact on them – *"talking to Joe on the planning day was brilliant... explaining it from his experience was a lot more beneficial and really insightful"*. The students also commented that the day also made them think carefully about what the young people *"can do"* rather than what they *"can't do"* –

"I was amazed how good some of the young people were at playing Boccia – they were really skilful"

"I have so much more respect … Boccia is really hard, really skilful – working with Joe and the others has really changed my view about it, I thought it would be easy but it wasn't. Joe and the others made me realise how it works and I really enjoyed the competition"

The Role of Sport and Physical Activity

During the process of reflection a number of students evaluated the role of sport and physical activity. After participating in the day one student reflected "*I realise what a tool sport and physical activity can be for everybody when used in the right way*".

As highlighted earlier in this paper students considered the responsibility of the teacher/coach in creating a learning environment in which all young people are given the opportunity to participate. The students also realised how much the day had meant to the young people and the impact the day had on them – "*I loved seeing the look on the young people's faces when they collected their medals at the end of the day – made me realise how much this day meant to them*". Considering that most of the students volunteering at the Hexathlon event were hoping to become physical education teachers, sport and physical activity coaches or sports development practitioners this experience will hopefully make them think about the role they play in promoting inclusive physical activity.

Conclusions

Although the students responded very positively to the programme it should be recognised that there were some specific issues that were raised. In particular a number of the students commented that they found it difficult "*communicating with the children, learning the best way in which they can understand and communicate together*". They also worried about using the correct terminology - "*knowing what to say – what was acceptable?*" Quite a few students found it difficult managing some of the challenging behaviours, for example one student commented "*When a girl with autism wouldn't take part in activities, it was hard to get her to take part – I didn't know how to manage the situation*". Taking these points into consideration the training day for next year's event will include sessions on Managing Challenging Behaviour and Terminology and Communication Techniques, which will be delivered by practitioners from the local community.

Kendall (1990, p. 40) stresses that "Service-learning programs emphasize the accomplishment of tasks which meet human needs, in combination with conscious educational growth." As highlighted in this chapter, students at the University of Gloucestershire are provided with a number of opportunities where they are encouraged to actively engage in activities that they may well find challenging but this ability to grow through experience provides them with an opportunity to start to reflect critically on their experiences. The impact of this type of pedagogical approach is highlighted in the quote blow:

"This experience opened my eyes to an area that holds so much reward
…this is the best thing that has ever happened to me … I have learned so
much"

Finally the students on this programme have been *exposed* to a disability sport
event and given the opportunity to *experience* this event first hand; the next step
is for them to fully embrace Lieberman and Houston- Wilson's (2002) levels of
disability by becoming *advocates* in the field of adapted physical activity.

References

Astin, A.W., Volgelgesang, L.J., Ikeda, E.K., Yee. J.A. 2000. How service
    learning affects students. Los Angeles, CA: Higher Education Research
    Institute, University of California, Los Angeles.
Avramidis, E. and Norwich, B. 2002. "Teachers Attitudes towards
    Integration/Inclusion: A Review of the Literature". European Journal of
    Special Needs Education, 17(2); 129-147.
Block, M. and Obrusnikova, I. 2007. "Inclusion in Physical Education: A Review
    of the Literature from 1995-2005". Adapted Physical Activity Quarterly,
    24; 103-124.
Carson, R.L. 2008. "Introducing the Lifetime Exercise and Physical Activity
    Service-Learning (LE PAS) program". Journal of Physical Education,
    Recreation and Dance, 79(1); 18-22.
Conville, R. L., & Weintraub, S. C. (eds) 2001. Service-learning and
    communication: A disciplinary toolkit. Washington, DC: National
    Communication   Association.   Available   at
    http://www.natcom.org/nca/files (Accessed October 4th 2012)
Dewey, J. 1963. Experience and education. New York: Collier
Eads, S. E. 1994. "The value of service-learning in higher education", In Kraft,
    R.J. & Swadener, M (eds.), Building Community: Service Learning in
    the Academic Disciplines. Colorado: Campus Compact.
Eyler, J., & Giles, D. E. 1999. Where's the Learning in Service-Learning? San
    Francisco, CA: Jossey-Bass Publishers.
Flick, U. 2009. An Introduction to Qualitative Research. (Edition 4). London:
    SAGE.
Gray, M. J., Ondaatje, E. H., Fricker, R.D. Jr., & Geschwind, S.A. 2000.
    "Assessing service learning". Change, 32(2); 30-40.
Hazelbaker, C.B. 2011. "Basis of Service-Learning", In Miller, M. P. and Nendel,
    J.D. (eds), Service- Learning in Physical Education and Related
    Professions - A Global Perspective. London; Jones and Bartlett
    Publishers.
Kendall, J. 1990. "Principles of Good Practice in Combining Service and
    Learning", In Combining Service and Learning: A Resource Book for
    Community and Public Service Vol. I, National Society for Internships
    and Experiential Education, Raleigh, N.C: NSIEE.
Kolb, A., and Kolb, D. 2005. „Learning styles and learning spaces: Enhancing
    experiential learning in higher education". Academy of Management
    Learning & Education, 4(2); 193-212.

Learn and Serve America's National Leading Clearinghouse. (n.d). What is service-learning? Available at www.servicelearning.org (Accessed October 4th 2012)

Lieberman, L. and Houston-Wilson. 2002. Strategies for INCLUSION: A Handbook for Physical Education. Champaign, IL: Human Kinetics.

Martin, K. and Kudlacek, M. 2010. "Attitudes of pre-service teachers in an Australian university towards inclusion of students with physical disabilities in general physical education programs". European Journal of Adapted Physical Activity, 3(1); 30-48.

Meegan, S. & MacPhail, A. 2006. "Irish physical educators' attitude toward teaching students with special educational needs", European Physical Education Review, 12(1); 75-97.

McAleavey, S.J. 1996. Service-learning: Theory and rationale. *Available at* www.mc.maricopa.edu, (Accessed October 2nd 2012)

Miller, M. P. and Nendel, J.D. 2011. Service- Learning in Physical Education and Related Professions - A Global Perspective. London: Jones and Bartlett Publishers.

Smith, A. and Green, K. 2004. "Including Pupils with Special Educational Needs in Secondary School Physical Education: A Sociological Analysis of Teachers' Views", British Journal of Sociology of Education, 25(5); 603-617.

Tsangaridou, N. 2008. "Trainee primary teachers' beliefs and practices about physical education during student teaching". Physical Education and Sport Pedagogy, 13(2); 131-152.

Vickerman, P. & Coates, J. K. 2009. "Trainee and recently qualified physical education teachers' perspectives on including children with special educational needs". Physical Education & Sport Pedagogy, 14(2); 137-153.

Chapter 3: Canadian Initiatives in Disability Sport and Recreation: An Overview of the Moving to Inclusion and Changing Minds, Changing Lives Programs

Douglas G. Cripps (University of Regina, Canada), Jennifer R. Tomasone (McMaster University, Canada) & Kerri L. Staples (University of Regina, Canada)

Introduction

Regular participation in moderate to vigorous physical activity is associated with a decreased risk of developing chronic diseases, including cardiovascular diseases, many types of cancer, and diabetes (Warburton et al., 2007). Particularly among individuals with a disability, engaging in physical activity is associated with positive physical, psychological, and social benefits (Martin Ginis et al., 2010; McVeigh et al., 2009; Wolfe et al., 2010), including a decreased incidence of secondary health complications (Heath & Fentem, 1997). Despite these benefits, only 3% of individuals with a disability in Canada participate in physical activity (Statistics Canada, 2007).

Tertiary prevention is a relatively new concept that underscores the importance of physical activity for individuals with disabilities (World Health Organization, 2011). Prevention at the tertiary level is directed towards reducing the impact of an already established disease by reducing complications that may be associated with a particular disability. As such, introducing and encouraging individuals with a disability to participate in physical activity may foster inclusion of individuals with a disability into the community and provide additional opportunities for them to achieve the many benefits of a physically active lifestyle. Implementing initiatives to educate Canadians about the importance of embracing diversity and fostering equity and inclusiveness in our society is imperative to promoting physical activity to individuals with a disability.

Moving to Inclusion (MTI) and *Changing Minds, Changing Lives (CMCL)* are two educational programs developed by the Active Living Alliance for

Canadians with a Disability (ALACD) and the Canadian Paralympic Committee (CPC), respectively. This article will provide an overview of these two unique Canadian initiatives designed to increase opportunities for Canadians with a disability to participate in sport, physical activity, and recreation.

Moving to Inclusion

History of MTI

Unlike the Adapted Physical Education certification that exists in the United States (http://www.apens.org/), Canada does not have programs for physical educators and community program leaders to gain the knowledge about the diverse learning needs of individuals with disabilities and skills necessary to help them achieve their physical activity potential. The ALACD rose to this challenge and developed *MTI*, a series of resources designed to help physical educators and activity leaders plan and lead a variety of inclusive programs.

MTI was developed in 1994 as a series of nine, disability-specific binders that were distributed to over 15,000 schools throughout Canada. As a means to promote the inclusion of students with disabilities in physical education, dozens of *MTI* leaders were trained to deliver on-site training in schools to teachers in physical education, special education, and traditional classrooms. Hundreds of training presentations were delivered throughout the 1990s and early 2000s. Since its initial dissemination, the *MTI* resource has evolved to become an online, interactive resource that emphasizes independence, self-determination, and choice as being characteristics inherent in the promotion of successful and meaningful participation for individuals of all abilities. *MTI Online* was launched in 2010 and continues to be extensively used throughout Canada.

What is the purpose of MTI Online?

The purpose of the *MTI Online* resource is to provide physical activity leaders with a tool that will help them facilitate inclusive opportunities in a wide variety of physical activity and sport programs. Regardless of the environment - recreational, competitive, educational, or fitness and wellness pursuits - one should expect and be ready to offer enjoyable and satisfying opportunities to all individuals, including those with disabilities.

Who is MTI Online designed for?

MTI Online is an excellent training and professional development tool for those who are working in or training for a career in the recreation, fitness, education, sport and active living fields. As a staff training tool, *MTI Online* can be used to provide a community organization with information and practical approaches to apply in a program setting. Teachers who complete *MTI Online* are equipped with tools, strategies, and creative adaptation ideas to use in a physical education setting. Universities, colleges, and other training institutions can use this interactive resource to complement the materials used in recreation, physical education, kinesiology, sport, health, teacher preparation, and other courses.

MTI Online provides a variety of resources to meet everyone's needs and learning styles, by providing examples of activities, case studies, tips to adapt activities, fact sheets about different disabilities and sports, and information about the use of terminology. The new format allows a greater number of teachers, coaches, practitioners, and other physical activity and community recreation leaders to gain the requisite knowledge and skills to influence best practices and ultimately plan and implement inclusive opportunities for physical activity.

What does MTI Online include?

The primary focus of the *MTI Online* resource is to identify general concepts, strategies, and practical approaches that can be useful in planning and leading physical activity situations. *MTI Online* includes 5 modules:

1. Introduction to Inclusion and Inclusive Physical Activity
2. Understanding Disabilities and their Impact on Performance
3. Planning an Inclusive Physical Activity Program
4. Activity Modifications
5. Situational Scenarios

What can I expect to learn from MTI Online?

The *MTI Online* resource has many learning outcomes, enabling participants to enhance their understanding of the needs of persons with disabilities and to develop appropriate programs and supports. After completing *MTI* Online, participants will:

- Have an increased awareness and improved understanding of why to include individuals in physical activity settings based on their abilities rather than focusing on their disabilities.
- Be able to create an inclusive environment for individuals with disabilities to achieve meaningful participation.
- Utilize information and practical strategies to better include persons with disabilities in physical activity settings.
- Have the knowledge to think critically and problem solve regarding potential barriers of inclusion.
- Be confident in their ability to implement the step-by-step process for inclusion.
- Collect tools, strategies, and creative adaptation ideas.
- Have increased confidence to take the leadership role in inclusive physical activity settings.
- Expand their awareness of resources that can support inclusion.
- Become part of a network for sharing, support, and ongoing learning.

How can I learn more about or participate in MTI Online?

The *MTI Online* learning resource is available through the ALACD. To learn more about using *MTI Online* in your program, please visit www.ala.ca. To request a temporary access code to review the *MTI Online* resource, please contact the ALACD at ala@ala.ca

Changing Minds, Changing Lives

History of CMCL

The Canadian Paralympic Committee (CPC) is a non-profit, private organization dedicated to strengthening the Paralympic Movement in Canada. With help from 43 member sports organizations, the CPC aims to create an optimal high-performance environment to support the success of Canadian Paralympic athletes at Paralympic and ParaPanAmerican Games. At the same time, the CPC strives to empower all Canadians with a physical disability to get involved in sport at all levels. Because of the low levels of physical activity participation among Canadians with a disability, part of the CPC's mandate is to increase the number of individuals with a disability who participate in sport in some capacity, in the hopes that a passion for long-term involvement in sport will flourish. As a result, the CPC established their *CMCL* program in 2005, and has continued to disseminate the program across Canada over the past seven years.

What is the purpose of CMCL?

CMCL is a seminar-based, professional development program with the goal of creating advocates on the 'frontline' in the lives of individuals with a physical disability. *CMCL* provides attendees with the information, strategies, and resources that they need to promote the use of sport and physical activity as a vehicle for rehabilitation and inclusion of persons with a physical disability in the community. *CMCL* is at the centre of the CPC's strategy to ensure every Canadian with a physical disability is given the opportunity to benefit from the empowerment and confidence that comes from participating in sport.

Who is CMCL designed for?

Because individuals with a physical disability view health care professionals (e.g., physicians, recreation therapists, nurses, kinesiologists, rehabilitation therapists, etc.) as influential sources of physical activity and health information (Faulkner et al., 2010), *CMCL* is designed to be delivered to health care professionals; however, educators and those involved in the disability sport and recreation community would also benefit from the presentation. Since the program's inception, the CPC has delivered *CMCL* seminars to over 3000 health care professionals across Canada.

What does CMCL include?

Currently, there are seven Provincial Coordinators (representing eight Canadian provinces) who are responsible for scheduling and organizing *CMCL* seminars in their respective provinces. These Coordinators also provide training and ongoing support to local Presenters who deliver the *CMCL* content. Each presentation is delivered by both a Peer Presenter (health care professional) and an Athlete Presenter (current or former Paralympic or parasport athlete). The number of Presenters in each province depends on the demand for *CMCL* seminars in different areas within the province. For example, the seminars in the smaller provinces of Nova Scotia and Prince Edwards Island are delivered solely by one Provincial Coordinator, whereas other provinces have a number of trained Presenters who are each assigned to specific geographic region within province.

What can I expect to learn from CMCL?

The *CMCL* curriculum is consistent across Canada, with a single, hour-long PowerPoint presentation as the foundation for all seminars. The presentation begins with a discussion of how attending the *CMCL* seminar will help health care professionals fulfill their role as a key influencer in the lives of people with a disability. Information about the benefits of physical activity and risks of physical inactivity are included, along with up-to-date statistics about the low prevalence of physical activity and sport participation among individuals with a physical disability in Canada. Parasport is then introduced as the ideal means of physical activity, with an emphasis on the breadth of options for participation that are available in order to drive home the message that there is an opportunity for everybody, regardless of interest or ability. Presentation of the Canadian Sport for Life (2007) "Active for Life" and "Long-Term Athlete Development" models reiterates this notion of inclusivity and helps point to health care professionals' important role in generating awareness of parasport among their patients/clients.

Following these models, three different vignettes of current parasport participants are presented, each with a picture of the participant using their adapted sport equipment and a quote specifying how their health care professional influenced their parasport involvement. At this point in the presentation, the Athlete Presenter shares his/her individual story of how sport and/or physical activity has influenced their life. The Athlete Presenter discusses the nature of their own disability and shares their experience with sport, including the role that health care professionals have played in shaping their involvement in achieving and maintaining a physically active lifestyle.

In the last section of the presentation, the Peer Presenter provides the attendees with a three-step strategy for creating awareness of and discussing parasport with their clients with a physical disability. The strategies include:

- Advocating for clients' participation by focusing on what they CAN do, sharing the benefits of physical activity and sport, and encouraging that a disability is not a barrier to participation.

- Talking to clients about the importance of physically activity during their routine visits. Important topics to discuss include common barriers to participation and the amount of physical activity necessary to meet evidence-based physical activity recommendations and achieve health-related benefits (Canadian Society for Exercise Physiology, 2011; Martin Ginis et al,. 2011).
- Providing clients with resources pertaining to opportunities for physical activity and sport in their respective communities. These resources include contact information for the *CMCL* Provincial Coordinator and local sport organizations and opportunities. Health care professionals are also encouraged to use and direct their clients to the CPC's website (http://www.paralympic.ca/) which houses the Get Involved Portal, a comprehensive listing of parasport clubs, organizations and opportunities across Canada.

Throughout the presentation, both the Peer and Athlete Presenters interact with the attendees who are encouraged to share their experiences and thoughts. Finally, each presentation ends with a question and answer session.

While the curriculum's foundation remains consistent across the country, the Presenters are encouraged to make adaptations to the content to highlight local resources, opportunities, and Paralympians or parasport participants. For example, Peer Presenters often provide *CMCL* attendees with the contact information of local accessible facilities or community organizations that provide opportunities for people with a disability to get involved in sport. If the seminar room permits, the Provincial Coordinator will arrange for adaptive sport equipment to be presented during the seminar, and Presenters will leave time at the end of the seminar for attendees to try using the equipment. While a *CMCL* presentation is designed to be delivered in a one-hour time slot, Presenters are able to modify these additional components to suit the time allocation and audience interests.

How can I learn more about or participate in CMCL?

For more information about the *CMCL* program or to schedule a presentation in your health care centre or community, please visit the *CMCL* section of the *CPC* website at http://www.paralympic.ca/en/Programs/Changing-Minds-Changing-Lives.html. Contact information for each of the Provincial Coordinators can also be found on this website.

References

Canada Sport Centres, LTAD Expert Group and Groves, J. 2007. Canadian Sport for Life: A Sport Parent's Guide.

Canadian Society for Exercise Physiology. 2011. Physical activity guidelines 2011. Available at www.csep.ca (Accessed 13th April 2013)

Faulkner G, Gorczynski P, Arbour K, Letts L, Wolfe D, Martin Ginis KA, 2010. Messengers and methods of dissemination health information among individuals with spinal cord injury: A scoping review, In Berkovsky TC (ed.), Handbook of Spinal Cord Injuries. Nova Science Publishers, Inc. New York: 349-374.

Heath GW, Fentem PH, 1997. "Physical activity among persons with disabilities: A public health perspective". Exerc Sport Sci Rev 25:195-233.

Martin Ginis, K.A., Jetha, A., Mack, D.E., & Hetz, S. 2010. "Physical activity and subjective well-being among people with spinal cord injury: A meta-analysis". Spinal Cord, 48; 65-72.

Martin Ginis, K.A., Hicks, A.L., Latimer, A.E., Warburton, D.E.R., Bourne, C., Ditor, D.S., Goodwin, D.L., Hayes, K.C., McCartney, N., McIlraith, A., Pomerleau, P., Smith, K., Stone, J.A., & Wolfe, D.L. 2011. "The development of evidence-informed physical activity guidelines for adults with spinal cord injury". Spinal Cord, 49; 1088-1096.

McVeigh, S., Hitzig, S., & Craven, C. 2009. "Influence of sport participation on community integration and quality of life: A comparison between sport participants and non-sport participants with spinal cord injury". The Journal of Spinal Cord Medicine, 32(2); 115-124.

Statistics Canada. 2007. Participation and Activity Limitation Survey Tables 2006. Ottawa: Statistics Canada.

Warburton DER, Katzmarzyk PT, Rhodes RE, Shephard RJ. 2007. "Evidence-informed physical activity guidelines for Canadian adults". Appl Physiol Nutr Metab 32; S16–68

Wolfe, D. L., Martin Ginis, K. A., Latimer, A. E., Foulon, B. L., Eng, J. J., Hicks, A. L., & Hsieh, J. T. C. (2010). Physical activity and SCI. In Eng, J. J., Teasell, R. W., Miller, W. C., Wolfe, D. L., Hsieh, J. T. C., Connolly, S. J., Mehta, A., & Sakakibara, B. M., Eds. Spinal Cord Injury Rehabilitation Evidence (Version 3.0). Vancouver: ICORD. Retrieved from "http://www.scireproject.com" www.scireproject.com'

World Health Organization 2011. World Report on Disability. Geneva, Switzerland; WHO.

Chapter 4: Disability, Sport and the Millennium Development Goals (MDGs): Disability in the Context of Development in the Asia-Pacific Region

Jackie Lauff (Sport Matters, Australia)

This article explores an international perspective on disability and sport by examining disability and sport in the context of development in the Asia-Pacific region. Disability has gained prominence in the international development landscape in the Asia-Pacific region with strong leadership from government and non-government organisations. In the efforts to eradicate global poverty, sport is under-utilised as a development tool to engage, connect and empower people with disabilities in their communities. Despite the progress in the region, there is still a long road ahead to ensure that people with disabilities are included not only in sport for development initiatives but also in broader development programs.

People with disabilities in developing countries have poorer health, lower educational achievements, less economic participation and higher rates of poverty and inequality than people without disabilities. People with disabilities are more likely to be unemployed and often face discrimination in employment, limited access to transport, and lack of access to resources to promote self-employment and livelihood opportunities (World Health Organisation & World Bank, 2011; p.11). As a result, a disproportionate number of people with disabilities live in extreme poverty.

Disability is a growing issue as a result of population growth, ageing and lifestyle diseases, conflict, malnutrition, traffic accidents and injuries, HIV/AIDS and medical advances that prolong and preserve life. According to the latest World Disability Report released from World Health Organisation and the World Bank, 15% of the world's population has a disability and over 80% of those live in developing countries (World Health Organisation & World Bank, 2011). That is approximately a billion people and that global percentage has increased by 5% from previous estimates. Disability is a cause and a consequence of poverty, particularly in developing countries, and disability is a significant cross-cutting theme in international development.

The global push in international development is to achieve the Millennium Development Goals (MDGs) that were established in 2000 at the Millennium Summit with a view to eradicating poverty by 2015. The MDGs are global targets to eradicate or reduce poverty, hunger, child mortality and disease, and to promote education, maternal health, gender equality, environmental sustainability, and global partnerships by 2015. With 2015 fast approaching, there is increasing debate and discussion about if, and to what extent, the MDGs will be reached by their expiry date in 2015 and what a post-MDG framework might look like. What is critical to understand is that the MDGs, and their successor, will never be attained without the systemic inclusion of people with disabilities in mainstream development. The relationship between poverty and disability is of course not limited to developing countries, however, it has direct implications for development and the global efforts to achieving the MDGs.

Disability, the MDGs and sport for development are too often viewed as separate and unrelated themes. For many decades sport has been well recognised internationally as a tool for development and peace, and an effective and powerful instrument for social change. Whilst sport does not have the capacity to tackle the MDGs on its own, it can be very effective when used purposefully as part of a broader development strategy. Sport for development and peace refers to the intentional use of sport, physical activity and play to achieve specific development and peace outcomes, including the Millennium Development Goals (MDGs). In the context of development, sport takes on a broader definition than competitive sport. Sport in a development context is understood as so much more than sport competition and it encompasses indigenous games, dance and any type of physical activity that promotes physical, social and mental well-being (International Working Group on Sport for Development and Peace, 2003).

Similarly, the application of sport for people with disabilities in development is not centred on pathways and performance in disability sport. For people living with a disability, sport and physical activity can reduce stigma and discrimination, and promote social inclusion and well-being. It is about changing attitudes surrounding disability and about changing the way people with disabilities think and feel about themselves. Elite athletes with disability can become positive and important role models and contribute to development strategies.

For people with a disability, access to sport, recreation and leisure activities is a fundamental right in accordance with Article 30.5 of the United Nations Convention on the Rights of Persons with Disabilities (CRPD). Sport and physical activity can break down stigma towards disability, promote social inclusion and bring people with and without disabilities together on a level playing field. Sport and physical activity is not a luxury, or an optional extra – it is a human right.

The application of sport in development can be conceptualised as 'purposeful physical activity', where sport and physical activity is applied and adapted to address specific development outcomes, that might lie, for example, in health, education or economic development. In terms of disability-inclusive development, sport can be used to promote access to, and opportunities for, participation as mandated in Article 30.5 and it can also be used to promote other areas of the CRPD such as access to education, employment and health.

Internationally, sport is well recognised as a tool for development and sport also featured at the Millennium Summit when the MDGs were agreed. One of the outcomes of the Summit was the establishment of the UN Office of Sport for Development and Peace. Shortly afterwards (2003), that office released a landmark publication that set the scene for the role sport has to play in development and clearly articulated the relationship between sport and the MDGs (International Working Group on Sport for Development and Peace, 2003). One of the functions of the UN Office of Sport for Development and Peace is to advocate for the use of sport as a tool for development across the UN system. In the Pacific, for example, there are a number United Nations Country Teams that embrace the potential of sports to effectively convey messages and influence behaviour.

On the international landscape, the International Olympic Committee (IOC) also embraces the use of sport as a tool for development. The IOC has identified 5 development goals it believes it can help advance through sport in association with its partners, and these include:

- Eradicating extreme poverty and hunger
- Promoting gender equality and empowering women
- Combating HIV/AIDS, malaria and other diseases
- Ensuring environmental sustainability
- Developing a global partnership for development

Internationally, disability-inclusion within sport and development is starting to attract attention. In June 2012 an interactive panel discussion was held at United Nations Headquarters with the goal of drawing greater attention to the role of sport as a platform and catalyst for fostering the inclusion and well-being of persons with disabilities in society and development. The panel discussion centred on using sport to promote the rights of persons with disabilities, as well as using sport as a catalyst for implementing the CRPD.

Focusing now on the Asia-Pacific region, there have been a number of recent initiatives that are important points of leverage for both the disability sport movement and also for international development. Action is being taken at a policy level and at a program level from both government and non-government players with substantial potential to make an impact on development and improve quality of life for people with disabilities.

The Australian Government has invested in sport and development for a number of years and established programs across the region. In terms of disability-inclusion, the Australian Agency for International Development (AusAID) is fast becoming recognised as an international leader for its disability-inclusive development strategy, 'Development for All: Towards a Disability-Inclusive Australian Aid Program 2009 – 2014.' (AusAID, 2008). The Development for All strategy has been a catalyst for mainstreaming disability within AusAID and their country programs and is also having an influence on its partners. In 2011, AusAID went a step further and included disability as one of ten key development objectives - 'enhancing the lives of people with disabilities'.

AusAID's investment and leadership in development through sport is making an impact within country programs across Asia and the Pacific. AusAID funds a number of Pacific Sports Partnerships that supports sport-related partner organisations to contribute to agreed development priorities that need to be addressed. That includes initiatives using rugby league, football, rugby union, netball and cricket across the Pacific. Another initiative is the Australian Sports Outreach Program (ASOP), managed by the Australian Sports Commission, which delivers development through sport activities and grants in Fiji, Kiribati, Nauru, Samoa, Solomon Islands, Tonga, Vanuatu and the Caribbean. The ASOP Fiji program has a specific emphasis on disability and there are elements of disability inclusion within the Vanuatu program.

AusAID announced in October 2012 a commitment of AUD$2 million over four years to use sport as a vehicle to improve quality of life for people with disability in the Pacific (FaHCSIA, 2012). That is a positive step forward but there is a long road ahead to see sport increase its legitimacy as a development tool within the international development sector in the region and also to ensure that all development through sport activities have a component of disability-inclusion in line with both AusAID's policy and also the CRPD.

At the regional level, disability-inclusion is making it onto the agenda at the government level as a result of intense advocacy from organisations like the Pacific Disability Forum that work to support signing and ratification of the CRPD. Papua New Guinea recently hosted the second Forum Disability Ministers Meeting in Port-Moresby that brought together government delegations from 14 Pacific Island nations. It was the second time such a gathering took place to address policy frameworks and promote the rights of people with disabilities throughout the Pacific. Whilst the focus of the meeting was on human rights and development, sport and culture was recognised in the outcome statement as a priority for the region. There is much to be done to ensure that the statement becomes more than words on paper and stimulates action at a national policy level, however, changing attitudes at that level can never be under-estimated.

The strong leadership from the Australian Government is coupled with innovation and advocacy from the non-government sector. There are non-government organisations (NGOs) taking positive action towards disability-inclusion in development and also embracing the potential of sport to make a difference in the lives of people with disabilities.

The Australian Disability and Development Consortium (ADDC) is an example of an organisation embracing sport and development and including the field within broader advocacy efforts. ADDC is an Australian-based international network focusing attention, expertise and actions on disability in developing countries building on a human rights platform for disability advocacy. ADDC has over 550 members both in Australia and overseas and provide regular publications, conferences and events promoting disability-inclusive development.

ADDC has included sport in a number of programs and activities raising awareness among practitioners and researchers about the power of sport to make an impact on disability-inclusive development. In February, ADDC hosted a practitioner interest forum titled Disability, Sport and Development. The forum was hosted in Canberra, as part of the quarterly forum series, and brought together professionals with an interest in the application of sport in this setting.

This was the first time ADDC embraced sport and development and in doing so connected like-minded professionals from diverse academic backgrounds and also developed supporting literature (ADDC, 2012). Continuing this momentum, ADDC included a sport-based case study as part of a poster series hosted at the University of Sydney to celebrate International Day of People with a Disability in 2012.

Connecting professionals and publishing supporting resources is essential to support organisations and individuals to harness the power of sport within inclusive development programs. The Christian Blind Mission (CBM) recently released a new publication to assist development professionals. The resource 'Inclusion Made Easy' is open-source and is an informative toolkit written to guide aid and development agencies on their journey towards disability-inclusion (CBM, 2012a). Whilst not specifically referring to sport and physical activity, the guide is an excellent tool and the first of its kind aimed at breaking down some of the barriers at an organisational level that prevent full inclusion of people with disabilities in development activities.

To harness advocacy efforts and create social change on a larger scale, a new NGO was introduced in 2011 called Sport Matters. Based in Australia, Sport Matters aims to enhance aid and development strategies using sport as a tool for development. Disability is one of ten core development themes which are strategically designed to ensure Sport Matters can provide flexible responses to the needs of target communities. A key approach of Sport Matters is to create innovative partnerships that bring together aid and development organisations, with the sport sector and community groups. Through this partnership approach, Sport Matters strives to use sport in places it hasn't been applied before towards specific and measurable outcomes.

One example of that partnership approach is a project that Sport Matters established in Laos that brings together ChildFund Laos, Lao Rugby Federation and Sport Matters. The sport and play component of that project sits within a broader strategy of ChildFund Laos called Child and Youth Participation for Development. The project uses sport and play to support life skills development and develop voice, power and agency among children and youth in twelve target villages in the north of Laos. The project is designed to be inclusive of people with disabilities in terms of program content, including youth leaders with disabilities and including disability-inclusive development within professional development training.

Reinforcing the need for partnerships on an international level, just before the Beijing Olympic Games opened in 2008, IOC President Jacque Rogge said,

> "The IOC is aware that we can never do enough to support humanitarian and environmental issues today. However, the IOC is a sports organization. We must rely on the expertise and influence of the UN to define goals and determine how they can be best met through sport." (IOC, 2008)

This quote highlights the importance of bringing together the development and sport sector and working together to create sustainable and responsive sport for development solutions. Our challenge is to ensure that disability remains on the agenda both in sport and also in development. With so many competing priorities in development, it can be challenging to get disability on the agenda and an even bigger challenge is overcoming the assumption that sport is a luxury.

An argument that repeatedly surfaces in terms of disability, sport and development is that if people do not have access to health care, rehabilitation and even assistive devices that they are not in a position to participate in sport until those needs are met. On the contrary, sport becomes a reason for people with disabilities to come out of their homes, interact with their communities, build friendships and participate in society. That is possible in the absence of an appropriate wheelchair, with physical barriers such as steps in their homes and limited support from parents and families.

There are countless examples of people with disabilities overcoming barriers in their lives through sport. It is not a luxury but a right. In the absence of access to rehabilitation services, employment or formal education there is much idle time and sport and physical activity can have enormous impact on individuals and communities providing a sense of purpose and a connection to society. However, in many developing communities, people with disabilities are simply unaware of the opportunities available to them. Advocacy is of critical importance to inform people with disabilities of their rights and also to inform service providers of their obligations under the CRPD to include people with disabilities in leisure, recreation and sport.

What is clear is that there is more than enough demand in terms of people with disabilities in need of support in developing countries. In the Pacific for example, there is a major health crisis in non-communicable diseases (NCDs). NCD rates are higher in the Pacific than anywhere in the world causing 75% of all deaths. Risk factors are: diets heavy in fats, salt and sugar; smoking; insufficient amounts of daily activity. More than 15% of Pacific Island countries population has diabetes, which is over a third higher than any other region in the world. Diabetes is the most common cause of amputation in Fiji and anecdotal evidence suggests that on average one amputation is occurring every day. In the Western Division of Fiji alone from 2004 to 2008 the number of diabetes-related lower limb amputations was 1160 (Patel et al., 2011). Physical inactivity is a major risk factor for diabetes.

Access to sport, leisure and recreation is a human right, not an optional extra and sport is a powerful catalyst for change that has been largely un-tapped in international development. Sport has developed a solid reputation as a development tool and strong evidence exists to support its application in broader development initiatives. The challenge is to refine program design and measurement tools to better communicate the effectiveness of sport-based initiatives and given the diverse settings and thematic areas, building the evidence base will continue to be the biggest challenge for sport and development. Sorely needed are tools that are designed to capture and monitor changes and impact in the lives of people with disabilities and their families and friends, and of course those tools need to be available in different languages and in accessible formats as necessary.

With the year 2015 fast approaching, the world is starting to think about a framework for action after the MDG era. For disability-inclusive sport for development that presents a number of challenges, but also a number of opportunities. Given that disability lacked prominence and focus without its own

MDG or targeted thematic area, there is a push to increase the focus of disability within the post-MDG framework. In the context of disability, the world has changed significantly since 2000 when the MDGs were developed and there are current issues such as climate change and the global economic crisis that further increase the inequality of people with disabilities in developing countries (CBM, 2012b). Regardless of what the post-MDG framework looks like, the eradication of poverty will never be achieved without targeted and systemic inclusion of people with disabilities in mainstream development.

Conclusion

This paper has examined the intersection of disability, sport and development in the Asia-Pacific region and highlighted some of the latest developments in the region. There are a number of exciting developments from both government and non-government organisations in the Asia-Pacific region and new players stepping up to the plate, taking an interest in and making positive steps towards using sport as a tool for development and improving quality of life for people with disabilities.

The challenge is to ensure that disability is systematically included as a cross-cutting theme in broader development programs but also in targeted sport for development initiatives. Until mainstream development agencies recognise the potential of sport to make a difference in the lives of people with disability, disability-inclusive sport and development activities will remain the domain of a select few specialist organisations.

Sport is a human right for everyone, regardless of where they live or what their ability and sport has enormous potential that is largely un-tapped to make an impact on poverty alleviation.

References

Australian Disability and Development Consortium. 2012. Sport, development and disability resources. Available at www.addc.org/wp-content/uploads/2009/11/Sport-and-Development-Resources.doc. (Accessed 9th November 2012)

Christian Blind Mission (CBM). 2012a. Inclusion made easy. Available at www.cbm.org/Inclusion-made-easy-329091.php. (Accessed 9th November 2012)

Christian Blind Mission (CBM). 2012b. CBM's position paper on the post-2015 Millennium Development Goals (MDGs) global framework. Available at www.cbm.org/CBM-MDG-position-paper-338656.php. (Accessed 10th November 2012)

FaHCSIA. 2012. Improving the lives of people with disability in the Pacific. Available at www.janmclucas.fahcsia.gov.au/node/289. (Accessed 10th November 2012)

International Olympic Committee. 2008. UN Secretary General visits the IOC. Available at www.olympic.org. (Accessed 10th November 2012)

International Working Group on Sport for Development and Peace. 2003. Sport for development and peace: Towards achieving the Millennium Development Goals.

Patel, R, Vanualailai, N, Kubuabola, I & Wainiqolo, I (Lautoka Hospital, Ministry of Health). 2011. "Diabetes related lower extremity amputation in Western Division of Fiji", in Pacific Islands Health Research Symposium: NCD Crisis, Nadi, Fiji: 10.

The Australian Agency for International Development (AusAID). 2008. Development for All: Towards a disability inclusive Australian Aid Program 2009 – 2014, Canberra.

World Health Organisation & World Bank. 2011. World report on disability, WHO Press; Geneva: 10-12.

Chapter 5: 'Sports For All': Handicap International's Experiences Promoting Social Inclusion in Developing Countries through Inclusive Sport, Leisure and Cultural Activities

Steve Harknett (Handicap International, Sri Lanka)

The Position of Sport within HI

Handicap International (HI) is an independent, international non-governmental aid organization working in situations of poverty and exclusion, conflict and disaster. Created in 1982 in Cambodian refugee camps in Thailand, HI now works alongside persons with disabilities and other vulnerable groups in over 60 countries worldwide.

HI's interventions fall in six thematic areas: emergencies, physical rehabilitation, landmines and cluster munitions, health, local inclusive development, and inclusion. Within these areas, HI has long recognised the value of sport and physical activity to persons with disabilities, and sport has featured in many of its programmes, especially as a component of physical rehabilitation. In more recent years the wider value of sport has increasingly been recognised. Nowadays sports activities are likely to feature in HI's projects as a means to social inclusion, mental health and inclusive education, as well as physical rehabilitation. In 2004 sport was reinforced as a specific sector of expertise within the organisation.

Recent and current sports projects include projects in Tunisia, Mozambique, Senegal, Nicaragua, Bangladesh and Sri Lanka. The focus of these projects has experienced a reorientation in recent years. Projects used to address mainly national-level, elite disability sport, including specific, disability-focused sports, but it was found that this approach tended to reach a relatively small and privileged number of persons with disabilities, and those living in urban areas or near specialised centres. There has now been a shift towards inclusive sport/physical activity: supporting community-based practices to become inclusive of persons with disabilities. Working at community level enables sport, leisure and cultural initiatives to be accessible to the most vulnerable, including those in remote rural areas, where there is the greatest need for social inclusion and access to such activities. HI works with community-level actors who may be mainstream or disability-focused, as long as they are open to including both people with and without disabilities.

It should also be noted that one constant throughout this shift, however, has been HI's specialism in developing practical and user-friendly manuals for community members, sports and mainstream educators, and rehabilitation professionals in many countries.

To illustrate HI's reorientation, this paper will briefly describe two recent projects, from Tunisia (more elite, national-level) and Bangladesh (community-level, inclusive sport/physical activities), before discussing in more detail a current project in Sri Lanka, and its successes and challenges.

Tunisia: Football for Persons with Disabilities

HI's involvement in Tunisia centred on disability and sports-specific projects, including horse-riding, football and goalball. HI has worked with the Fédération Tunisienne des Sports pour Handicapés - (FTSH) since 2003. HI's FIFA-funded football development project (2008-2010) had the goal of developing the practice of football for persons with disabilities as a means of social inclusion and personal development. Although the stated goal was social inclusion, the approach taken was not inclusive sport with mixed participants; instead it promoted disabled-persons only football for groups such as people with mobility impairment, hearing impairment, visual impairment and intellectual disability.

The project trained sports clubs, physical education specialists and referees in coaching football for people with different impairments. A training manual, *Football et Handicap: les pratiques adaptées*, was developed in Arabic and French, coaching provided and national and international-level tournaments were organised, including the first ever regional (North Africa/Mediterranean) Futsal Tournament for deaf football players, with teams coming from five countries. Each tournament was accompanied by a media campaign to increase public awareness and promote subsequent social inclusion.

An external evaluation found that the project impacted on national-level sports service-providers such as the FTSH, making them aware of a wider range of sporting opportunities for persons with disabilities. It also increased the number of persons with disabilities playing sport. The number of clubs for persons with disabilities registered for football increased by 38% during the project, and the number of licensed football players increased by 43%. In many cases, people with visual and physical impairments (for whom adaptations are particularly necessary) gained access to adapted football for the first time. However access still remained limited only to those persons with disabilities who were members of specialised centres and sports clubs (an estimated 15% of all persons with disabilities in Tunisia), rather than people living in the wider community. The project was unable to make inroads into mainstream sports clubs, to make their sports services accessible to persons with disabilities.

Still, the project had a great impact on public awareness of persons with disabilities in sport. It was remarked that media coverage of sports events became "more focused on the abilities and sporting achievements of persons with disabilities, and much less based on the 'curiosity' of disabled sports that could often be presented from a more 'charitable' angle" (Handicap International, 2010), thus reflecting greater understanding among the public of disability issues. The quality and quantity of media coverage also rose, and the media's use of appropriate terminology describing persons with disabilities improved. The organisation of events at national and regional level also had an effect on persons with disabilities themselves. Sports clubs reported that people with visual impairments and cerebral palsy in particular began expressing the desire to play football, having been made aware that the possibility existed in the country.

Hence, despite the successes of the project, two lessons learned were (1) the need to take sports opportunities down to the local level and (2) to aim for true social inclusion and avoid the trap of designing sporting/physical activities exclusively for people with disabilities. One project which began from the start with local-level initiatives and a mixed-participant approach was a project by HI Bangladesh.

Bangladesh: Inclusive Sport and Leisure Activities

Sport, leisure and cultural initiatives for persons with disabilities in Bangladesh were considerably less developed than in Tunisia prior to the launch of HI's project, especially at the local level. While national-level games organised by the 'National Federation of Organizations Working with Disability' have been held annually since 2000, local level sports activities that were provided by a few disabled people's organisations (DPOs) were extremely limited.

HI began a project in 2006 in response to this gap, which ran until 2010. The project worked through three disabled people's organisations in rural, geographically isolated areas – Manikganj, Mymensingh and Tangail. Facilitators were trained in each DPO to promote inclusive sport, leisure and cultural activities. Following training of these facilitators, sports and games equipment was provided to the three DPOs, which then began organising weekly games and sports sessions for children with and without disabilities. Sports trainers and disability professionals were involved in these sessions to introduce adaptations to physical and social settings, and to games' methodologies and rules. Games were adapted to create challenges for people of different abilities and to promote cooperation. Each games session was preceded by an 'interactive learning session', (i.e. recounting the history and achievements of the Bangladesh national cricket team), to provide motivation to the children and youth. Because the goals of the project extended beyond sport, these learning sessions covered wider topics such as disability rights, empowerment, health and hygiene. Local level sports tournaments were organised, which doubly served as advocacy events promoting inclusion of disability. A small number of children and youth were also helped to participate at national level disability sports events.

One product of the Bangladesh project, for example, was a colourful, illustrated manual targeted at sports coaches, DPOs, rehabilitation professionals and communities, and packed with ideas for games, adaptations and tips on inclusion, which has been of great use in subsequent projects such as the one launched in Sri Lanka.

The project succeeded in changing social attitudes towards disability by showing the abilities of children with disabilities: 'family members and community people [were] surprised to discover the strength of their child and after seeing their performance in the field started believing that their child can be included in a team, in a community (Mandal, 2010).' The project also helped to build friendships between children with and without disabilities; for example children without a disability were paired with children with a disability to travel together to the games sessions. Due to the recurrent frequency of the sessions, children were able to develop social skills and social engagement over an adequate period of time. Functional psychological and social impacts on the children/youth were reported. The project also succeeded in engaging with local government and sports associations, and in promoting the concept of inclusive sport to other NGOs and the corporate sector.

Limitations observed by project staff stemmed from the rural, isolated base of the project. Since the project was located far from the central government, it was unable to be as visible as needed to impact upon government policy at central and higher levels. Also, few persons were disabilities were able to benefit from national-level sports opportunities through the project.

Sri Lanka: Sports for All

The design of the Sri Lanka 'Sports For All' project was modeled on the Bangladesh project and follows the same strategic focus on community-level sport and leisure, although with some national-level linkages.

Sri Lanka prides itself on being a sporting nation and there is considerable political effort to develop sport, perhaps as part of nation-building following the recent end of the thirty-year civil war. Despite this, there is evidence that persons with disabilities are being excluded from sports and other physical activities: one survey found that only 14% of persons with disabilities had ever engaged in sport (Government of Sri Lanka, 2003a).

Prevalence of disability in Sri Lanka is highest in the Northern Province, where the civil war has left a legacy of numerous war injuries. Many people, including children and youth, have war-related impairments, resulting from landmines and gunshots, while the destruction of health and rehabilitation services in the region has also contributed to a high prevalence of disability.

It is probable that the participation of persons with disabilities in sport in the North is lower than in the rest of the country. Baseline assessments conducted by HI Sri Lanka 2011, found some evidence of physical inactivity among many children and youth with disabilities (see fig. 1). 168 children and youth with disabilities were asked 'how often do you play sport?' Although a large number of children and youth appeared to be active every day, a quarter played sport less than once a month ('rarely' or 'never').The survey did not make a comparison with children/youth without disabilities, but field experience has suggested that the number of those without disabilities who participate daily is higher than the 42% of those with disabilities.

Figure 1: Sport participation of children/youth with disabilities (n=168)

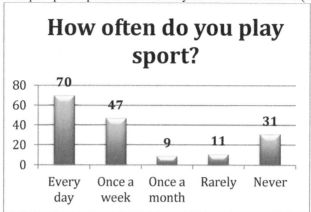

Some of the reasons for this low participation are common to all children and youth, e.g. the lack of sports facilities and equipment in Northern Sri Lanka due to the war, and widespread poverty: for many youth, gaining a livelihood is the main priority and they have little time for leisure or sports. For young women, sports participation is low for cultural reasons such as parents' concern about their daughters' safety in public spaces. Other reasons for the low physical activity and sports participation of children and youth with disabilities are related to the personal, social and environmental constraints resulting from the disability:

Personal factors:
- Low self-esteem and low self-confidence. Youth with disabilities have reported being shy about joining sports clubs, and believing that sports clubs have nothing to offer them anyway.
- Some children and youth with disabilities have also shown reluctance to participate in sports activities, which may be due to misplaced worry about failure or injury.

Social/Environmental factors
- Transport difficulties – transport to sports grounds is particularly difficult and expensive, especially in rural areas with unrepaired roads and limited public transport.
- Lack of awareness/training of sports personnel. A handful of sports coaches in Northern Sri Lanka have received training on disability or adapted sport. In schools, there is also a lack of teacher training related to disability and sport. Adapted physical activity is not covered in special education teacher training, and mainstream PE teachers do not learn about disability during their teacher training.
- For children with disabilities, parents may not see the value of sport for their child, and be overly worried about the risk of injury or bullying from other children.

In response to the low participation of persons with disabilities in sport in the North, and to address the underlying causes, HI began a two-year 'Sports For All' project in 2011, funded by the European Union. The project is based in Vavuniya District and reaches into the neighbouring districts of Mullaitivu, Kilinochchi and Mannar. It serves children and youth (aged 7 to 30) with war-related physical disabilities, as well as other physical disabilities, mental, cognitive/intellectual and sensory disabilities. Being an inclusive sports project, children and youth without disabilities also participate.

Activities

The project first trained personnel working in sport or disability: physical education teachers, special education teachers, sports officers, sports club members, youth workers, social workers and NGO workers. During this training, two models of inclusive sport were found to be particularly useful: the 'Inclusion Spectrum' (Stevenson and Black, 2011) including 'STEP' (modifying Space, Task, Equipment and People in a sport or game), and the 'Continuum of Inclusion' (Winnick, 1987).

Following the training, Sports For All staff conducted three 'Assessment Days' in different parts of Vavuniya District. The prime goal of these public events was to identify children and youth with disabilities who could be involved later in sport activities, and to conduct baseline assessments on them. Because the project was working towards achieving a range of impacts, a variety of assessment tools were needed:

- Physical impacts – the Assessment Days involved a physiotherapy assessment, using tools developed by HI such as the manual from the Bangladesh project (Handicap International, 2006)
- Functional impacts – the project is aiming to increase children and youth's physical function, fitness and sports ability. A battery of fitness tests were used, many of them based on the Brockport Physical Fitness Test (Winnick and Short, 1999) to assess fitness in terms of aerobic capacity, strength, endurance and flexibility
- Social impacts – tools used to measure social impact included a Rosenberg Self-Esteem Scale (translated into Tamil) and a self-efficacy questionnaire, based on a tool used in a recent sport-for-development study in Africa and India (Coalter, 2010).

Each Assessment Day was conducted by a multi-disciplinary team created by the project, which uniquely brought together individuals with sports skills (e.g. sports officers and PE teachers), together with persons with a disability background (e.g. social workers, special education teachers and physiotherapists).

Another base-line activity in the project has been attitude surveying. A self-completed, 26-article questionnaire was developed aimed at high school students (without disabilities), about their attitudes towards disability and children with disabilities' participation in sport. The survey has been administered to 110 children so far in three schools and one children's club. The aim is to conduct a

Mandal, N.H. 2010. Inclusive Sports and Leisure Activities: Experience of Inclusive Approach facilitation in rural Bangladesh (Handicap International PowerPoint presentation)

Stevenson, P. and Black, K. 2011. The Inclusion Spectrum incorporating STEP. Available at http://www.icsspe.org/documente/Ken_Black_-_Inclusion_Spectrum_summary.pdf (Accessed 13th April 2013)

Winnick, J.P. 1987. "An integrated continuum for sport participation". Adapted Physical Activity Quarterly, 4;158.

Winnick, J.P. and Short, F. 1999. The Brockport Physical Fitness Test manual. Champaign, IL: Human Kinetics

Chapter 6: Sport as a Tool for the Rehabilitation and Social Inclusion of Children with Disabilities in Developing Countries

Isabel de Vugt (Sport 4 Socialisation, Zimbabwe)

Introduction

Sport 4 Socialisation is a non-profit organisation working towards improving the quality of life and promoting social inclusion of youth and children living with disabilities in Zimbabwe. This is done through implementation of the Social Inclusion Programme (SIP) developed in 2005. This programme has a holistic and family orientated approach. The programme was developed after a one year research period, with a pilot project carried out in Kenya. Since early 2008 the Social Inclusion Programme has been running in Mutare, Zimbabwe where the organisation works with over 500 children living with disabilities and their immediate families.

Statement of the Problem

Over 650 million persons around the world live with disabilities of which 80% live in developing countries. Add to that their extended families, and a staggering two billion people are daily confronted with disabilities. In every country in the world, persons with disabilities often live on the margins of society, deprived of some of life's fundamental experiences.

On November 29th 1998 the United Nations adopted the Convention on the Rights of the Child. Special attention was paid to the needs of children, adolescents and youth with disabilities in article 23. These children are guaranteed:

- The right to a full and decent life, to ensure dignity, self-reliance and active participation in the community;
- The right to education, training and preparation for life skills and employment;
- Access to health services;

3. Through the participation in adapted physical activities coaches and physiotherapists can also identify additional needs with regards to the disability, like the need for medical interventions, counselling, educational assistance etc.

4. Involving the immediate family of the child creates understanding and increases the chances of the child being accepted as a full member of the family at home. Creating understanding by the family can be done through involving them in the implementation of the adapted physical activities and events and create support groups around the adapted physical activities where parents can meet and start projects that create economic empowerment so they can foresee the needs of their child. Organising special information days about the different disabilities and adapted physical activity has also proved beneficial.

5. To create more commitment by the care givers it is important to involve them throughout the programme development and implementation. We hold quarterly evaluation workshops where we discuss the activities for their children and their own programmes, like the parent support group programme and the livelihood development programme. We furthermore involve them continuously in organising the weekly community adapted physical activity programme and any special events that we organise throughout the year.

6. To create more understanding between the different Parent Support Groups we organise monthly overall Parent Support Group meetings which are attended by the chairperson and secretary of each suburb.

7. To create more commitment by the children we have found it very important to let them partially decide on the activities they would like to include in their programmes.

8. Coaches should receive full training on disability issues but also about creativity when organising activities for children living with a disability. The education system in developing countries is very different from the European system and often coaches are less creative and find it hard to think 'outside the box'.

9. In developing countries there is not a variety of equipment available and also organisations have to work with the basics. It's important to teach coaches how to make their own equipment and work with what is available locally. This can mean adapting the games to what is available.

Recommendations

1. Sport for development organisations, health care organisations and other NGOs need to start working together to provide a holistic approach in the rehabilitation of children living with disabilities. Too often organisations run their own programmes, sometimes venturing into areas which are not their expertise. Therefore a good collaboration between a variety of organisations focussing on different parts of the holistic rehabilitation process increases the chances of success.

2. Share best practices and challenges between organisations. Organisations can learn from each other's success and failures and build

on them to strengthen existing programmes. This could be done through periodic sector group meetings.

3.   Before implementing (adapted) physical activity projects assessments need to be conducted with individuals to generate enough information on the person's abilities and plan activities accordingly. Without proper assessments adapted physical activity programmes can do more damage than good if the individual abilities and limitations are not taken into consideration.

4.   Proper training for coaches and parents/care givers to conduct adapted physical activities is a necessity in order to provide good quality activities.

5.   Listen to the needs of the family in the care of their disabled child. What are the real challenges and what are the needs? Through group focus discussions and individual interviews one can find out the needs and together with the parents/care givers address these issues.

6.   Involve the target group from the planning process, the implementation process all the way through to the evaluation stages. Their input is valuable to deliver the services that best serve their needs as well as keep the target group motivated to participate in the organisation's programmes.

Monitoring and Evaluation

Monitoring and evaluation is a vital part of any organisation working in the development sector. Funders, supporters, stakeholders and the organisation itself all want to know what the impact is of any given programme and the investment made for it. S4S has designed a monitoring tool in the online platform on www.salesforce.com. Every child and parent/care giver attending this programme is being entered into the system after which every activity attended (adapted physical activity, training, Parent Support Group meeting, physiotherapy session) and every medical intervention conducted are entered too. This gives the organisation good knowledge about the numbers of people who are reached through each specific activity within the Social Inclusion Programme, but also allows the organisation to monitor and follow up on each person's attendance and progress.

What the actual impact is that each individual activity within the Social Inclusion Programme has or the combination of all these activities together has on the lives of the children with disabilities and their families, is a different thing to measure. S4S is currently developing an impact assessment tool that provides evidence that the programme is indeed improving the quality of life and stimulating social inclusion other than the observations by staff members and parents/care givers and the group focus discussions that S4S holds quarterly.

Sustainability of the Social Inclusion Programme

For the implementation of the Social Inclusion Programme activities S4S is dependent on donor funding. Fundraising is part of the tasks of the CEO and project coordinator in Zimbabwe. Currently most institutional donor funding comes from organisations in The Netherlands whilst a smaller part comes from organisations in Zimbabwe.

S4S however has the aim to make the projects more self-sustainable with own income streams to become less depended on donor funding. This is a very challenging situation as by doing so, an organisation must be aware not to lose focus of what its goals and focus areas are. Also in order to develop your own income it is necessary to obtain additional funding and expertise to set up an income generating project for the organisation. S4S is currently mapping out a strategy to develop a project(s) that could generate sustainable income for the organisation.

The Social Inclusion Programme runs on a US$200.000,- budget per year. This amount could fluctuate per country. The costs of living in Zimbabwe are extremely high due to the political and economic climate under the Mugabe regime. The country has lost its own currency and production of goods came to a standstill in the period 2006-2009 which has resulted in goods being imported from South Africa or other countries.

(Adapted) sport equipment, medical equipment and assistive devices are not readily available in Zimbabwe and need to be imported.

Challenges

Priorities in rehabilitation

One challenge for smaller organisations like S4S is the bigger NGOs that often come into an area for a shorter period of time. In S4S' experience in Zimbabwe these organisations have little to no experience with disability issues but have a project outline and budget which often needs to be spent within a limited time frame. Unfortunately this often means that these organisations interfere with the rehabilitation process of children with disabilities because of their short term solutions. For example, they give out wheelchairs without thoroughly assessing the disability of the child and without involvement of a physiotherapist or doctor. The same child and caregiver would be in the Social Inclusion Programme with S4S, where a lot of resources are being used to provide this child with the care to be able to improve physically, socially and mentally. Since the start of the Social Inclusion Programme in 2008 it happens quite regularly that children who are assisted in a lengthy and costly rehabilitation process with S4S suddenly appear with an assistive device which further disables the child in the long run, because both the care giver and the bigger NGO chose the easy option. The care giver chooses the wheelchair because it solves the issues of today, while the NGO chooses to give out a wheelchair because it has a target number to reach and a budget to spend. Unfortunately, what the care giver and NGO fail to consider with this approach is that due to these short-sighted choices the child may never improve.

Salaries

Another challenge for smaller organisations is the fact that they are competing with the bigger NGOs for staff members. In the experience of S4S in Zimbabwe the smaller organisations invest a lot of resources in the capacity building of staff members but cannot afford the high salaries that bigger NGOs are offering to their staff. What often happens is that the smaller organisations have a large turnover in staff, because they get headhunted by the bigger NGOs, which puts a lot of pressure on the smaller NGOs to use their limited resources for capacity building and recruitment. This staff turnover also affects the continuity of programme activities.

References

Choruma, T. 2007. The forgotten tribe: People with Disabilities in Zimbabwe, Progressio; London.

Delnooz, P., 2006, Creative Action Methodology, What is it all about? What does it mean in practice? NHTV Breda University of Applied Sciences. Available at
http://www.nhtv.nl/fileadmin/user_upload/Documenten/PDF/Onderzoek_en_advies/AcademicStudies_04.pdf (Accessed 11th April 2013)

de Vugt, I., 2012, Social Inclusion in Zimbabwe, Disabled Children Initiative of Zimbabwe (Available from author upon request)

de Vugt, I., 2005, Sport as a means of acceptance and integration of disabled children in developing countries: a case study in Kenya, NHTV Breda University of Applied Sciences (Available from author upon request)

United Nations, 2009, Why Sport? Available at
http://www.un.org/wcm/content/site/sport/home/sport (Accessed 11th April 2013)

Chapter 7: Tackling Stigma towards Disability: Using Sport to Break Down Barriers in Developing Countries

Jackie Lauff (Sport Matters, Australia)

Introduction

Sport can play a unique and powerful role in changing attitudes, breaking down barriers experienced by people with disabilities and promoting social inclusion (SDP IWG, 2008). In the context of developing countries, social stigma towards disability is for many people one their biggest challenges and a barrier that isolates people within their communities. The application of sport and physical activity in this context is about changing the way people think and feel about disability and also changing the way people with disabilities think and feel about themselves.

Two approaches will be explored in this paper using case studies of disability-inclusive sport for development projects in South Africa and Fiji. The projects were selected because they both use sport as a tool towards improving the quality of life of people with disabilities in developing countries and because Sport Matters, an Australian-based NGO, contributed to both projects. The discussion will include an analysis of the key strengths and weaknesses of the projects and recommendations that can be drawn from these approaches. The case studies differ significantly in size and scale, however, they offer interesting approaches to influence attitudes surrounding disability in developing countries.

According to the latest estimates in the World Report on Disability (WHO & World Bank, 2011) approximately 15% of the world's population lives with some form of disability. The global prevalence of disability is higher than previous estimates due to factors such as the ageing population, rapid spread of chronic diseases and improvements in measuring disability. Given rising prevalence of disability, catering for people with disabilities is going to be of increasing concern for development practitioners working towards achieving the Millennium Development Goals, and also for organisations delivering sport for development programs.

Both South Africa and Fiji are recognised as developing countries as they both appear on the latest list produced by the Organisation for Economic Cooperation and Development (OECD) of countries that receive official development assistance. The latest list released by the Development Assistance Committee of OECD is based on per capita gross national income in 2010 and is effective for reporting on aid flows for 2011, 2012 and 2013. South Africa is classified as an Upper Middle Income Country by the OECD and Fiji is classified as a Lower Middle Income Country (OECD, 2012). South Africa and Fiji are also signatories to the United Nations Convention on the Rights of Persons with Disabilities which South Africa signed and ratified in 2007, and Fiji signed in 2010 and has not yet ratified.

Sport is well recognised internationally as a low-cost and high-impact tool for development and a powerful agent for social change. There are few definitions of sport and development in the literature; however, the term is generally accepted as "the use of sport to promote and address specific societal goals. These goals include areas such as health, economic development, gender, peace, disability, trauma and child development" (Lauff, Meulders & Maguire, 2008; p.457). The terms 'sport and development', 'sport for development' and 'development through sport' are used inter-changeably and reflect the emphasis of a particular program or organisation towards sport-based outcomes or development outcomes. This paper will use the term 'sport for development'.

The link between disability, sport and development is not new. Disability is one of the thematic areas of the International Platform on Sport and Development, which is an international portal and information hub for the sport for development community hosted by the Swiss Academy for Development. Disability is one of the key themes of the United Nations Office of Sport for Development and Peace, and the Sport for Development and Peace International Working Group has a thematic working group on 'Sport and Persons with Disabilities'.

Sport can play an important role in "improving the inclusion and well-being of persons with disabilities and, in so doing, help to advance the Millennium Development Goals." (SDP IWG, 2008: p173). Parnes & Hashemi (2007) published a literature review on sport and development for the International Working Group on Sport for Development and Peace that included a chapter on disability. More recently, Comic Relief (2011) commissioned a mapping exercise of research in the area of sport for development to help understand the nature of the evidence base. The report refers to a survey of 246 users of the International Platform for Sport and Development (www.sportandev.org) who were asked to rate their main area of thematic focus. The results revealed that 'disability' rated only slightly higher than 'crime' at the lowest end of the scale, and there was slightly more interest in the area of disability, compared with interest in research into disability (Comic Relief, 2011: p36).

There is very little academic literature available that addresses approaches and methodology towards including people with disabilities in sport for development programming, although there are an increasing number of programs being developed internationally. As someone who has worked in this area I have no doubt that sport has great potential to make a difference in the lives of people with disabilities and that "sport is an ideal tool for raising awareness, addressing stereotypes and fostering the inclusion of people with disabilities in society." (Farkas et al., 2012; p.255). This article attempts to capture the learning from two case studies and offer a critical analysis of each approach to help build on the available literature in this space.

Case Study 1: South Africa

The first case study features a community-based approach funded by an international NGO where Sport Matters worked in partnership with RESPO International (a Dutch NGO) to deliver a train-the-trainer basketball program in South Africa. The case study will focus on the key outcomes relating to changing attitudes of people with disabilities and changing attitudes of decision-makers. Mitchell's Plain is one of South Africa's largest townships commonly associated with gangsterism and methamphetamine addiction among its youth. Mitchell's Plain, Khayelitsha and surrounding townships are densely populated and also are a hub for a range of sport for development initiatives for able-bodied populations in sports such as football, boxing and surfing, yet few that cater for people with disabilities.

RESPO International developed a program in Cape Town in 2010 with a specific focus on using sport to promote the inclusion of people with disabilities. The basketball component was part of a larger Sport and Physical Activity Trainer (SPAT) program that featured a series of workshops including basketball, tennis, circus skills, recreational games and play and sign language. The basketball workshop was delivered by Liesl Tesch, who has represented Australia in five Paralympic Games in wheelchair basketball and Jackie Lauff, a content specialist in adapted physical activity. This was the second basketball workshop delivered by Sport Matters in Cape Town by the same presenters and more than half of the participants had also attended the training one year earlier.

Twenty-three people attended the three-day basketball workshop (19 men and 4 women) from four local communities – Ravensmead, Khayelitsha, Mitchell's Plain and Delft. They were predominantly people with disabilities who were reformed gangsters (with spinal cord injuries as a result of shooting or knife attacks) or people with physical disabilities as a result of car and train accidents. There were also a number of people without disabilities that attended who had an interest in getting people of all abilities active in their community and most of the participants were unemployed. The training was delivered in English with translation into Tsutu, Xhosa and Afrikaans as required and basketball wheelchairs were provided by the Greater Bulls Wheelchair Basketball Club of Mitchell's Plain.

The workshop content focused on three areas: the principles of coaching; including people with disabilities in sport; and the basic skills necessary to play, coach and referee basketball. Importantly, the training also included sessions on attitudes surrounding disability and how to use sport to promote the rights of people with disabilities. An essential part of Sport Matter's train-the-trainer programs is a practical session where participants work together in small groups to plan and deliver an hour-long coaching session to a targeted group of either children or adults from the local community.

The outcomes of the workshop were measured using RESPO's pre and post workshop questionnaires and for the basketball component, confidence scales were used to measure perceived confidence in three areas; coaching, including people with disabilities and basketball. Each participant designed their own scale before and after the training and presented it to the group with an explanation of their choices, using a scale from 1 to 10 (with 10 being the highest).

	Coaching	Including PWD	Basketball
PRE	45%	65%	56%
POST	73%	81%	78%

> "I started off very badly but I think I ended up off nicely. I started with a 3 and I ended with an 8. I started with a 4 and I ended off with a 7. I started with a 2 and I ended with a 7. I'm confident because I can play the game. I've outdone myself." Vanessa (Ravensmead Disability Forum)

All but one participant showed an increase in their confidence across the three key markers, and the one outlier explained that his scores decreased after the training because he realised that the more he learnt, the more there was to know.

Changing Attitudes of People with Disabilities

A series of participatory learning activities were delivered to encourage workshop participants to speak up, become strong advocates and explore different methods to use sport as a way to break down negative community attitudes. The role model athlete begins by sharing their story, some of their challenges and how they have overcome different barriers in their life. A large group discussion is then facilitated to bring out some of the local challenges for people with disabilities and attitudes towards disability in the community. During one of those discussions in South Africa, the participants initially felt that for the coaching session, the able-bodied coaches should do the talking because school children would not listen to people in wheelchairs. The workshop sessions provide an opportunity to explore and challenge those perceptions from a human-rights framework.

In preparation for the community coaching session, one girl was given the task of introducing the discussion about attitudes and she said:

> "People tease me everyday and it's like water off a duck's back. I'm proud to have my disability and I want to show everyone what I can do."

This moved most of the group to tears and for many people in the group it was the first time they had considered being proud of their disability. The community coaching session was delivered to 11 in-patients of the Western Cape Rehabilitation Centre (WCRC), participating in sport for the first time since acquiring their spinal cord injury. It is during this session that the most powerful transformations occur as participants gain confidence and experience leading, speaking and coaching.

At the end of the workshop a sample of the participants were interviewed and below are some of their responses:

> "I do believe that sports keeps a healthy body and a health mind, especially when you've got a disability in the late age. Secondly, it helps

to wipe the fears away because most of us are shy of ourselves because when you are involved in sports you're not always in a hidden place. Lastly, it also helps you to know your disability and how much sense do you have on yourself." Michael (Khayelitsha)

One participant from Ravensmead Disability Forum was interviewed after the workshop for a magazine and he demonstrates strong advocacy skills sharing his perspective on the challenges he faces,

"People in my area behave badly or react negatively towards people with disabilities ... When I use public transport, I find that people don't know how to behave towards me ... Some of the challenges I face from non-disabled people are rudeness, violence and being intimidated in the workplace. They think we can't speak for ourselves or contribute positively," Paul January (Destiny Man, 2012).

During the basketball workshop in Mitchell's Plain, a meeting was held in one of the breaks during which the participants decided to form their own NGO and voted on the name Mandla Sport 4 Change (Mandla means power in Afrikaans). Mandla now has 14 members and has received community funding, donations of equipment and hosted a number of mini basketball tournaments in their townships.

Influencing Decision-Makers

The 3rd annual Cape Town Wheelchair Basketball tournament was hosted at the University of Cape Town on the weekend preceding the Train-the-Trainer Basketball workshop. RESPO International had formed a link with the City of Cape Town and they supported t-shirts, catering and transport for the tournament and representatives from the City of Cape Town were invited to open the tournament in 2010 and 2011.

In 2010, Counsellor Brett Herron spent a short time at the tournament, was invited to sit in a basketball chair and meet some of the players. His opening address began with, "Today my eyes have been opened!" He acknowledged that the City had long been focused on racial and ethnic divides and building social inclusion in Cape Town post-Apartheid, and realised that they had neglected people with disabilities and took immediate action after the tournament. The following year there was new representative from the city, Samuel Festus who after a very short opening address, cancelled his prior engagements and stayed at the tournament for the day. In his address during the closing ceremony he said:

"This is my first wheelchair basketball tournament that I watched for the whole day. It was very exciting and I enjoyed it. Half the time I didn't know what you were doing but it looks like you were having fun. Hopefully we'll do this next year again. We must talk about getting a league organised ... That's only going to happen if we organise ourselves. We have to work together collectively to make it happen." (Samuel Festus)

Two new teams made their debut in the tournament in 2011, from Ravensmead and Delft, after having the opportunity to participate regularly in basketball activities through RESPO's programs in Cape Town. After the tournament, the City of Cape Town created full-time jobs for people that had completed RESPO's training. Their role was to deliver inclusive sport and play programs within their Recreational Hubs across the city. Nine people have completed their first three month contract and for the next term that number is expected to increase to twelve people. The partnership with the City of Cape Town has made an enormous impact and inviting decision-makers to the sport event was the catalyst for very positive change within the City of Cape Town.

Case Study 2: Fiji

The next case study focuses on the Australian Sports Outreach Program (ASOP) Fiji, a national program funded by the Australian Government. Sport Matters was engaged by the Australian Sports Commission to support the re-design of their Australian Sports Outreach Program in Fiji (ASOP Fiji) in 2011. Fiji is a country of over 300 islands with a population of over 800,000 people, and a national baseline disability survey revealed that there are over 11,400 people with disabilities in Fiji (FNCDP, 2010). Fiji has a strong sporting landscape and a small number of existing sport for development activities addressing HIV/AIDS prevention and awareness, peace-building and post-disaster intervention through sport.

The ASOP Fiji program has been implemented since 2005 by the Australian Sports Commission in partnership with the Fiji Paralympic Committee (FPC) and enhancing the lives of people with disability is a priority of the Australian Aid program in the Pacific, along with non-communicable disease prevention. The program is well recognised in Australia and internationally and is featured in the World Report on Disability as a good practice example of "creating an environment which enables people with a disability to flourish." (WHO, 2011; p224). The program has achieved some progressive outcomes through its two main programs; Matua Sports which is a child-focused program for children with disabilities from Fiji's 16 special schools, and Duavata Sports which is an education and awareness program that promotes the rights of people with disability and advocates for their greater inclusion in society. As the World Report on Disability recognised, the efforts of the Fiji Paralympic Committee (FPC) see over 1000 children with a disability playing sport each Friday afternoon across the country.

Sport Matters conducted two in-country consultations in November and December 2011 with the goal of expanding the partnership approach of ASOP Fiji. Rather than have the responsibility of disability-inclusion sit solely with the Fiji Paralympic Committee, the intention of the re-design was to foster disability-inclusive strategies within three new partner organisations;

- Fiji National Council for the Disabled (FNCDP)
- Fiji Disabled People's Federation (FDPF) and
- Fiji Association of Sport and National Olympic Committees (FASANOC)

The consultation process included a sport for development workshop with Disabled People's Organisations (DPO's), a presentation at FASANOC's Board of Management meeting, a survey of national federations, and one-to-one meetings with selected sports and DPO representatives.

Changing Attitudes through Disabled People's Organisations

The DPO workshop was hosted in partnership with the Fiji Disabled People's Federation – an umbrella body for DPOs in Fiji - where many participants were learning about the potential of sport to make a difference in the lives of people with disabilities for the first time. The DPO representatives came from all over Fiji including 7 regional branches of FDPF and representatives from FDPF's member organisations including; the Spinal Injury Association, United Blind Persons of Fiji, and the Psychiatric Survivors Association.

DPO's play a major role in promoting the rights of people with disabilities and the workshop highlighted the rights for people with disabilities to access leisure, recreation and sporting opportunities as mandated in the CRPD. Many of the DPO representatives were unaware of the opportunities available through sport and their point of reference was the main sports they see at the village level, which in Fiji is predominantly rugby, football and volleyball. The following statements highlight the impact of the workshop:

- "The most important thing I have learned today is the number of new sports that members in my organisation can take part in. Nothing is impossible if you are ready."
- "To empower people with disabilities in our area about sports. If others can do it why can't they?"
- "All DPOs must collectively work together in creating advocacy and awareness to all levels of society in promoting sports and equal participation for all people, able-bodied or a disability."

Having choice and opportunity for participation in sport and physical activity is essential and DPOs are important stakeholders with strong networks to inform and empower people with disabilities about their rights to participate in sport.

Changing Attitudes through National Sport Federations

National Sport Federations were introduced to the importance of creating inclusive opportunities for people with disabilities. A survey of national federations revealed some interesting data to help start the national planning process and overlay the strengths, assets and readiness of local partners. To highlight some examples from responses collected in the NF surveys:

- Cricket Fiji has over 15,000 members, 7 development staff located in the main towns and regional areas, already work in 12 special schools with their own adapted cricket equipment and are very interested in becoming more inclusive.

- Surfing Fiji has 100 members, no staff, is moderately interested in becoming more inclusive and commented that "it's difficult to surf with a disability (even to swim)."
- Women's Golf Fiji has 100 female members, no paid staff, no inclusive programs but are very interested in becoming more inclusive.

This planning process highlighted that sport partners need support and assistance on their journey towards disability-inclusion and advocacy is a strong starting point in the consultation process. The outcomes of the ASOP Fiji re-design will see the Fiji Disabled People's Federation (FDPF) manage three Community Outreach Festivals in rural areas from December 2012 to June 2013. Among other aims, the festivals will have DPOs and selected national sport federations working together to:

- Use sport and education/advocacy activities to engage all members of targeted communities, including people with disabilities; and
- Deliver specific activities to educate people with disabilities and their families about their potential and provide them with practical strategies to increase their inclusion in the community.

This case study presents the first step in changing attitudes of DPOs, National Sport Federations and local government counterparts to spread the ownership and responsibility for disability-inclusive sport in a national framework.

Discussion

The two case studies had very different partnership approaches. Programs are a product of the vision and foresight of policy makers, however, "their fate though ultimately always depends on the imagination of practitioners and participants. Rarely do these visions fully coincide. Interventions never work indefinitely, in the same way and in all circumstances, or for all people." (Pawson & Tilley, 2004: p3.) Finding the right partners requires a flexible approach but one that considers combinations of sport, development, disability, government and community partners.

Inviting decision makers to events can be a very powerful way to influence the attitudes of decision-makers. Downs (2011) puts this down to empathy and adds that it is impossible to predict who will have empathy as people relate very differently to the experience of seeing and feeling the importance of participation for people with disabilities (Downs, 2011). The CRPD is very clear in terms of where the responsibility lies for disability-inclusion as 30.5 (e) states, "ensure that persons with disabilities have access to services from those involved in the organisation of recreational, tourism, leisure and sporting activities." (United Nations, 2008) Those unpredictable outcomes should become predicable as we move beyond empathy to legal responsibility within national policy as more countries ratify the CRPD.

In the South African case study, wheelchairs were an important consideration and the curriculum included strategies for adapting the game of basketball for any situation and not relying on a standard game with ten wheelchairs required on the court. Access to sport specific equipment is an essential consideration in enabling people with disabilities to participate in sport, depending on the sport and the needs of individuals, based on their functional ability. With technology and innovation in sport-specific equipment in disability sport advancing rapidly, the "gap between participation and performance of developed and developing countries is likely to continue." (SAD, 2009: p18). Accessible equipment is much more than wheelchair provision but adaptive equipment is essential to enable participation in sport, not an optional extra.

The South African case study has clear strengths in offering a multi-sport approach, empowering communities to lead, and providing employment opportunities. That model could be enhanced by engaging local role models and forming partnerships with the local sporting community. The greatest strength of the Fijian case study is the partnership approach bringing together national bodies representing Government, DPOs and sport and the systematic approach of using sport as a tool for advocacy. As the strategy is rolled out, having facilitators with and without disabilities working together would enhance the delivery model.

Recommendations

- **Active and Central Role for People with Disabilities**
  In line with the principles of the CRPD and also the 'Nothing about us without us' slogan of the disability rights movement, people with disabilities must be actively involved in planning and decision making about disability-inclusive approaches in sport for development. "Role models with disabilities can challenge stereotypes and have a positive impact on community perceptions". (SDP IWG, 2011: p169) Empowerment, advocacy and leadership skills can be fostered through participatory learning activities that help people with disabilities find their voice and use their story to advocate for their needs. Discussions and feedback in South Africa and Fiji highlighted the importance of having people without disabilities also engaged in program delivery. Training together and modeling positive attitudes and social inclusion goes a long way towards breaking down negative stereotypes.

- **Selecting the Right Tool**
  The Fijian consultations with DPOs highlighted that outreach must begin with advocacy so that people can make informed choices about what sports and activities are appropriate for their needs and aligned with their interests. The challenge, particularly in less-resourced settings, is to ensure that ongoing opportunities are created at the local level and that support is provided to local providers and community leaders on how to include people with disabilities in sport and physical activity. Sport in this context is defined as much more than competitive sport and includes dance, indigenous games and any physical activity that stimulates physical, mental and social well-being (SDP IWG, 2003). At the community level much sport and physical activity takes place outside of

structured clubs and competitions so opportunities for informal participation should also be fostered. The South African case study also highlights the value of wheelchair basketball to give people without disabilities exposure to disability sport through a fun and interactive learning experience that lasts a life-time.

- **Monitoring and Evaluation**
  A strong focus on identifying program theories and articulating how programs are meant to work is a critical step to enhance monitoring and evaluation and capture impact of sport for development programs (Coalter, 2010: p5). Measuring community attitudes before and after sport-based interventions would provide meaningful insights, along with community development tools such as participatory rural appraisal, participatory video evaluation and the Most Significant Change method. Access to information is a key consideration and questionnaires/surveys and other data collection tools and program reports should be available in formats that are accessible to the target population. That may include for example; large print versions, sign language interpreters, or hosting focus groups/interviews in accessible venues.

- **Sport as a Development Priority**
  One of the challenges in developing new initiatives is the list of competing development priorities for people with disabilities, and also for sport organisations in a developing country context. For people with disabilities those priorities can include access to housing, transport, rehabilitation, employment, education and health care. In the absence of opportunities for education and employment, there can be a lot of idle time. With nothing to do many young people with disabilities are vulnerable and in the South African context, for example, many are recruited to local gangs or can be found begging on street corners or in shopping malls.

  "Sport is important for the children because most children are drunk now or they are gangsters and that is not the most important thing but sport is the most important thing for anyone's life. If you are older, or you are younger, or very tall or short, it doesn't matter because sport is a very good thing for you to do." (Lorenzo, Ravensmead)

Sport can become a reason for people with disabilities to leave their homes, an outlet for socialisation, and for some people it is their only connection to the community. Rather than think of sport as only possible at the expense of other priorities, consider that people with disabilities will overcome some of the challenges and barriers in their lives to play sport. In Cape Town, for example, one participant pushes his wheelchair 15 kilometres each way between his home and the basketball stadium. Another lives very close to the stadium but has a flight of stairs leading to the door of his house and his girlfriend provides assistance every time he enters and exits his house. People with disabilities demonstrate high levels of resilience in overcoming obstacles they face in their communities.

These two case studies in South Africa and Fiji highlight different approaches combining empowerment, leadership and advocacy to influence the attitudes of people with disabilities, decision-makers, Disabled People's Organisations and national sport federations. Through structured learning activities, engaging positive role models, and showcasing ability through sport events, these case studies have highlighted a range of mechanisms for using sport to address attitudinal barriers in two developing countries.

There is no doubt that sport has enormous potential to make a positive impact on the quality of life of people with disabilities in developing countries and addressing attitudes towards disability is an integral step in creating opportunities for participation and development. As Joshko Wakaniasa, President of Spinal Injury Association of Fiji said,

> "It has no bounds. The opportunities that sports presents is limitless from health, to sustainability, to employment, to education. The opportunity that's given in regards to things that you thought you're not capable of ... I challenge you to take up a sport and make your lives better."

References

Coalter, F. 2010. Sport for development: An impact study. Available at http://www.uksport.gov.au/docLib/MISC/ExecutiveSummary.pdf (Accessed December 10th 2012).

Comic Relief, 2011. Comic relief review: Mapping the research on the impact of sport and development interventions. Available at http://www.orlacronin.com/wp-content/uploads/2011/06/Comic-relief-research-mapping-v14.pdf (Accessed November 28th 2012).

Destiny Man. Men fulfilling their destiny (May-June edition). 2012. Available at www.destinyman.com (Accessed December 7th 2012).

Downs, P. 2011. Where opportunity knocks, The Inclusion Club, Available at http://theinclusionclub.com/resources/ (Accessed December 8th 2012).

Farkas, A., Karr, V., Wolff, E. & A. Lachowska. 2012. Inclusive sport for development, In Gilbert, K. & W. Bennett (eds.). Sport, peace and development, Illinois, U.S.A; Commonground Publishing, 255-267.

Fiji National Council for Disabled Persons (FNCDP). 2010. Making women with disabilities visible: National baseline disability survey. September, 2010, Suva, Fiji.

International Working Group on Sport for Development and Peace. 2003. Sport for development and peace: Towards achieving the Millennium Development Goals. Available at http://www.un.org/wcm/webdav/site/sport/shared/sport/pdfs/Reports/200 3_interagency_report_ENGLISH.pdf (Accessed November 30th 2012).

Lauff, J., Meulders, B. & Maguire, J. 2008. Sport and development, In Borms, J. Directory of Sport Science – 5th Edition: A journey through time – the changing face of ICSSPE, Human Kinetics.

Organisation for Economic Cooperation and Development (OECD). 2012. DAC list of ODA. Available at http://www.oecd.org/dac/aidstatistics/48858205.pdf

Parnes, P. & Hashemi, G. 2007. Sport as a means to foster inclusion, health and well-being of persons with disabilities, in Sport for Development and Peace International Working Group, Literature reviews on sport for development and peace. Available at http://righttoplay.com/news-and-media/Documents/Policy%20Reports%20docs/Literature%20Reviews%20SDP.pdf (Accessed November 22nd 2012).

Pawson, R & Tilley, N. 2004. Realist evaluation. Available at http://www.communitymatters.com.au/RE_chapter.pdf

Sport for Development and Peace International Working Group (SDP IWG). 2008. Sport and persons with disabilities: Fostering inclusion and well-being, in Chapter 5, Harnessing the power of sport for development and peace: Recommendations to Governments, Available at http://www.righttoplay.com/International/news-and-media/Documents/Policy%20Reports%20docs/Harnessing%20the%20Power%20-%20FULL/Chapter5_SportandDisability.pdf

Swiss Academy for Development. 2009. Sport and disability, International Platform on Sport and Development. Available at http://www.sportanddev.org/en/learnmore/sport_and_disability2/ (Accessed November 27th 2012).

United Nations. 2008. United Nations convention on the rights of persons with disabilities. United Nations. Available at http://www.un.org/disabilities/default.asp?id=259 (Accessed November 30th 2012).

World Health Organisation & World Bank. 2011. World report on disability. WHO Press, Geneva. Available at http://www.who.int/disabilities/world_report/2011/report/en/

Chapter 8: Fighting the Stigma of Persons with Disabilities in Haiti

Albert Marti (Swiss Paraplegic Research (SPF)), Michael Baumberger (Swiss Paraplegic Centre (SPC)) & Carwyn Hill (Haiti Hospital Appeal (HHA))

Background

According to the 2011 World Report on Disability, about 1 billion persons live with disabilities (PWDs) which equates to 15% of the global population (WHO, 2011). Of this group 80% are living in developing countries with only 2% receiving appropriate rehabilitation and support (WHO, 2011). Haiti is one example that reflects the desperate situation of the correlation between disability and poverty (Wolbring, 2011). Even before the devastating earthquake in 2010 that killed about 220,000 people (Brown et al., 2012), 10% of the Haitian population had been living with a disability (Burns et al., 2010). Exact numbers of PWDs as a result of the earthquake remains unknown. Estimates for persons who acquired a disability after the earthquake vary between 250,000 and 1.1 million people, which equates to nearly one seventh of the Haitian population (Burns et al., 2010; Arie, 2012). Infrastructure was widely destroyed, 245,000 buildings collapsed and left 1.5 million Haitians homeless (Burns et al., 2010). The earthquake, but also other frequent natural disasters such as hurricanes intensify the level for basic needs in Haiti and increase the number of persons in challenging life situations.

All over the world PWDs face discrimination and stigma in many areas of everyday life (WHO, 2011). In the developing world the problem is more accentuated and the consequences of stigma can be severe. The report of the international working group "Sport for Development and Peace" reveals, that in some cultures having a family member with a disability makes it difficult for the woman in the same family to marry (UNOSDP, 2008). Mothers may be blamed when a child with a disability is born and then abandoned by their husbands. Often unable to work full-time and care for their child(ren), they may be denied help by their own families because of their child's disability. Parents, driven by shame or fear for their child's safety, may confine a child with a disability at home. This leads to the fact that only 2% of children with a disability living in developing countries receive education (UNOSDP, 2008). As a result of this discrimination, a disproportionate number of PWDs live in extreme poverty (UNOSDP, 2008).

Also in Haiti, prejudice against PWDs is seen as a major problem for their integration into society (Wolbring, 2011, Schure, 2010). In a recent local survey, conducted through the community rehabilitation workers of Haiti Hospital Appeal (HHA) and in collaboration with the project "The Dream", among 66 families with a disabled child, living in the northern part of Haiti, 77.3 % of respondents expressed that their family faces discrimination and abuse (figure 1). Of these persons, 93% stated that they face daily discrimination and abuse. The participants reported that verbal abuse and discrimination were most frequent, but that also physical and sexual abuse was committed (figure 2). The survey supports the findings in the international literature (UNOSDP, 2008), that it is the circle of friends and acquaintances or even the family, driven by cultural and religious barriers as well as by shame, who commit discrimination and abuse against the disabled child. Most frequent discrimination is committed by neighbours (24.4%) followed by friends (22.8%). Family and community members (18.9% and 18.1% respectively) were also mentioned as being a source of discrimination (figure 3).

Figure 1

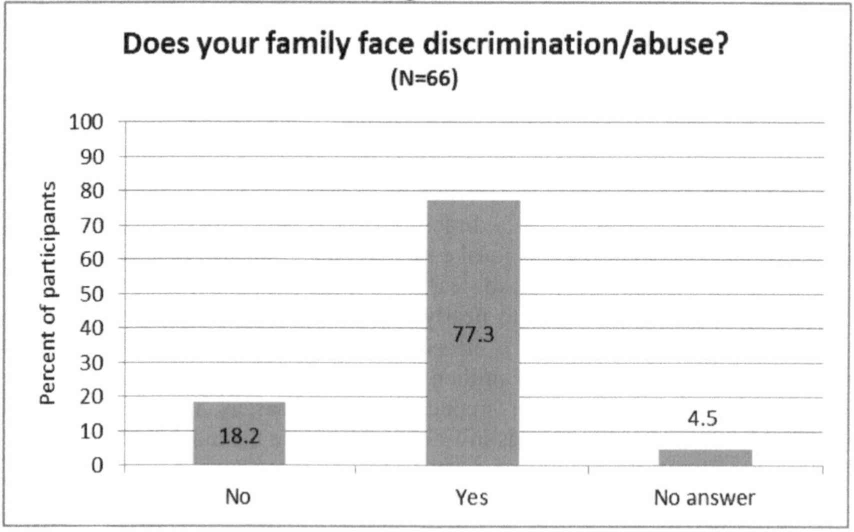

Does your family face discrimination/abuse? (N=66)

Figure 2

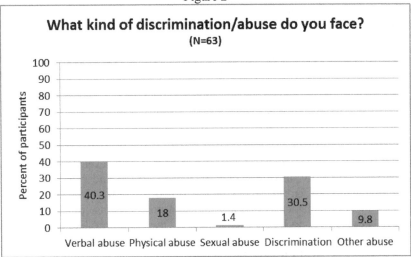

Figure 3

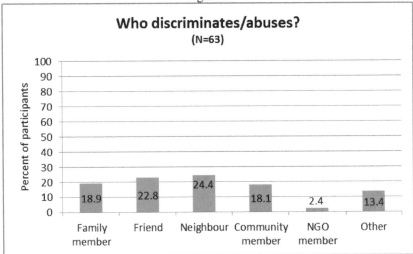

The preliminary report "Sport for Development and Peace" highlights the value of sport programs to empower and promote the inclusion of marginalized groups such as women, migrants and PWDs (UNOSDP, 2008). The report states that sport for PWDs is not a new concept, but its full potential as a powerful, low-cost means to foster greater inclusion and well-being is only beginning to be realized. Sport is known to improve the inclusion and well-being of PWDs in two ways — by changing what communities think and feel about PWDs and by changing what PWDs think and feel about themselves (UNOSDP, 2008).

To change what the community thinks and feels in relation to PWDs it is necessary to reduce stigma and discrimination. Sport is highly visible and it touches almost everyone as a participant, spectator or consumer. Sport changes community perceptions because it focuses attention on abilities rather than disabilities (DePauw and Gavron, 2005). Through sport, persons without disabilities encounter PWDs in a positive context (sometimes for the first time) and see PWDs accomplish things previously thought impossible (Parnes and Hashemi, 2007). Their assumptions about what PWDs can and cannot do are profoundly reshaped by this experience. Moreover, the tendency to see the disability instead of the person is greatly reduced, in part because of the common experience of sport that persons without disabilities and PWDs share (UNOSDP, 2008).

Sport also empowers PWDs. Through sport, PWDs may recognize their own potential and advocate for positive changes in society. Sport can provide opportunities to develop social skills, develop friendships, develop independence, exercise responsibility, learning team work, cooperation and goal setting, self-discipline and take on leadership roles (Fukuchi, 2007, UNOSDP, 2008). Through this peer interaction, PWDs develop a positive sense of self and group identity because they no longer feel set apart – they are more like everyone else (UNOSDP, 2008).

To sum up, by focussing on abilities rather than disabilities, sport can considerably improve the community perception and help reduce the isolation of PWDs. Secondly, through sport PWDs can improve their self-confidence and self-esteem and become empowered to lead and make change happen.

"The Dream" Project

Having seen the devastating results of the discrimination survey in north Haiti, and having experienced the desperate reality and need for greater support, the chairpersons of the English NGO, Haiti Hospital Appeal (HHA), developed the project "The Dream". The Dream is a sports project which is dedicated to support a team of disabled Haitian athletes seeking to qualify for and participate in the Paralympic Games. The goals of the project are to enhance the empowerment and social inclusion of the athletes and PWDs and to establish long-term sports infrastructure in Haiti.

The project aims to:

- help fight against stigma regarding PWDs
- support and empower PWDs
- provide infrastructure for long-term inclusive sport activities
- help establish support for Haitian communities to provide services to PWDs

In the beginning of 2011 HHA bought the first handbike for their spinal cord injury (SCI) rehabilitation unit and started to implement a sport program during rehabilitation of persons with a SCI. A few months later The Dream set up a collaboration with the National Paralympic Committee (NPC) in Haiti, BMS World Mission and Global Hand UK and started to provide support to athletes in Port-au-Prince and Cap-Haitien. The project facilitates access to proper equipment, balanced sport nutrition and technical and training advice. Alongside the development of the sport projects, The Dream together with the NPC Haiti, sought for universal wildcards to participate in the Paralympic Games in London 2012.

Leon Gaisli

Leon Gaisli is a 44 year old Haitian handcycling athlete, who sustained a SCI and lost his wife and 8 children during the 2010 earthquake. Before the earthquake, SCI rehabilitation did not exist in Haiti and persons sustaining a SCI were not expected to survive more than one or two years after the injury. However, there has been an increase in knowledge and training of staff. Persons with a SCI now survive much longer (Arie, 2012). Leon Gaisli received rehabilitation in the SCI unit of HHA in Cap-Haitien. During rehabilitation Leon learned the importance of sport for his physical functioning and independence. After having realised the new thrilling possibilities that handbiking could give him, Leon came to be a dedicated sportsman. He enjoyed himself riding through the streets of Cap-Haitien and realising how people in the streets, who had never seen such a thing as a handbike, reacted and cheered for him. When the project The Dream started, the "Swiss Paraplegic Foundation" donated 2 additional handbikes and sent a trainer to Haiti to teach the patients in the SCI rehabilitation unit how to ride a handbike and to instruct on basic training principles. From that time on, Leon has been using sport as a tool to help him cope with his tragic past and to develop new goals in life.

In November 2011 Leon left Haiti for the first time in order to participate in the two handbike events at the Parapan Games in Mexico. The participation at the Parapan Games was a requirement to have any chance for a starting slot at the Paralympic Games in London 2012. Although it was a substantial financial burden to send Leon and his coach to the Parapan Games – which often is an insurmountable barrier for low resource countries – The Dream facilitated Leon's participation. This was an important initial event for the sports movement of PWDs in northern Haiti.

Since then, Leon has been helping to lead a movement of change in Haiti. During training in the streets around Cap-Haitien, the locals recognise him and his fellow handbikers and cheer them on. Instead of being socially excluded, he is talking at public events and challenging the population on Haitian television. The UN's "Community Violence Reduction Team" chose Leon as the face of Cap-Haitien (Haiti's second largest city) in 2011, which gave him publicity never seen before. Finally, Leon was leading the 2011 UN Peace Marathon in Cap-Haitien. The recognition Leon received would never have been possible without sport as a tool to overcome barriers. The reactions of the Haitians after Leon's first international competition encouraged The Dream to continue their work.

Paralympic Games in London 2012

Four days before the opening ceremony of the Paralympic Games in London, the project leader of The Dream received a call from the International Paralympic Committee (IPC) informing that Leon would be allowed to participate in the

Paralympic Games in London. As it was at the Parapan Games, Leon would compete in London in the handbike Time Trial and Road Race. During the games, his story has inspired many people and got immense recognition. Leon's story was voted 7 out of "The 50 best moments in the Olympic and Paralympic Games", well ahead of such famous athletes as tennis player Andy Murray or wheelchair racer David Weir (Lewis, 2012). Another national British newspaper stated that the story of the Haitian athletes, Leon's Gaisli and Josue Cajuste (who received at the Paralympics for the first time in his life a prosthetic for his shortened right leg), were the most inspiring individuals of the Paralympic Games 2012. (Maughan, 2012)

Aside from media interest in the UK, in collaboration with a number of groups including Haiti's Secretary of State for The Inclusion of PWDs, it was decided that purchasing the TV rights for the Paralympics would be a positive step, for the overarching objective to see national change in the attitude towards PWDs. Through Haiti's National Television company, TNH, three highlight packages were broadcast on three separate days across Haiti, the first time the Paralympics had ever been shown in Haiti. Using a network of Haitian Rehabilitation NGO's, groups were informed of the initiative so as to spread the coverage of the Haitian athletes at the Paralympics as widely as possible.

Implications

As research shows, media coverage of sports events involving PWDs can play a major role in creating more accurate perceptions of PWDs (Blauwet, 2007). The growing profile of the Paralympics has contributed to the increased recognition of PWDs all over the world. Although it is difficult to see immediate implications on the everyday life in Haiti, there seems to be momentum to empower PWDs in Haiti. The Haitian government signing the "Declaration on Policy for the Disabled" on October 4th, 2012 is one major event likely driven by this momentum (Caribbean, 2012). But there are other promising signs of an increased recognition of PWDs. When Leon returned home for the first time after the Paralympics, he was greeted with an enthusiastic reception by his local community, with children running beside him, cheering him on, and adults surrounding him to ask questions and congratulate him on his success. This level of inclusivity has been increased through television coverage. In 2011 HHA ran a two day training course for amputee football players that was greeted by the local community with scepticism, and in some cases, discrimination. Having witnessed the increased capacity of PWDs in the last few months, successful joint training sessions with able bodied and disabled individuals have taken place. It is these small but promising steps which make the chairpersons of The Dream project confident that change can happen.

A central part of the project is a documentary following Leon and the other Paralympic athletes from Haiti. The broadcast is planned for the end of 2013. The Dream documentary will be translated and transported by a mobile cinema team to all ten of Haiti's regions, accompanied by a community based rehabilitation team. It is planned to show the documentary on Haitian as well as European TV channels. With the documentary, it is hoped to see an even greater impact of the project on the social inclusion of PWDs in Haiti. By making Leon's story public not only in Cap-Haitien but all over Haiti, The Dream hopes to contribute to a change in the recognition of PWDs in Haiti.

Empowerment

Leon's positive example persuaded other PWDs of the importance of physical exercise for their health as well as to experience new exciting activities they had never thought to be possible. Seeing Leon on the TV competing at the Paralympic Games, was an incredible moment for the rehabilitation patients at HHA. For the first time they saw that a peer was able to achieve his goals and that his achievements were recognised by the Haitian population. Leon's participation also inspired other athletes at HHA to start training seriously and setting themselves the goal to become a Paralympian as well. But also for Leon himself it was a stimulating experience. When Leon was back in Haiti he gave an interview to the UN "Mission des Nations Unies pour la stabilisation en Haïti" (MINUSTAH). During this interview he emphasized that it was important for him and the other PWDs in Haiti, that he was able to compete in the London Paralympic Games (Boudre, 2012). The following parts of the interview underline this statement:

What is the difference between Leon Gaisli before and after the Paralympic Games?

> I feel like another person because now everybody (the whole world) knows me. And I have met a lot of people. Ah.... if only I could have hoisted the Haitian flag higher! I hope that one day I'll bring an Olympic medal to Haiti. But anyway, I feel like a complete man now because I represented my country.

How did your friends at the rehabilitation centre welcome you when you came back from London?

> Everybody was happy to see me again. I told them everything. [...] I told them not to give up, because I could participate at these games only thanks to their support.

Do you have a message for the disabled and the people in general in Haiti?

> I would like to tell the persons with a disability: Have courage! Don't think life is over only because you are stuck in the chair. You can accomplish the same tasks as a person being able to use all his limbs. Let us turn to the future. It is important that the authority offers better conditions for persons with disabilities. A person with a disability can contribute to the development of his country like everybody else. You only have to give him the opportunity. And above all, I wish that the government would support persons with disabilities to win medals at international competitions.

Most astonishing is how much more self-confidence Leon got through the participation in the Parapan and the Paralympic Games. In that interview, Leon is exactly expressing what the project leaders had been hoping would happen. After having seen at these games what other, even more disabled persons achieve and how other countries include their PWDs, Leon is not only challenging his peers to not give up, he is also asking the government to improve the situation of PWDs in Haiti. It seems that Leon, in relation to empowerment, can become a role model for other PWDs in Haiti.

Sport infrastructure

Integrated sport participation is only slowly becoming more accepted and is not yet routine. Individuals with a disability who are able to compete among able bodied persons are considered an exception rather than the rule (DePauw and Gavron, 2005). On November 16th, 2012, the inclusive sport centre at the campus of HHA, financed by the MINUSTAH UN mission, was opened. The sport centre consists of a gym with equipment for both PWDs and able bodied persons. The centre also includes a tennis and basketball court where inclusive, adaptive sport will be facilitated. The Dream is now employing a full-time sport coach who is starting to teach sport to all patients at the rehabilitation unit and who introduces, amongst others, inclusive sport sessions with a local football club.

Conclusion

Although it is difficult to see changes in perception of PWDs in Haiti, The Dream project is a starting point that has already had many positive impacts. The combination of having Leon as a role model, having the sport centre, where persons with and without disability can train and having the publicity of the documentary with Leon's story, seem to be promising steps towards a more inclusive society in Haiti. The next steps will be to build grassroots sporting opportunities and infrastructure for PWDs as well as gaining support to ensure the sustainability of the project.

Acknowledgements

We would like to thank Mirjam Brach from Swiss Paraplegic Research for the possibility to work with the Haitian handcyclists during the last year. We also thank the Swiss Paraplegic Foundation and the Swiss Paraplegic Centre for their various supports. Finally we thank all the supporters of The Dream who have made this incredible dream become a reality.

References

Arie, S. 2012. "Work of 125 aid agencies failed to create lasting rehabilitation services in Haiti, study shows". BMJ, 344; e2952.

Blauwet, C. 2007. Promoting he Health and Human Rights of Individuals with a Disability Through the Paralympic Movement. Available at http://www.toolkitsportdevelopment.org/html/resources/CE/CEF58F28-3786-4AE9-B9C3-887E0397E24C/Health_as_a_Human_Right_Final_Long_Version.pdf (Accessed 28th October 2012)

Boudre, S. 2012. Léon Gaisli, athlète paralympique haïtien : «J'en suis convaincu, un jour notre pays va évoluer». *Mission des Nations Unies pour la stabilisation en Haït* Available at http://minustah.org/?p=37591. (Accessed 13th April 2013)

Brown, C., Ripp, J. & Kazura, J. 2012. "Perspectives on Haiti two years after the earthquake". Am J Trop Med Hyg, 86; 5-6.

Burns, A. S., O'Connell, C. & Landry, M. D. 2010. "Spinal cord injury in postearthquake Haiti: lessons learned and future needs". PM R, 2; 695-697.

Caribbean. 2012. Haiti's Government Signs Declaration on Policy for Disabled Caribbean Journal. Available at http://www.caribjournal.com/2012/10/04/haitis-government-signs-declaration-on-policy-for-disabled/ (Accessed 4th October 2012)

DePauw, K. P. & Gavron, S. J. 2005. Disability sport, Champaign, Ill., Human Kinetics.

Fukuchi, K. 2007. My Hope for an Inclusive Society. Sport in the United Nations Convention on the Rights of Persons with Disabilities. Available at http://iris.lib.neu.edu/cgi/viewcontent.cgi?article=1023&context=sport_staff_pres (Accessed 28th October 2012)

Lewis, J. 2012. The 50 Best moments from the London 2012 Olympic and Paralympic Games The Independent, September 10th.

Maughan, M. 2012. In Haiti we lost our children and homes. Now we train in the rubble - but we're showing g what disabled people can really do' THE WORLD'S MOST INSPIRATIONAL PARALYMPIAN STORIES It's not what you can't do.. it's what you can do. Sunday Mirror, 2nd September 2012; 34-35.

Parnes, P. & Hashemi, G. 2007. Sport as a Means to Foster Inclusion, Health and Well-Being of People with Disabilities.

Schure, T. 2010. Haiti's Rising Urgency. Available at http://www.worldpress.org/Americas/3514.cfm (Accessed 25th October 2012)

UNOSDP. 2008. Harnessing the power of Sport for Development and Peace: Recommendations to Governments. *In:* PEACE, I. W. G. S. F. D. A. (ed.) Sport and Persons with Disablities.

World Health Organisation. 2011. World report on disability. WHO Press, Geneva

Wolbring, G. 2011. "Disability, displacement and public health: a vision for Haiti". Can J Public Health, 102; 157-9.

Chapter 9: Identity of the Warrior and the Impact of Spirituality through Disability Sport for Traumatically Injured British Service Personnel

Sarah Green (Coventry University, UK)

Introduction

More and more casualties are returning from Afghanistan with traumatic, life-changing injuries. Yet, to what extent do traumatic personal injuries impact the identity and the meaning of life for injured Service personnel? In Iraq and Afghanistan, there has been a change in tactical warfare, whereby an increasing number of Improvised Explosive Devices (IEDs) have a tendency to remove limbs or damage them so severely that they have to be amputated. Advances in field medicine, as well as defensive and protective equipment, has meant that an unprecedented percentage of Service personnel are now surviving traumatic wounds or injuries (Chivers 2009). This means that increasing numbers of personnel are therefore returning home with injuries that present significant changes to their life. Within Great Britain, statistical representation of the amount of injuries and the type of injury sustained is difficult to come by due to the British military's rather complicated classification system of very seriously injured or wounded, which means that there is imminent danger to life and seriously injured or wounded, which means that there is no imminent danger to life (British Army, 2011).

Nevertheless, in order to place this into some context, the USA report that in Operation Iraqi Freedom and Operation Enduring Freedom, for every US soldier killed, seven have been wounded. Combined, over 48,000 Servicemen and women have been physically injured in the recent military conflicts (Wounded Warrior Project, 2012). Because of this the defense community is striving to ensure that the aftercare provided is of the highest possible standard and the use of disability sport in this process is highly valued (The Australian Army, 2012; British Army, 2011). In direct relation to this, there are a number of military-based initiatives that use disability sport as a central part of their rehabilitation programmes. Across the globe these initiatives are known as, the USA's

'Wounded Warrior Project', Canada's 'Soldier On' programme, the 'Australian Defence Force Paralympic Sports Program' and Great Britain's 'Battle Back' programme. All of these initiatives consider disability sport to be extremely important for injured Service personnel, as a way for individuals to come to terms with their traumatic injuries. Fundamentally, for people to understand what they are still able to achieve – focusing on ability rather than inability (British Army, 2011; Wounded Warrior Project, 2012; CFPFSS, 2012; The Australian Army, 2012).

This recognition is largely due to the fact that disability sport, in the rehabilitation process, is considered to have psychological benefits such as improved self-image, self-esteem, leadership, camaraderie and quality of life (Groff *et al.*, 2009). This recognition also draws on the fact that sport[1] is innate to military life, where fitness has and continues to be essential, to not only meet the physical demands of the job but also encourage discipline, focus, determination and achievement in the military arena (Sporner *et al.*, 2011). It is due to the fact that sport and fitness are so important to military life, that the aforementioned military-based initiatives encourage the continuation for injured Service personnel to take part in almost any sport or fitness activity (British Army, 2011). Thus it can be considered that, from the military's perspective, sport is seen as an extremely positive component to the rehabilitation of traumatically injured Service personnel.

For example, Great Britain's 'Battle Back' initiative aims to encourage sports and adventurous training to aid "physical, psychological and social recovery (mind, body and soul)" (British Army, 2011). Building on Guttmann's legacy, the universally accepted founder of the modern day Paralympic movement (Brittain and Green, 2012: 2), 'Battle Back' aims to improve and formalise the use of adventurous training and sport in the aftercare of seriously injured service personnel. They recognise the pioneering work of Guttmann, who first introduced sport to help rehabilitate World War II veterans (Lomi *et al.*, 2004). In order to facilitate this, 'Battle Back' is in fact funded by both The Royal British Legion and Help for Heroes and 'Battle Back' now plays a central role in the new initiative 'Front Line to Start Line', which aims to help the injured make the progression to Paralympic sport. It is said that 'Battle Back' is important for three reasons: equality, morality and ability (British Army, 2011). Equality, because it provides seriously injured Servicemen and women the same adventurous training as their non-disabled colleagues; morality because the defence community has a moral obligation to ensure that the aftercare of its wounded is of the highest possible standard and ability because it is felt that when one is first coming to terms with a life-changing injury, it is essential to understand what one is able to achieve – focussing on ability rather than inability.

Recognising this, the importance of sport is heavily present in the British military's rehabilitation model, a model that centres on recreational therapy and the importance of getting some level of fitness back for all involved (Datta and Nicol, 2006: 105). The military's rationale for this is that injured or ill personnel need to know that they can still achieve physical endeavours (British Army, 2011). This relates to the fact that sport is extremely important in military life and it is through active doing that a sense of normality is often restored. The findings of Brittain and Green's (2012) study confirm this, that disability sport is a central and indeed important component to the rehabilitation of injured military personnel, which is considered to take us once again back to Guttmann's original claims of the physiological and psychological values of sport in the rehabilitation process (McCann, 1996). Brittain and Green's (2012) findings are also in agreement with other previous research that acknowledges disability sport as an important rehabilitative tool (Sakic *et al.*, 2007; Weaver *et al.*, 2009). So how can we increase our understanding on the importance of disability sport in the rehabilitation process?

My current research looks at the deeper impact that disability sport has, specifically in the identity adaptation process and the influence it can have on an individual's meaning in life. Some recent findings underpin this research and relate to the fact that fitness is important for the military on lots of levels, as a necessity for the job, so that personnel can function. Therefore, injured and ill personnel are constantly reminded that there is a need to be fit (Datta and Nicol, 2006: 106). My research has uncovered that it is due to this and the cultural demands surrounding fitness and the military's view of injury, that personnel feel neither worthwhile nor a worthwhile person immediately post-injury. So, when personnel start rehabilitation and recreational therapy, participants report that there is a significant positive development in mind-set and they become more confident in their own ability, as well as experiencing increased levels of interaction with others through exercise - a finding that is supported by the work of Sporner *et al.* (2009: 414). This therefore helps individuals build confidence, esteem and morale, facilitating individuals to gain back camaraderie.

It is important to consider however that this research has uncovered that within the military, there are significant levels of fear surrounding injury and illness. These are multifaceted in that there are practical, physical, psychological and emotional implications (Brittain, 2004). When personnel find themselves injured or ill, they are denounced as being 'not fit for purpose', 'out of duty', 'redundant', 'defunct'. This denunciation also occurs on a day-to-day basis if personnel are sick or ill, they are called a "biff". So, within the military set up, there is an overwhelming fear of being a 'biff' or 'biffed'. It can be recognised therefore that life-changing injuries and disability are, in most cases, considered to be negative and something that needs to be fixed or overcome through sporting endeavours. Throughout rehabilitation, physical endeavours are a chosen tool to motivate individuals to fight against disability, as they see the need to move beyond their injury by proving themselves to still be physically able. With this, within the military context, it is significant to look at the psychosocial impact of participation in recreational therapy. In line with Goffman's work on stigma (1963: 20), my research data has highlighted that recreational therapy relates to the ways in which injured personnel, the stigmatised, attempt to correct their condition indirectly through activity associated with their shortcomings.

Yet, as it has already been noted, from the military's perspective, sport is seen as an extremely positive component to rehabilitation, thus acting as a central facet of their initiative. That said, such initiatives could place added pressure on individuals who have received traumatic, life-changing injuries and do not find participation in sport of value and/or interest. Lack of involvement in sport does not however 'fit' with the military's rehabilitation model. Since spring 2012, injured service personnel are now obliged to participate in sport as part of their recovery at the recently established National Sports' Centre (Sport England, 2012). There is a growing concern that the lack of choice to partake in sport will remove feelings of enjoyment and fulfillment, as well as a sense of control at a time when traumatic injuries have done just that. So although the military feel that the 'Battle Back' programme is building on Guttmann's legacy, we have to question whether his pioneering message has been lost in the mists of time. This is especially the case as Guttmann stressed the importance of enjoyment. He declared that the restorative power of disability sport may in fact be lost if participation is not enjoyable (Brittain and Green, 2012: 246).

Identity of the Warrior

For some time it has been recognised that traumatic, life-changing injuries often require a re-adjustment or adaptation of identity (Wright, 1983). This incorporates the idea that the experience of psychosocial adjustment is an adaptive response to a significant life change (Hamill, Carson and Dorahy, 2010: 729). My research supports the work of Hamill, Carson and Dorahy, as participants recognised the impact of self-identity in the adaptation process. Fundamentally, the struggle to come to terms with a new 'disabled' identity. Identity adaptation is multifaceted and has to be considered in order to discuss the transitional process wounded Service personnel need make from a warrior, to an injured veteran, to an athlete.

In relation to this, 'Identity' is a term that is widely used and therefore has different meanings to different people (Deaux, 2001: 1). The term 'social identity' indicates the aspects of an individual that are defined by his or her group membership. Tajfel and Turner (1986) first introduced social identity theory, claiming that the individual has more than one identity. They claim that the individual draws on a certain identity depending on the environment or situation that they find themselves, hence the term social identity. It is the individual's response to 'Who am I?' derived from perceived membership of social groups. Tajfel and Turner declare that such groups influence how an individual sees themselves, their self-concept, which is dependent on "the meaning the individual attaches to group membership" (Griffith, 2009: 41). In other words, social identity relates to the individual's self-concept that comes from his or her membership of a social group or groups, as well as the way in which the individual values and places emotional importance on such membership. Although most people belong to a number of social groups, only some of them are meaningful when they define themselves.

Therefore, it is acknowledged that people cogitate about what links them to the rest of society as a means of developing life meaning, a role and a purpose. The experience of traumatic injury can affect this because an individual's external, relational identity and internal, spiritual identity is, post-traumatic injury, different to their pre-injury status. During an interview, one former marine stated that, "going from a fit, healthy, fully able-bodied marine, to some midget in a wheelchair is difficult". This indicates the ways in which individuals have to challenge and face up to their own prejudices and judgements that acted as an inherent belief before they themselves were injured. Another injured soldier described to me how he sees himself, through categorisation and personal identification, as two separate people, pre- and post-injury. He acknowledges that he has changed externally and internally. Fundamentally his life course has changed and his relationship with society has changed from a soldier, to a blind veteran. It is therefore pertinent to consider the ways disability sport could increase the experience of wounded Service personnel. Specifically those who are in the process of re-defining their position in society and choose disability sport as a vehicle to break through, what the military see to be, the 'shackles of injury'[2]. In other words, to move beyond the societal identification of an injured veteran to that of an athlete who is able to achieve and accomplish individual and/or team goals.

It is necessary to question whether the "Identity of the Warrior" impacts the ways in which people come to terms with their injuries? As it has already been mentioned, injury and subsequent disability is often perceived as something that is negative. In connection to this, it may be the case that some injured Service personnel feel that they have to prove themselves to still be physically able. An injured soldier's opinion highlights this as he says, "okay, I've lost my leg, but I'll get a new one in a few weeks and I'll be running around and walking about and it's not going to affect me." Many more choose sport as a tool to achieve this. Disability sport can be thought of as an individual therapy to aid a person's rehabilitation and help them come to terms with their injuries and their re-adjustment in lifestyle. Terry Byrne, a cyclist who was injured in Afghanistan by an IED, explains this in a news story, "sport has aided me, I don't worry about my leg, I think about my times" (Razzall 2011). His opinion highlights how cycling has benefitted what can be called his physical and cognitive rehabilitation, showing that this achievement has assisted him to adapt to his injury as he states that he does not worry about the loss of his leg, but the focus and determination required of his sport. In his own words, it is through the absence of "worrying" about his injury, that Byrne views cycling as a tool to assist his identity adaptation, what is fundamentally a transition from a warrior, to an injured veteran, to an athlete.

Spirituality through Disability Sport

It is now pertinent to take a look at how sport provides purpose, meaning and direction as a means to ascertain whether participation in disability sport post-traumatic injury can be a spiritual endeavour. It has already been recognised that meaning, purpose and direction are ultimately lost because of traumatic injury (Brittain and Green, 2012). Therefore, it is now time to add to this discussion and provide new insights into the impact of disability sport in the recovery from life-changing injuries. In order to consider the spiritual experience of disability-sport-rehabilitation, we must first recognise the nebulous nature of the term 'spirituality' as something that is contextual and subjective (Jamison 2006). It is reported that spirituality is a nebulous term that is historically associated to religion, yet now has a wider significance in 21st-century western society, where there is space for nontheistic spiritualties (King, 2009: 28; Collicutt McGrath 2011). Specifically, there is space for spirituality to have its own standing in 21st-century western society, where spirituality is no longer contained by a theistic, God-orientated understanding. As a result, some key understandings are suggested as integral to an embryonic, secular, postmodern and existential understanding of spirituality.

Specifically in a nontheistic sense, these are: connectedness, well-being, meaning, purpose, awareness and experience (Hunt 2001).

An individual's spirituality can change post-traumatic injury. This is because it is recognised that traumatic disability affects an individual's spirituality, which can be thought of as an individual's meaning in life and sense of purpose (Collicutt McGrath, 2011: 84). As a result, my current research reveals how participants seek to re-establish their purpose and meaning in life through disability sport. This process was identified as goal striving, the identification of a goal and goal attainment, the fulfilment of said goal. It has already been noted that a re-assessment or re-adjustment of identity is often required post-traumatic injury. This is because the experience of life-changing injuries often requires the need to gain a new understanding of oneself and the world in which we live. With this, traumatic injuries can change the way individuals identify themselves, as well as the way in which society identifies the individual. As an integral part of the rehabilitation and re-integration process, this transition can be difficult (Emmons 2005).

In support of extant research, this current work is in agreement with a number of qualitative studies that looked at the impact of trauma within a civilian context. They indicate that when faced with life-changing injuries, it is frequently through partaking in sport and active doing, that individuals are able to re-connect or indeed deepen a connection with the self (Emmons 2005; Faull and Hills 2006; Smith and Sparkes 2008). And, in relation to the recognition of goal striving and goal attainment, many individuals are said to develop and define their meaning and purpose in life through achieving personal sporting goals (Schulz 2005). This research indicates therefore that goal setting is crucial in the rehabilitation process and it is through achieving sporting goals that the injured are able to gain direction, meaning, purpose and enjoyment. A former marine describes it as "every time you reach a goal, you're bettering yourself and it's good for my spirit".

In my current research, participants expressed clearly how they use disability sport to re-enter their world. This can be understood as the way in which participation in disability sport helps individuals find purpose, meaning and a place within their society. This relates heavily to the ideas on perceptions of disability that were expressed earlier - participants feel the need to come to terms with the physical change to their body, which is (initially) an extremely negative change. My current research would suggest that this is largely due to inherent preconceptions of disability as 'unnatural' and 'abnormal'. In order to overcome this, participants identify how they use disability sport as a tool to alter the perception of being disabled and present mediating effects on their newly disabled identity (Tasiemski *et al.* 2004). Another important recognition in the relationship between spirituality and disability sport is the way in which participants use disability sport as a tool to perceive the world. In other words, disability sport provides individuals with increased levels of self-awareness and understanding that positively contribute to their recovery. Findings such as these relate to a previous study carried out by Cordova *et al.* (1998), who investigated the influence of the national disabled veterans' winter sports clinic on self-concept and leisure satisfaction. Their findings claimed that sport participation increased self-concept and self-satisfaction. The current findings, as well as previous research therefore indicate that disability sport has a transformative and liberalising power (Andrews, 1993; Cordova *et al.*, 1998; Ashton-Shaeffer *et al,.* 2001).

Key Points

Significance

We can conclude that disability sport once again plays a significant role in the rehabilitation of traumatically injured Service personnel. The reasons for this relate heavily to the modern day British military's perception of disability and the need for some personnel to prove that they are still physically able.

Identity

Identity adaptation is multifaceted and it is important to recognise that life-changing injuries often require the re-adjustment of identity. Current research supports the idea that disability sport can act as a tool to help individuals come to terms with their traumatic injuries.

Spirituality

An individual's meaning in life and sense of purpose can change post-traumatic injury. Partaking in disability sport can have spiritual meaning as a tool to bring back meaning and purpose to the lives of traumatically injured service personnel.

Notes

[1] Sport can encompass adventurous training, physical training, team sport and individual sport (British Army, 2011)
[2] The motto 'to break through the shackles of injury' is used at Headley Court, the main rehabilitation centre for British Service personnel in Surrey, United Kingdom (DMRC, 2006)

References

Andrews, D. 1993. "Desperately seeking Michel Foucault's genealogy, the body, and critical sport psychology." Sociology of Sport Journal 10: 148-167.
Ashton-Shaeffer, C., Gibson, H. J., Autry, C. E. and Hanson, C. S. 2001. "'Meaning of sport to adults with physical disabilities: A disability sport camp experience." Sociology of Sport Journal 18: 95-111.
British Army. 2011. Battle Back [online] Available at www.army.mod.uk/events/sport/16263.aspx (Accessed 3rd June 2011)

Brittain, I. 2004. "Perceptions of disability and their impact upon involvement in sport for people with disabilities at all levels." Journal of Sport & Social Issues 28(4): 429-452.

Brittain I. and Green, S. 2012. "Disability sport is going back to its roots: Rehabilitation of military personnel receiving sudden traumatic disabilities in the twenty-first century." Qualitative Research in Sport and Exercise 4(2): 244-264.

CFPFSS. 2012. Soldier On Fund [online] Available at https://public.cfpsa.com/en/SupportOurTroops/OurFunds/Pages/Soldier-On.aspx (Accessed 17th July 2012)

Chivers, S. 2009. "Disabled Veterans in the Americas: Canadians "Soldier On" after Afghanistan – Operation Enduring Freedom and the Canadian Mission." Canadian Review of American Studies 39(3): 321-342.

Collicutt McGrath, J. 2011. 'Posttraumatic Growth and Spirituality after Brain Injury." Brain Impairment 12(2): 82-92.

Cordova, J., Miller, J., Leadbetter, G., Trombetta, S., Parks, S. and O'Hara, R. 1998. "Influence of the national disabled veterans' winter sports clinic on self-concept and leisure satisfaction of adult veterans with disabilities." Palaestra 14(1): 40-44.

Datta, S. and Nicol, E. 2006. "Military Sports and Rehabilitation Medicine." JR Army Med Corps 153(2): 105-110.

Deaux, K. 2001. Social Identity [online] Available at http://www.utexas.edu/courses/stross/ant393b_files/ARTICLES/identity.pdf (Accessed 11th December 2012)

DMRC. 2006. Headley Court [online] Available at www.headleysurrey.org.uk/hc.htm (Accessed 19th April 2012)

Emmons, R.A. 2005. "Striving for the Sacred: Personal Goals, Life Meaning and Religion." Journal of Social Issues 61(4): 731-745.

Faull, K., Hills, M.D. 2006. "The Role of the Spiritual Dimension of the Self as the Prime Determinant of Health." Disability and Rehabilitation 28(11): 729-740.

Goffman, E. 1963. Stigma: Notes on the management of spoiled identity. Englewood Cliffs, NJ: Prentice-Hall.

Groff, G.D., Lundberg, N.R., Zabriskie, R.B. 2009. "Influence of adapted sport on quality of life: perceptions of athletes with cerebral palsy." Journal of Disability and Rehabilitation 31(4): 318–326.

Hamill, R., Carson, S., and Dorahy, M. 2010. "Experiences of psychosocial adjustment within 18 months of amputation: an interpretative phenomenological analysis." Disability and Rehabilitation 32(9): 729-740.

Hunt, C. 2001. "A way of Wellbeing? Approaching Spirituality through reflective Practice." Adult Learning 12(3): 7-9.

Jamison, C. 2006. Finding Sanctuary: Monastic Steps for Everyday Life. London: Weidenfeld and Nicolson

King, U. 2009. The Search for Spirituality. Norwich: Canterbury Press

Lomi, C., Geroulanos, E., Kekatos, E. 2004. "Sir Ludwig Guttmann – The de Coubertin of the Paralysed." Journal of the Hellenic Association of Orthopaedic and Traumatology 55(1):

McCann, C. 1996. "Sports for the disabled: the evolution from rehabilitation to competitive sport." British journal of sports medicine 30(4): 279–280.

Razzall, K. 2011. Paralympics: War veterans aim for sporting glory. [online] Available at http://www.channel4.com/news/paralympics-war-veterans-aim-for-sporting-glory (Accessed 11th April 2011)

Sakic, V.A., Sakic, D., Badovinac, O. and Pjevac, N. 2007. "Importance of kinesiologic recreation beginning in early rehabilitation in Zagreb." Acta medica croatica 61(1): 75–76.

Schulz, E.K. 2005. "The Meaning of Spirituality for Individuals with Disabilities." Disability and Rehabilitation 27(21): 1283-1295.

Smith, B., Sparkes, A.C. 2008. "Changing bodies, changing narratives and the consequences of tellability: a case study of becoming disabled through sport." Sociology of Health & Illness 30(2): 217-236.

Sporner, M.L., Fitzgerald, S.G., Dicianno, B.E., Collins, D., Teodorski, E., Pasquina, P.F., Cooper, R.A. 2009. "Psychosocial impact of participation in the national veterans games and winter sports clinic." Disability and rehabilitation 31(5): 410–418.

Sport England. 2012. Battle Back Centre at Lilleshall to support wounded troops. [online] Available at: http://www.sportengland.org.uk/about_us/our_news/battle_back_centre_at_lillesha.aspx (Accessed 12th August 2012)

Tajfel, H. and Turner, J. C. 1986. "The social identity theory of inter-group behavior." In Psychology of Intergroup Relations. ed. by Worchel, S. and Austin, L.W. Nelson-Hall: Chicago

Tasiemski, T., Kennedy, B., Gardner, B. P. and Blaikley, R. A. 2004. "Athletic identity and sports participation in people with spinal cord injury." Adapted Physical Activity Quarterly 21: 364-378.

The Australian Army. 2012. Australian Defence Force Paralympic Sports Program. [online] Available at: http://www.army.gov.au/Army-life/Wounded-Injured-and-Ill-Digger/Sport/ADF-Paralympic-Sports-Program (Accessed 17th July 2012)

Weaver, F.M., Burns, S.P., Evans, C.T., Rapacki, L.M., Goldstein, B. and Hammond, M.C. 2009. "Provider perspectives on soldiers with new spinal cord injuries returning from Iraq and Afghanistan." Archives of physical medicine and rehabilitation 29(3): 517–521.

Wounded Warrior Project (2012) Wounded Warrior Project. [online] available from <www.woundedwarriorproject.org/> [17 July 2012]

Wright, B. A. 1983. Physical disability: a psychosocial approach. New York: Harper and Row.

Chapter 10: Print Media Inclusions and Omissions in Sport and Disability: Disability and Gender in the 2011 International Sport Press Survey (Canada)

Jill M Le Clair (Humber College, Canada)

Introduction

Over the past twenty years there has been a shift globally from government policies and sport based on a medicalised view of disability, to a social construction, rights-based framework symbolised by the 2006 UN Convention of the Rights of Persons with Disabilities (CRPD), the first Convention to include benchmarks (Rioux, 2012). It is often forgotten, but approximately 10% of the world's population has some form of impairment. Disability statistics vary and UN Enable (2012) reports there are 650 million persons with disabilities whereas the 'World Report on Disability' by the WHO and the World Bank (2011) states there are a billion. This population wants inclusion in all aspects of society - in public spaces, in organisations, and in sport. It is thought that the 20th century images of jaunty, white, able-bodied moustachioed men that in the past exclusively represented sporting excellence and nationhood have vanished. However perceptions about this expected change are sometimes mistaken.

The media play an important role in framing national, social and individual identities (Brookes, 2002). Who is, and what is included in the press is usually determined by those who hold power to impose their perspective (Foucault, 1995), have financial interests, and topics are politically framed, whether narrowly as in 1930s Nazi Germany (Gellately, 2001) or more broadly as in Canada in the 2010s (Le Clair, 2011). Stereotypes about abilities lead to exclusion and omission regardless of the historical period and regardless of who is the target for discrimination, and who is defined as an outsider. Definitions may change over time, but there is an ongoing dominance of the 'normal', and stigma associated with disability. In turn this leads to the management of disability and how the self is presented by the individual (Goffman, 1963) and overseen by the often powerful medical 'gaze' of others (Foucault, 1994); this liminality and marginalisation of the so-called 'different' are then sometimes seen to be 'polluting' (1984) because the 'outsiders' are not positioned as within the 'normal' category (Titchkosky, 2007). It is in this context that justifiably researchers have been critical of media representations of disability (Schantz and Gilbert, 2001; Brittain, 2004), of the few images of disabled female athletes (Pappous, de Léséleuc, & Marcellini, 2012), and of the media's 'production' of the meaning of disability within the Paralympic Games themselves (Howe, 2008).

In order to debate the nature of representation, images have to be examined and it is helpful to document what is happening at a particular time period and that is why the 2011 International Sport Press Survey (ISPS) was established. Rather than impressions, evidence-based research allows us to further discuss another issue about representation, and that is omission. This paper examines the Canadian coverage of sport and who is included and excluded, in a study that was part of the 2011 ISPS. It analyzes three national, regional and local Canadian newspapers and the findings provide some surprises related to omissions tied to disability (and gender) in spite of considerable changes in inclusive policies, programs and legislation, based in disability rights.

The 2011 International Sport Press Survey (ISPS)

Dr. Thomas Horky, in the Journalism Department of the Macromedia University of Applied Sciences (MHMK) in Hamburg, and Dr. Jörg-Uwe Nieland at the Communications Institute at the German Sport University in Cologne are the directors of this international survey, and they have brought together researchers in twenty countries, from a variety of disciplines. The aim of the study is to obtain nation-based data that will provide a detailed comparative analysis of press coverage and the representation of sport over a wide range of topics to better understand what was taking place in 2011.

ISPS Methodology

To obtain a comprehensive perspective the newspapers analyzed in each country included a national newspaper, a regional paper and a tabloid paper, and in order to include a wider time frame the period surveyed was conducted for two 'artificially' constructed weeks for a total of 14 days that included Monday to Saturday, and Sunday papers if published, during the period from April 15 to July 2, 2011. The survey covered all sport topics in the different sections of the paper. The parameters of the study were defined to ensure all researchers used the same criteria and the analysis of the articles was thorough.

> The concept 'article' is understood as a text (or an integrated combination of text and picture/fact box/illustration) constituting a separate piece/item that can be read and understood without reading other articles or items on the page.... All texts will be coded as different articles. An article constitutes a story in its own right (Nieland & Horky, 2011; p.1).

Stand-alone pictures, boxes, illustrations, statistical results, pages covering betting or bookmaking and news briefs, notes, telegrams and digests were not included (ibid, p.1).

Each article throughout the newspapers was coded and the section noted, so any sport article in the business or politics section was included, as was the prominence of the article, the form of the article such as news, report, interview, and the sources. In addition the gender of the journalist was recorded and the sport itself, the topics of the articles themselves, the nature of the event (international or not), the actor or person (such as an athlete or coach etc.) and their gender, and the sources cited in the article such as an athlete, news agency, TV etc. (ibid 3-12). Although the variables of disability and the global disability sport organizations (Paralympic Games, Special Olympics & Deaflympics) were not included as variables by all the participating researchers, these topics were covered in the Canadian study to shed light on how disability is presented in the press.

Canadian Results

The three Canadian papers analyzed were *The Globe and Mail* which is a national paper. The *Toronto Star* which by title seems to be a city-based paper, but in fact it directly serves not only the Greater Toronto Area (GTA) which includes an amalgamation of adjacent cities with a population of 5.5 million, but is also a regional paper that is read across the province and to some degree across the country. The *Toronto Sun* is a tabloid newspaper which stresses its sport coverage and always has a photograph that covers almost the entire front page on a topic that is usually tied to the most provocative or key issue of the day, and often sport linked.

The total number of newspapers analysed was 42 and the total number of sport articles in all sections of the newspapers was 837. This did not include lists of results or stand-alone photographs. Perhaps one unique feature of Canadian sport is the fact that Canada shares a border and many sport activities with the United States. American based professional sport teams such as basketball, baseball and hockey have teams in Canada, and many amateur sport organisations compete in the USA. Also young student athletes often go to train and study in American colleges and compete on their teams. This meant that the Canadian definition of international is somewhat different from the definition and experiences of European athletes.

Those familiar with Canada will immediately ask: 'How does the weather, or the time of year, impact on the results?' There are extremes of severe cold and heat so sport and recreational activates vary considerably through the year. In Canada it was the end of the NBA basketball season, the start of the MLB baseball season and a time of NFL and CFL football tryouts, and the start of the soccer season. There was some coverage of horse-racing, tennis (as Wimbledon took place during part of this time), lacrosse and golf events. However this period also covered the end of the hockey season when teams are competing for the annual Stanley Cup championship. Of the 837 articles 351 or 42% of the total were on hockey. (See Table 1: Total articles.) It is probably no surprise to Canadians that 42% of all the articles (351 of 837) were about hockey. In addition to the Stanley Cup finals, the news coverage of riots in the streets of Vancouver with car burnings and looting after the finals received considerable coverage in this period, and also skewed the results. Stories that were tied to hockey discussed the problems of youth violence, hockey violence, safety and criminality that would not otherwise have been present. Extensive coverage in the press and on-line footage came with headlines such as 'Riots erupt in Vancouver after Canucks loss: dozens injured amid scenes of violence, looting' dominated the media (Canadian Broadcasting Commission, 2011). Photos of Vancouver rioters and looters were in all newspapers as the country was shocked that thousands rioted, and some set fires and broke into stores (Globe and Mail, 2011). Once the hockey season was over in June the focus switched to other sports.

International Sport Press Survey: 14 Days from 15 April–2 July, 2011

Table 1: Total articles

	Total number
Newspapers	42
Sport articles	837
NHL hockey	351= 42% of total

In 2011 there were also some sports new to Ontario. The Ultimate Fighting Championship events (http://ultimatefightingclubs.com) were previously banned because of the potential injuries to competitors who use both their hands and feet in fights that mix the skills of boxing and wrestling, but in 2011 were no longer outlawed. The first event was covered by all three papers, and to the horror of many was immensely popular and almost immediately the events sold out in the biggest venues in Toronto and Montreal.

Disability

Historically the social sciences and media studies included only a very limited discussion and analysis of disability. Some researchers argue that the representation of disability is still "pretty much the same as it has always been: clichéd, stereotyped, and archetypal.... (with a recent) increase in impairment imagery" (Darke, 2004, p.100). Anthropologists Rapp and Ginsberg as recently as 2010 asked: "Given the centrality of diversity to our epistemology, why has the subject of disability not been a central topic for our discipline?" ... our students raised these questions: Why isn't disability being taught in every introductory anthropology class? Why isn't it part of graduate training?" (2010, p. 517). Funding for disability research is hard to obtain and there are few senior scholars in Canada who are familiar with disability issues in sport. Disability is still rarely a part of textbooks in many subjects. This is important because often research results are the focus for press articles presenting new research such as concussions in sport, better training methods etc and the absence of research results means fewer articles on disability in sport. Successful organisational and participation growth internationally, and at all levels, are assisted by a better understanding of the science and social context of disability in sport.

Disability itself can be both visible and invisible and we find this same reality in the media. It is only in the last few years that we see both male and female reporters in wheelchairs conducting interviews, on location, and interviewing athletes with disabilities, but they are few in number. Even at the Paralympic Games in Athens "over 95% of the journalists in both the media centre and the IBC were able-bodied" and Howe found numerous physical barriers in spite of accessibility promises (Howe, 2008, p.141).

Fortunately the framing of the Games is changing since then. The 2008 Games in Beijing promoted the Paralympic Games as the new national inclusive disability policies were championed (Sun & Le Clair, 2011). It was a requirement of the 2012 Olympic and Paralympic Games bid that the Games would be promoted together. These shifts in perceptions and in the organization of sport and disability in both the global south and north are reflected in the introduction of national and regional disability rights policies such as the Accessibility for Ontarians with Disabilities Act (AODA, 2005) and there is increasing support for integration of high performance sport, and mainstreaming at the local level in the context of both recreation and organised sport.

Another factor was that the general public and the media became much more engaged in disability sport during the 2010 Vancouver Paralympic Games. The new Olympic consortium using different technologies 'television, radio, digital and print'was formed to provide 'the biggest and most robust coverage ever in Canada of a Paralympic Games':

> Canada's Olympic Broadcast Media Consortium is a unique relationship between leading media conglomerates CTV Inc. and Rogers Media Inc., which together will provide unprecedented coverage and consumer choice in English, French and multi-languages on multiple platforms for the Vancouver 2010 Olympic and Paralympic Winter Games and the London 2012 Games of the Olympiad. Official brands include CTV, TSN, RDS, RIS Info Sports, Rogers Sportsnet, OMNI, OLN, TQS, APTN, ATN, CTVOlympics.ca, RDSolympiques.ca, *The Globe and Mail* and select Rogers' radio stations across the country (Channel Canada, 2009).

In addition the IPC's Internet TV channel (www.ParalympicSport.TV) provided 150 hours of coverage (Levitz, 2010). The media provided more coverage and the public had a greater interest as 1.1 million viewers watched the sledge hockey game against Italy as the country hoped for a gold medal, and a total of 13.6 million Canadians watched some part of the Paralympic Games (Bell Media, 2010). Reflecting this new interest, when the Canadian television networks hosting the Games did not include live coverage of the Closing Ceremonies in their schedule there was vigorous criticism from across the country. This resulted in the network reversing its decision and in the end 1.5 million viewers watched the Closing Ceremonies (Bell Media, 2010). Part of the difference in media coverage is tied to the significant financial differences between the Olympic and Paralympic Games; it was reported that CTV Rogers paid US$ 93 million for the rights to the Olympic Games and only $50,000 for the Paralympic Games (Levitz, 2010). Also even though the *Globe and Mail* newspaper was part of the 2010 Olympic Broadcast Media Consortium neither it, nor the other newspapers and media provided much coverage of disability in sport during the following non-Paralympic year.

With increased access to sport opportunities for persons with disability, the growth in disability sport and in integrated sport events it might be expected that the press coverage of disability in sport would have much increased also. This proved not to be the case. Out of 837 articles only five were on disability. (See Table 2: Articles on disability by newspaper.) Two newspapers, the *Toronto Star* and the *Globe and Mail* had one article each, and the Sun had three (including the article on the event they sponsored). Also the content of the articles was not primarily on sport itself. One article had a direct focus on the sport of sledge hockey and it was a promotional event supported by the newspaper itself – the *Toronto Sun*. The other four articles had a health focus that included pulmonary fibrosis, Ride 4 Heart, a broken neck and neurofibromatosis. The individuals participating in their sport events had a connection to a health issue such as the athlete participating in the Ride 4 Heart who had a heart attack and was participating to raise funds for research. Typical articles show a disabled person completing a run with headings such as 'A day of triumph at waterfront marathon.' This 2012 story was about a seven year old with cerebral palsy; his mother explained, "Nobody thought he could do the whole thing" (Hinkson, 2012 p. GT1).

Table 2: Articles on disability by newspaper

		National paper	**Tabloid**	**Regional (GTA) Greater Toronto Area**
		Globe& Mail	*Toronto Sun*	*Toronto Star*
Total sport		236	358	242
Daily average		16.8	25.5	17.2
Total on Disability		1	3	1

Gender

Today as there are many women and persons with disabilities in the workforce, on television, and participating in sport in numbers not seen before, it is often assumed that there has been an increasing coverage of women's sport and physical activities in the media, however, this is not the case in the United States and Canada. Messner has analysed gender and sport for over twenty years. His studies on the coverage on women in sport on television news and highlight shows in Los Angeles, California found in 1990 that women's sport represented 5% of the coverage, that 9% of TV airtime in 1999 was on women athletes, but only 1% in 2006 (2010). Surprising the percentage has gone down from 1990! In Canada the 2011 print media coverage were similar to Messner's 1990 television figures.

The statistics on gender are also interesting in the context of the changes in Canada over the past 20 years where many more competitive sports have become available to girls and women. Rowing, ice hockey, ski jumping and boxing are examples of choices that are now available, often after legal battles for inclusion and legislative change such as the repeal of Section 19(2) of the Ontario Human Rights Code where differential treatment for females in the use of sport facilities was ended. There are many more female participants across the country even if overall participation rates in physical activity are declining. To the disappointment of some in 2011 there was coverage (mainly on television) of the new 'sport', Lingerie Football League (www.lflcanada.com) *with young* women playing American NFL style football in skimpy underwear.

The results show there is little coverage of women's sport of all kinds. Only 5.8% of the articles were on women's sporting activities. (See Table 3 Percentage of all sport coverage by gender.) Some were on tennis, ice skating, and a little on golf and amateur sport. Often the press and academic articles assume that media coverage has changed from the 'bad old days' back in the 1990s when coverage was almost exclusively on male sport. However the initial global results that Horky and Nieland have received show that little has changed in twenty years, and Canada, in spite of rights legislation and greater sport opportunities, is no different.

Table 3: Percentage of all sport coverage by gender

	Total number	On males	On females	Gender not specified
Newspapers	42			
Sport articles	837	748	48	41
Percentage		89.4%	5.8%	4.9%
NHL hockey	351= 42% of total			

The results show that there is not much difference between the total number of articles on female sport in the broadsheets and the tabloid. *The Sun* stresses its sport coverage and so it is not surprising to see that *The Sun* has more articles on a daily basis than the other two papers with a total of 358 articles versus 242 for *The Toronto Star* and 236 for the national *Globe and Mail*. However the total numbers of articles on females in sport is low for all the papers; the *Globe and Mail* had 15 articles out of 236, the *Toronto Sun* 15 articles out of 358 which is lower proportionately, and the *Toronto Star* had 18 out of 242 - for a total of 5.8% of newspaper articles on females and 4.9% not specified. (See Table 4 Articles on females by individual newspaper.) The focus in all papers is on professional male sports.

Table 4: Articles on females by individual newspaper

		National paper	Tabloid	Regional (GTA) Greater Toronto Area
		Globe& Mail	*Toronto Sun*	*Toronto Star*
Total sport		236	358	242
Female totals		15	15	18
% of total		6.35	4.19	7.44
Daily average of articles		16.8	25.5	17.2

Issues of limited representation are not restricted to the print press and television, but also found in the film industry. In spite of the extensive coverage of female 'movie stars' in celebrity magazines about who they are, and what they do, 'only 11 percent of 'clearly identifiable protagonists' in 2011's top movies were women, according to one recent study - down from 16 percent in 2002' (Fortini 2012, p. 44). When we examine the presence of women with disabilities in film there are virtually non-existent and in newspaper sport coverage we find few images (Pappous et al, 2012). In spite of the considerable success of Canadian Paralympian athletes on the world stage during the period covered within the 2011 ISP Survey there were no images of women with disabilities.

Social   Change and the Growth of Disability in Sport: Strategies to Support Awareness

Globally there has been a considerable increase recently in the participation of women with disabilities in international sport, although the rates of participation vary widely by region (Lauff, 2012). First, this Canadian data makes it clear that there are few articles on disability issues and on disability in sport in the context of an historical absence of education about disability in journalism, the social sciences and sport programmes, and hence limited disability research. Often the few articles on disability in sport are linked to health or medical issues. For those committed to support sport for all and the inclusion of persons with disabilities it is important that literature, research and curriculum include information and research on disability in sport that will allow for better media coverage.

Second, there are few mentors, senior journalists or scholars, with disability knowledge to support newcomers. Collaboration across a variety of disciplines has been one of the ways the limited number of researchers in disability have been able to collaborate. Support from others - non-researchers or those who are wear two hats as researchers and fulfil other roles as educators, and others who are also advocates active in furthering opportunities in sport for athletes with disability as administrators, coaches, umpires, classifiers, and, in addition, many are active within sport and disability organizations as well. This discipline and practitioner diversity it is hoped will lead to the greater support for students who might be considering doing graduate work or research in the disability area. One hopeful development is the growing aging populations and rising health care costs in many countries has led to an increase in the interest and demand for evidence-based research on the part of governments and not-for-profit NGOs to service disability populations.

However the traditional print media exists in a changing landscape for media and disability. New technology and social networks are un-mediated by traditional publishers and media. This was not part of the ISPS study, but there are thousands of people online who are using websites, blogs, Facebook, YouTube, LinkedIn, Twitter, and QR smartphones scans to present disability in new ways as sales of hardcopy 'traditional' newspapers decline and companies decide to offer 'free' daily tabloids and move to paid on-line subscriptions with multiple platforms (such as the *Globe Unlimited*). Also disability communities and advocates are pushing back and changing the role of the media and reframing disability information and disability in new ways in the new media (Haller, 2010). In addition coverage of athletes with disabilities increasingly includes 'traditional' press coverage with links to their newspaper's websites, videos, blogs, and You Tube as there is recognition of a greater ambiguity in images. While at the same time new publications and research about the Paralympic Games and sport challenges traditional perceptions (Brittain, 2010, 2012; Howe, 2008a; Le Clair, 2011; Legg and Gilbert, 2011) and are increasingly being quoted, or sourced in the media.

Conclusion

This study was part of the 2011 International Sport Press Survey and analysed Canadian national, tabloid and regional newspapers (the *Globe and Mail*, the *Toronto Sun* and the *Toronto Star*) and found that the papers primarily covered professional male sports. Ice hockey and the National Hockey League (NHL) dominated with 42% of the total 837 articles on hockey. The growth of the Paralympic Games, children's and youth soccer, and female ice hockey and sledge hockey is not reflected in the press. There was virtually no coverage of disability in sport in a non-Paralympic year, and coverage of all women's sport represented only 5.8% of the articles. These populations are almost invisible in the press. However evidence-based research can provide analysis that can challenge assumptions and help raise awareness about exclusions to support social change and increased inclusion. Also change is already taking place as disability communities and advocates are framing disability in sport themselves in new ways with new technologies un-mediated and directly reaching out to the general public and scholars.

References

AODA. 2005. Accessibility for Ontarians with Disabilities Act, Available at http://www.mcss.gov.on.ca/en/mcss/programs/accessibility/ (Accessed 13th April 2013)

Bell Media, 2010. 13.6 million Canadians experience 2010 Paralympic Games through Canada's Broadcast media consortium. March 23. Available at http://www.bellmediapr.ca/olympics/releases/release.asp?id=12408&yy yy=2010 (Accessed 13th April 2013)

Brittain, I. 2012, From Stoke Mandeville to Stratford, Champaign, Illinois; Common Ground Publishing.

Brittain, I. 2010, The Paralympic Games explained. London; Routledge.

Brittain, I. 2004, "Perceptions of disability and their impact on involvement in sport for people with disabilities at all levels". Journal of Sport and Social Issues, 28: 429-452.

Brookes, R. 2002. Representing sport, New York; Bloomsbury.

Canadian Broadcasting Commission (CBC). 2011, Riots erupt in Vancouver after Canucks loss: Dozens injured amid scenes of violence, looting. June 16. Available at http://www.cbc.ca/news/canada/british-columbia/story/2011/06/15/bc-stanley-cup-fans-post-game-7.html. (Accessed 13th April 2013)

Channel Canada. 2009. Canada's Olympic Broadcast Media Consortium to deliver record hours of coverage of Vancouver 2010 Paralympic Winter Games. June 17. Available at http://www.channelcanada.com/olympic-broadcast/canadas-olympic-broadcast-media-consortium-to-deliver-record-hours-of-coverage-of-vancouver-2010-paralympic-winter-games. (Accessed 13th April 2013)

Darke, PA. 2004. The changing face of representations of disability in the media, In J Swain, S French, C Barnes & C Thomas (eds.), Disabling barriers – enabling environments, London; Sage, 100-105.

Douglas, M. 1984. Purity and danger: analysis of the concepts of pollution and taboo. London; Routledge.

Fortini, A. 2012. "You've got male: why women writers are creating the most convincing men on the big screen". Details. August; 44.

Foucault, M. 1995. Discipline and punish: the birth of the prison, New York; Vintage.

Foucault, M. 1994. The birth of the clinic: an archaeology of medical perception, New York; Vintage.

Gellately, R. 2001, Backing Hitler, Oxford; Oxford University Press,.

Globe and Mail. 2011. Photos of Vancouver rioting. June 16. Available at http://www.theglobeandmail.com/news/british-columbia/photos-of-vancouver-rioting/article635951/ (Accessed 13th April 2013)

Goffman, E 1963, Stigma: Notes on the management of spoiled identity, London; Routledge.

Haller, B.A. 2010. Representing disability in an ableist world: essays on mass media, Louisville, Kentucky; The Avocado Press.

Hinkson, K. 2012. Scotiabank Toronto Waterfront Marathon: a day of triumph for many. Toronto Star, October 14, p.GT1.

Howe, P.D. 2008. "From inside the newsroom: Paralympic media and the 'production' of elite disability", International review for the sociology of sport, 43(2); 135-150.

Howe, P.D. 2008a. The cultural politics of the Paralympic Movement: through an anthropological lens, New York; Routledge.

Lauff, J. 2012. Participation rates of developing countries in international disability sport: a summary and the importance of statistics for understanding and planning, In JM Le Clair (ed.), Disability in the global sport arena: a sporting chance, London; Routledge, 212-216.

Le Clair, J.M. (ed.) 2012. Disability in the global sport arena: a sporting chance. Routledge, London.

Le Clair, J.M. 2011. Inclusive Research: Dis/ability, Difference and the Paralympic Games, In K Gilbert, O Shantz & D Legg, 'Essays on the Paralympic Movement: certainties and doubts,' International Council of Sport Science and Physical Education [ICSSPE] Bulletin 61; 1-81.

Legg, D & Gilbert, K (eds.) 2011, Paralympic Legacies. Champaign, Illinois; Common Ground Publishing.

Levitz, A. 2010. Paralympic TV coverage to set new records. The Canadian Press, March 13. Available at
http://sports.ca.msn.com/olympics/article.aspx?cp-documentid=23638343 (Accessed 13th April 2013)

Messner, M. 2010. "Dropping the ball on covering women's sports". Huffington Post, June 3 Available at http://www.huffingtonpost.com/michael-messner/dropping-the-ball-on-cove_b_599912.html (Accessed 13th April 2013)

Nieland, J-W & Horky, T 2011, Survey of the sports press 2011: principles and definitions of coding parameters'. Personal correspondence, pp.1-12.

Pappous, A, de Léséleuc, E and Marcellini, A. 2012. "Contested issues in research on the media coverage of female Paralympic athletes". In Le Clair. J.M. (ed.) Disability in the global sport arena: a sporting chance, London; Routledge, 114-123.

Rapp, R & Ginsberg, F. 2010. "The human nature of disability", American Anthropologist, 112(4); 517.

Rioux, M. 2012. Disability rights and change in a global perspective, In Le Clair. J.M. (ed.) Disability in the global sport arena: a sporting chance, London; Routledge, 28-35.

Sun, S & Le Clair, J.M. 2011. Legacies and tensions after the 2008 Beijing Paralympic Games, In D Legg & K Gilbert (eds.), Paralympic Games: legacy and restoration. Sport and Society, Champaign, Illinois; Common Ground Publishing, 111-129.

Schantz, OJ & Gilbert, K. 2001. "An idea misconstrued: newspaper coverage of the Atlanta Paralympic Games in France and Germany", Sociology of Sport, 18(1); 69-74.

Titchkosky, T. 2007. Reading and writing disability differently: the textured life of embodiment, Toronto; University of Toronto Press.

United Nations Enable. 2012. 'Factsheet on persons with disabilities'.
http://www.who.int/disabilities/world_report/2011/en/index.html

World Health Organization (WHO) and the World Bank. 2011. 'World Report on
        Disability'.
        http://www.who.int/disabilities/world_report/2011/en/index.html

Chapter 11: Spanish Media Coverage of the Beijing Paralympic Games

Josep Solves Almela (Universidad CEU Cardenal Herrera, Spain)

Introduction

There can be little doubt that the media may help to perpetuate stereotyped representations of disability by conveying sensations of pity, weakness and dependence, or on the other hand, promote more positive images, thus contributing to the social inclusion process (Pappous, *et al.* 2011).

The GIDYC[1], or Group for Research into Disability and Communication of the Universidad CEU Cardenal Herrera in Valencia, Spain, has since 2005 been analysing the way Spanish media treat disability, and has already made a systematic study on the news coverage of the Paralympic Games in Beijing in the Spanish media. Several articles from this have been published and its final monograph was presented in June 2012 (Rius & Solves, 2009; Sánchez & Mercado, 2011; Solves, 2012). At the present time we are getting ready to make an analysis of the reporting of the London Paralympic Games which has been backed by the International Paralympic Committee. We believe that this research could be a good testing ground for later European-scale studies on sport, disability and the media.

This text will briefly explain the methodology and conclusions of our study of the Spanish press coverage of the Beijing Paralympic Games.

Methodology

Hypothesis

Our study covered three major aspects of interest:

    a.   The conduct of the media as production agencies, that is, their economic conduct in respect of the event as goods. The basic hypothesis in this respect was that its interest would be meagre, taking into account its history, and that the involvement of the Spanish Paralympic Committee, through advertising or of other kinds of proposals, would be *vital* for

guaranteeing the presence of the Games in current events making the news.

b. The way the media work as regards the event as a newsworthy item. We understood that the Paralympic Games had good news value, i.e., that this was a relevant news event, but we also thought that the news organisations would be discouraged from handling it properly for two reasons: the high cost entailed by this and the competition of other sports events with a foreseeably higher audience.

c. The differences that would be seen when comparing the coverage of the Beijing Games with the treatment of the previous Paralympic Games in Athens, as well as that of the Olympic Games themselves in China, which had been held a few weeks before. We assumed that the news coverage of the Olympic Games would have been much greater and much better than the treatment given to the Paralympics.

We also expected the daily sports newspapers to be the ones giving the event most space and resources, and that the radio and television would devote very little time to the Games, except for the *RTVE* –the public channels– which had the broadcasting rights. We thought that the competition of other sports events taking place on the same dates as the Beijing Paralympic Games –the football league, the Davis Cup Tennis etc.– would have an enormous influence on this. It all led us to expect that the treatment of the Games would be very similar to the coverage of the Athens event in 2004, unless any new aspects were involved, for example, the implementation of a different and more "aggressive" communication policy by the Spanish Paralympic Committee.

Universe and Sample(s)

The option chosen as regards the period covered by the analysis was to include the material published by the media in the sample or samples from 5th to 18th September 2008, both inclusive, these being the days on which the Games were held, as well as the day before and immediately after, which would give us a greater guarantee for monitoring the coverage observed.

The option chosen for sampling was to set up a specific sample for each major support. The press items chosen were the references published during the period stated in the newspapers *El País, El Mundo, El Periódico, Abc, La Vanguardia, La Razón* and *Público* – the nationwide Spanish general press with the largest circulation. It also included the state-wide sports publications *Marca, As, Sport*, and *Mundo Deportivo*, and the regional papers *Superdeporte* (in Valencia) and *Estadio Deportivo* (in Seville), a sample of the coverage in the specialised press, also coinciding with the six daily newspapers with which the Spanish Paralympic Committee had reached an agreement for covering the games, as will be explained below.

To observe the radio news coverage, the midday news programmes of *RNE-1*, the *Cadena SER*, the *Cadena COPE* and *Onda Cero* for the dates stated were used. For our analysis these represented the coverage of the most widely heard news programmes according to the General Media Study[2], for the stations with the greatest audience. The sample also included the possibility of analysing the differences between a more commercial *private* approach, and an (in theory) more *committed public* one. Since the first data analysed led to deducing a fairly scant radio coverage of the Beijing Paralympic Games, in the midday news on the stations observed, we opted for incorporating a specific survey of the coverage given by these same stations in their specialised nationwide sports programmes.

Lastly, the television sample was made up of the daily information slots of the six public and private nationwide networks, and the first channels of the six main regional stations, over August and September 2008.

Analysis of contents

Due to the nature of our study subject, the news on disability in the sports competitions at the Beijing Paralympic Games, the analysis should unquestionably be made with some *interdisciplinarity,* without failing to include a qualitative interpretation in any case.

To this end, we on the one hand accepted positivist theses, as we were dealing with reality from empirical premises, at the same time as collecting information on diverse variables with the aim of establishing their complex relations. In this respect we believe that the analysis of contents can be considered systematic without further discussion, as these were handled in the same way in the study of the variables and isolated elements, with exactly the same possibilities of being accepted and included in the analysis (Krippendorff, 2004).

Neither did we relinquish interpreting the data obtained with the aim of finding the ultimate response to our hypotheses in these interpretations. That is why we also included an analysis of the discourse from the conceptual categories which have been applied to the news items for a more qualitative analysis (Van Dijk, 2008).

Discussion

What image of the Beijing Paralympic Games did the Spanish media give? What was the *interest* displayed by news companies in the Games? How did the communication strategy of the Spanish Paralympic Committee affect that interest and the coverage of the events? Above all, did the media treatment abide by the usual canons of journalism, especially sports reporting, or are any major differences seen - stressing, for example, the athletes' handicaps, and tending to stigmatise them?

Results

Normalising Journalism, but Not Excessively So

Our research basically concludes that the media provided an integrating view of the Games, both in the sense of envisaging the event as another item in the agenda of current events, and through not tending to stress disability, either in the use of language or in the way illustrations were handled. Two qualifications to this *normality* should nevertheless be added, which we shall explain below: the *exceptional* treatment that the regional sports press gave to the events and their protagonists and the scant information about these in the other Spanish media.

Indeed, the exception to this *normalising* coverage of the Games was probably the press medium and very particularly the specialised regional (sports) press, by devoting much more space to the competitions and the athletes than the other media (radio and TV channels) and considering the facts and people involved from a much closer angle. What we have called *vicinity anchorage* –or news interest through geographical proximity and feeling of belonging– determined a specific model in the coverage of the Games. This involved a type of story of greater length and proximity, but above all, one which preferably tended towards *personalisation* of the events and inclusion of life stories in the narration. In this type of news story one can see more clearly than in any other the narrator's *involvement* as a result of two facets in the sports event itself: cultural identity and the impairment itself.

These features are found in the regional specialised press to such an extent that this developed a type of story that we have gone so far as to qualify as *epic*. This is characterised by the creation of heroes from the life stories of many of the athletes, distinguished by the aforementioned involvement of the narrator, and represented in the tendency to conclude in a happy ending which at least partly conceals any negative valuations that could have gone along with the sports details: failures or defeats.

In the case of the specialised press, and very markedly in the regional sports press, all of this forms a different narrative model to the usual one, the one found in the general press. But this is a *peculiarity* that we cannot consider negative, quite the opposite in fact. These papers built heroes and reported on their deeds to us perhaps with greater drive than they do with other sportspersons, but then again, since this involves adapted sports, and athletes with disabilities, how could this be considered unacceptable? The very circumstances, the athletes' lives and their daily efforts to get over their setbacks make it unavoidable –and, doubtlessly positive- to turn them into examples, good examples.

At the other end of the scale in the sports press a negative element could be seen: the negligible presence, sometimes absence, of any appearances of the Games in the media with greatest audiences, with the exception of *TVE* - state TV. Some companies, such as *Antena 3* and *Onda Cero*, did not give even a second to these games in their midday news. Most of them provided a token coverage in which it was considered enough to inform of certain medals or records, but certainly not all. A factor limiting this *process* was the communication strategy implemented by the Spanish Paralympic Committee.

A Vital CPE Communication Strategy

The CPE –Spanish Paralympic Committee– put an all-important communication approach into action which consisted on one hand of defraying the expenses of the special correspondents and also inserting advertising in six of these papers, four state sports papers and two regional ones.[3] This endeavour to a great extent conditioned the business and journalistic decisions of the papers affected, to the extent of becoming, in our view, one of the fundamental reasons for the proper treatment that we observed in the Spanish sports press.

The PCE strategy therefore managed to ensure that the state sports press gave the Games appropriate coverage and also helped the regional press to develop a type of narration of the Games and their protagonists which has proven to be highly beneficial for adapted sport and the persons practising this.

The Journalistic Epic Narration of the Regional Sports Press

In the press's case, our study concludes that three standardised forms of responding to the information challenge of the Games from a business and journalistic angle can clearly be seen, i.e. there are three models: the one found in the general state press, that of the specialised state press and that of the regional sports press.

Table 1[4]: News coverage, general press

Header	Lines	Pieces	Pictures
ABC	922	20	12
El Mundo	726	16	10
La Razón	507	14	10
El País	316	10	6
El Periódico	305	8	10
La Vanguardia	301	11	7
Público	117	13	15
Total	**3194**	**92**	**70**

The general country-wide press dealt with the Games as an event of little significance, which almost has to be included out of a sense of duty, but which does not arouse the interest found in major sports events. This can be seen in the analysis of the data, that is, the number of pages, pieces, lines of text or photos that this type of press devoted to the event, but also in the fact that the pieces were mostly brief or news items; there were very few reports and interviews, and the photos included were very small, and both these and the information itself went unsigned in most cases. We also found that the information was relegated to the back pages of the newspapers and very seldom seen on the cover, in spite of the great success achieved by the Spanish Paralympic athletes.

The positive aspect is the lexical and graphic normality with which the general press referred to the Games: the linguistic forms seem to have absolutely ruled out certain expressions, adjectives or nouns with pejorative connotations, and the photos tend not to stress any difference between the Paralympic athletes and other sportspersons, i.e., their disability is not stressed in the photos (Pappous *et. al.*, 2011). This trend can particularly be seen in the headlines, which basically cover the sports categories, i.e. are comparable to any other information of this sort.

Table 2: News coverage, sports press

Header	Lines	Pieces	Pictures
As	1494	40	35
Marca	1488	24	28
Mundo Deportivo	1384	23	30
Sport	2413	44	38
Total	**6779**	**131**	**131**
Superdeporte	2494	83	96
Estadio deportivo	3591	90	110
Total	**6085**	**173**	**206**
Total for all	**12864**	**302**	**337**

The nationwide sports press dealt with the Games somewhat better than the previously mentioned papers. This was first of all because their greater specialisation quite understandably meant that they had to include the Paralympics in their contents; secondly, because there was an agreement with the CPE binding them to do this, above all in the daily papers that we have examined. Taking into account nevertheless that a good deal of the cost of covering the Games was defrayed by the CPE, the information in these papers was fairly meagre, if this is compared with the coverage of other sports events, mainly football, in spite of the League not having started yet.

The sector that did indeed pull out all the stops for the Games was the regional sports press. We believe that the main reason for this is the proximity of these media, that is, their greater specialisation in events and people geographically and culturally closer to the audience. We looked at the newspapers *Estadio Deportivo* in Seville and *Superdeporte* in Valencia, but we consider that there are sound reasons for believing that these same characteristics in the other local press and especially the most local sports press make them inclined to produce a discourse with greater normalisation within the exceptional nature of Paralympic sport.

In these papers, apart from superior news coverage (more days' news, more pages, news items and lines written than the other daily papers) certain specific characteristics can be noted, such as drawing up exhaustive profiles of Paralympic athletes with possibilities of winning medals, the scarce attention to anecdotal news items or including reports of news interest in the setting of the Games.

As regards the genres used for narrating the stories, there were two ways of tackling the press information. One is the news item, with the same criteria as would be applied to any sports event. This provides the news normality which we have referred to so much. The other is what we call *journalistic epic narration,* in which the chronicle is mixed with the *life story* and *opinion* in more exaggerated terms than the sort normally found in sports press.

      Paralímpicos de Pekín 2008". Revista de Estudios de Comunicación, 16(31); 89-107.

Solves, J. (Coord.) 2012. Tratamiento de los Juegos Paralímpicos de 2008 en los medios españoles. CERMI-Cinca, Madrid. Available at http://www.cermi.es/esES/ColeccionesCermi/Cermi.es/Paginas/Inicio.aspx?TSMEIdPub=99. (Accessed 13th April 2013)

Van Dijk, T. 2008. Discourse and Power. Basingstoke, UK; Palgrave.

Chapter 12: A Great Leap: The Evolution of China's Involvement in the Paralympic Games

Joshua R. Pate (James Madison University, USA)

Introduction

China's quick ascent to become the world's leading power in the Paralympic Games is worthy of scholarly investigation considering it did not begin competing in the Games until 1984 in New York (Brittain, 2010). The nation established the Chinese Sports Association for Disabled Athletes in 1983, just prior to the 1984 Paralympic Games. Two decades later, China finished first in the 2004 Athens Paralympic Games medal count and hosted the Games four years later after winning the bid to land the 2008 Olympic and Paralympic Games. China, in fact, led the medal count in each summer Paralympic Games from 2004-2012, increasing the distance between itself and the second-place nation in each of the three Games.

The purpose of this paper is to explore China's evolution of participation in the Paralympic Games in comparison to its evolution of disability rights as a nation. Specifically, this paper explores China's evolution through the three stages of the Paralympic Games as identified by Prystupa, Prystupa, and Bolasch (2006). The three stages relay the Paralympic Games through establishment (1960-72), growth (1976-1992), and stabilization (1996-present) in accordance with quantity of events, types of competition, and disability classification. The remainder of this paper outlines the three stages of growth in the Paralympic Games, followed by a comparison of China's state during those three stages with regard to its treatment of and opportunities for people with disabilities.

The Paralympic Games: Three Stages of Growth

The Paralympic Games began as the Stoke Mandeville Games in 1948 when Ludwig Guttmann, director of the National Spinal Injuries Centre at Stoke Mandeville Hospital in Buckinghamshire, England, organized an archery competition between 16 competitors from his hospital and the Star and Garter Home, a facility for injured military veterans (Brittain, 2010; Gold & Gold, 2007). The archery competition was held the same day as the 1948 Olympic Games

Opening Ceremony in London. Guttmann extended invitations to individuals at five hospitals for the 1949 competition that included archery and wheelchair netball, and the event gained international traction over the following decade. Stoke Mandeville Games participants came from Canada, Finland, France, Israel and the Netherlands by 1953. The United States sent a team to the Games in 1955, and Australia began competition in 1957. The international recognition was solidified when the International Olympic Committee (IOC) awarded the Fearnley Cup to the Stoke Mandeville Games in 1956 for outstanding achievement in the service of Olympic ideals (Gold & Gold).

The international movement shifted the focus of the Stoke Mandeville Games away from competitions among hospital patients and toward the general population of people with disabilities. Furthermore, a committee was formed to formally organize a greater number of events and the 1960 Stoke Mandeville Games were held in Rome, the Olympic host city. Therefore, the 1960 Stoke Mandeville Games marked the beginning of the stages of Paralympic growth, according to Prystupa et al. (2006), with regard to the summer Paralympic Games.

Establishment (1960–1972)

The Establishment Stage is from 1960 to 1972, encompassing the first four Paralympic Games (1960, 1964, 1968, 1972). Major themes identified by Prystupa et al. (2006) within the Establishment Stage are an increase in quantity of sports and an increase in classifications. The number of sports offered at the Games increased from eight to 10 during this stage, and the number of sport competitions increased from 111 to 188 (Paralympic.org, n.d.a; Prystupa et al., 2006).

It was during this time that China operated as the "People's Republic of China" but was known internationally as "Communist China" or "Red China." The Chinese government set forth the Great Leap Forward in 1958, which was a social transformation focused on surpassing Great Britain in industry (Peng, 1987). The economic push was set in motion under the premise that lower-class society would organize as a production unit for the country. The social shift can be blamed for massive effects on China's people, as enhanced workloads, poor living conditions, and extreme poverty among peasants led to reduced fertility rates and nearly doubled the national crude death rate—both of which were reversed trends from what occurred prior to the Great Leap (Peng, 1987). This trend left people with disabilities somewhat of an afterthought in China at the time. A strong example, relating to this paper, came forth in 1960 when the invitation was extended to China to send a team to participate in the Stoke Mandeville Games in Rome. China's government officials declined (Gold & Gold, 2007).

Such response reiterated China's stance toward disability at the time, despite the nation claiming it has offered disability sport programming since the 1950s (Brittain, 2006). Discriminatory terms such as "can fei" were used in language toward the disability population, which translates as "handicapped" and "useless" (Zhang, 2007, para. 2). However, in the later years of Chairman Mao's rule and culminating with his death in 1976, China's Great Leap Forward slowed. In 1972, the People's Republic of China was admitted into the United Nations (U.N.), a key date progressing the country's acknowledgment of disability.

This first stage of the Paralympic growth process was a period of establishment for the Games while organizers began to manage an international competition. Yet, for China, it was a period of refusal. The government refused to participate on an international stage such as the Stoke Mandeville Games, which was in direct contradiction to China's embracement of sport. The Mao regime placed heavy emphasis on strong and fit bodies as a reflection of the country's strong and fit stature (Brittain, 2006). Therefore, sending a team to the Stoke Mandeville Games to show China had a population of people with disabilities would risk damaging the pristine perception Mao and the government aimed to send. In other words, China sending people with disabilities to take such an international stage shows weakness and that the Chinese people may not all be strong and fit, as Mao wanted to portray. Still, China's 1972 admission into the U.N. forecasted its transition into the second stage. For the Paralympic Games, it was a period of growth. For China, it was an accelerated combination stage of establishment and growth. As the country ignored disability sport on a global scale, other countries embraced a global establishment of disability sport. Such a refusal reinforced the critical perspective that China suppressed disability rights within its own walls. To combat such a perspective, the country shifted its outward embrace toward international disability sport and began competing—and winning—in the Paralympic Games.

Growth Stage (1976–1988)

The Growth Stage was from 1976 to 1988 and encompassed the second block of four Paralympic Games (1976, 1980, 1984, 1988). Prystupa et al. (2006) identified an increase in the number of athletes competing, an increase in impairment groups recognized in competition, a subsequent increase in classifications, and a greater awareness of inclusion within the Paralympic Games. Athletes with visual impairments and amputations as well as athletes with other physical disabilities were included in the Games of 1976, and athletes with cerebral palsy competed for the first time in the 1980 Games (Brittain, 2010). As Prystypa et al. (2006) noted, including more disabilities also increased the number of competitions and classifications. In fact, the 1976 Games doubled the number of competitions (376) compared to the previous Games in 1972 (Prystupa et al.).

With regard to China during this stage, the Communist party lost much of its power and control when Mao died in 1976. Just six years later, in 1982, China's constitution was enacted and the Law on the Protection of Disabled Persons was passed, both of which provide general principles of protection of the rights of people with disabilities for rehabilitation, education, employment, culture, welfare, access, and legal liability (Inclusion of People with Disabilities in China, 2009; Zhang, 2007).

Beyond general legislation for disability rights, China established the Chinese Sports Association for Disabled Athletes in 1983. The association was organized just as the nation was preparing for the 1984 Paralympic Games, which was the first time China competed in the Games. The 1984 Games were split between Stoke Mandeville (spinal cord impairments) and New York (amputee, cerebral palsy, les autres and visually impaired), and China earned 22 medals in its debut in New York (Brittain, 2010).

By the following Games in 1988, the Chinese government said its disability population was transforming into a self-sufficient segment of society. In a joint effort between the Chinese government and non-governmental organizations, the First National Sampling Survey on Disability polled the nation's population and found that 4.9% of the population had a disability (Zhang, 2007). Results showed that 50.2% of people with disabilities in urban areas (60.6% in rural areas) were employed in 1987. Similarly, a shift in language reflected the alleged cultural transition, as "can ji ren" became the term used in public and in government documents toward the disability population, a term that means "persons with disabilities" (Zhang, para. 2). Athletically, in the 1988 Paralympic Games, China earned 43 medals in Seoul, doubling its medal count from the previous Games.

China's development of supporting disability and performing in the Paralympic Games followed a similar pathway of growth during this stage as the Paralympic Games themselves. The Games nearly doubled in the number of competitors from approximately 1,600 athletes in 1976 to approximately 3,000 athletes in 1988 (Brittain, 2010). The number of sports and therefore competitions expanded, and the number of disabilities included grew. Similarly, China appeared to become receptive to disability within its borders at a rapid pace, positioning the nation in a role of playing catch up to the Paralympic Movement. As the Movement completed the Growth Stage, China combined its second stage into an Establishment and Growth Stage.

Such a rapid pace of acceptance, support, and ultimately success in Paralympic sport should be examined with a critical lens. Pockets of inequality and double standards emerge relating to Chinese government-funded organizations that serve people with disabilities, experiences of people with disabilities, and higher education opportunities for people with disabilities within the country (Brittain, 2006). As an example, Brittain (2006) cites evidence of disability organizations refusing the help of volunteers who also have disabilities as well as media evidence that education officials' support of medical and fitness exams as prerequisites for attending university may have prevented people with disabilities from attending and potentially encouraging others to attend. Furthermore, the motive behind China's enhanced dedication toward displaying the athletic successes of people with disabilities is questioned. Brittain (2006) argues that China, on one hand, strives to position itself as a world leader that protects all of its citizens; yet it could also be portrayed as a nation that is attempting to hide its social issues, particularly those of people with disabilities that are jobless and do not fit within the economic superpower's identity, and use those disability sport success stories to shame the remainder of the disability population for not reaching that level.

Socially, those questions remain. Athletically, China's dedication to competition at the international level and Paralympic Games positioned the nation to proceed into the third stage alongside the Paralympic growth, and surpass its peer nations.

Stabilization (1992–2000)

The Stabilization Stage began in 1992 and continued through the 2000 Paralympic Games, including the 1992, 1996, and 2000 Games. Prystupa et al. (2006) identified this period as one when the governance and classification system were stabilized for a more consistent and manageable Paralympic Games. The International Paralympic Committee (IPC) governing body was instituted and, in 2000, began working more closely with the International Olympic Committee (IOC) with regard to host cities and governance processes. In 2001, an agreement was reached between the IPC and IOC to host the Paralympic Games and Olympic Games in the same city and have the bidding process to include plans for both events. A functional classification system was also introduced, "allowing athletes with specific disabilities (amputee athletes, athletes with limb paralysis, athletes with different movement impairments and with cerebral palsy consequences) to compete against each other if they had similar levels of dysfunction" (Prystupa et al., p. 78). This shift reduced inflated competition numbers (from 792 competitions in 1988 to 490 in 1992), aligned many of the Paralympic sports with Olympic sports, and redefined classification from a medical-based model emphasizing disability to more of a social-based model emphasizing ability (Prystupa et al.).

This period of stabilization was reflective of an outsider's view in China offering rehabilitation services to 4.33 million people with disabilities (Zhang, 2007). Additionally, 77% of children with disabilities were enrolled in school (Zhang), which was below the national percentage of all children but still signified consistent service and opportunity for various ages of people with disabilities. The plateau that set China above other countries in terms of Paralympic performance came during the first year of the Establishment Period, 1992, which was also China's only Paralympic Games that it did not improve its medal count, possibly due to sending a smaller representation of athletes (Brittain, 2006). Following the 1992 Games, while the stabilization applied to China's services early within the stage, the nation surpassed expectations and moved into what this researcher calls an Advancement Period within this stage.

Considering the criteria Prystupa et al. (2006) used for stage classification, China's Advancement Period extends to the 2012 Paralympic Games in London to encompass China's ascent to the top-performing nation in the Games. Similarly, the nation outwardly claimed a dedication toward disability rights and went beyond that with its services toward disability sport. Athletically, in 2001, Beijing was awarded the 2008 Olympic and Paralympic Games. While some may argue the Olympic focus carries the bulk of the weight during the bidding process, potential host cities and venues must relay accessibility plans and designs throughout the bid. Therefore, that Beijing was awarded the bid reveals the vast distance that China traveled as a nation from its 1960 refusal to participate in disability sport to its 2001 bidding war victory to host the Paralympic Games.

Socially, this period was a time in which China appeared to focus on its services toward people with disabilities. From 2001 to 2005, 5.1 million people with disabilities received rehabilitation services, an increase of nearly 1 million people from the previous five years (Zhang, 2007). In 2003, all of the 30 provincial congresses issued disability regulations to preserve disability rights and ensure legal mandates were followed. That same year, according to the government, 83.9% of people with disabilities were employed (Zhang, 2007).

During this period, the Beijing Municipal People's Congress passed the first local legislation relating to physical accessibility in 2004, the Beijing Regulation on Construction and Management of Barrier-Free Facilities (Gold & Gold, 2007). The passage of legislation went beyond sport as it showed the nation was accepting and dedicated to providing accessible facilities for sport use, perhaps laying groundwork for welcoming the Olympic and Paralympic Games but also increasing public awareness of disability. Such legislation was likely an outward ploy to show the IOC and IPC the country was addressing accessibility concerns not because of landing both Games, but because the idea of inclusion needed work within the nation's walls. Additionally, this time period coincides with a period in the Paralympic Movement when the shift in athletic competition went from more traditional powers such as Australia, Canada, France, Germany, Great Britain, Japan, Sweden, and the United States to a period when first-time athletes from China, Egypt, Iraq, and Ukraine experienced success (Prystupa et al., 2006). China, perhaps, wanted to rise above all of those countries by displaying it was taking legislative action that other rising nations in Paralympic sport had not, and it was taking athletic action by putting the best product in the field of competition.

Performance in the Paralympic Games is where China's dedication toward people with disabilities can be measured and visible. China placed first in the medal count at the 2004 Paralympic Games in Athens, earning 141 total medals compared to the 94 earned by second-place Great Britain. Meanwhile, the dedication toward elite athletic performance continued as the China Disability Sports Training Center was built in 2007 and is the world's largest facility of its kind. As of 2012, approximately half of the Chinese Paralympic team members trained at the facility (Ru, 2012). Having the proper athletic training facilities assisted in the ascension of success as in 2008, when China hosted the Paralympic Games, it won 211 medals to place first, more than doubling Great Britain's 102 medals.

The Paralympic Games underwent a period of stabilization from 1992 to 2000 as China also made an attempt at social stabilization with regard to its treatment of people with disabilities through legislation and opportunities. Yet, China continued its accelerated trend well past the 2000 Paralympic Games by focusing on elite athletic training more than any other nation. Regardless of whether China's actual service of people with disabilities has been for legitimate assistance or propaganda to enhance perception, the country has become the world leader in Paralympic performance in the Games since the Stabilization Stage (Prystypa et al., 2006).

Conclusion

As of 2012, China had more than 83 million people with disabilities and approximately 6.2 million people with disabilities received rehabilitation services, yet another increase of 1 million people served in a five-year period (China Disabled Persons' Federation, 2008, n.d.). Sports are also part of the "national strategy of promoting equal enjoyment of basic public services and building social security and social service system for disabled persons" (China Disabled Persons' Federation, 2012, para. 1). China's performance in the Paralympic Games reflects sports' place in that national strategy. The nation sent 282 athletes to the 2012 Paralympic Games in London, ranging in age from 15 to 50 years (Ru, 2012). For the third consecutive summer Paralympic Games, China finished first in the overall medal count, earning 231 medals, and led with 95 gold medals. Great Britain was second in the overall medal count with 120, but was third in gold medals earned with 34. Russia had 102 overall medals, 36 of which were gold. The performance reveals China's continued acceleration—or Advancement Period—in accordance to athletic commitment as each of the last three Paralympic Games has been dominated by China, and the nation has increased its margin of victory each time.

It may not be noteworthy that a nation is consistently outperforming all other nations at the Paralympic Games, but the fact that China is the world leader in Paralympic performance is certainly cause for examination considering its history. China followed the traditional path of Paralympic sport growth, but in a delayed manner. While the world was in the Establishment Stage with regard to Paralympic sport—and disability rights, for that matter—China was in a Refusal Stage. The government refused to support a disability population to compete on an international stage as deaths resulted from the Communist government rule. As the rest of the world was in the Growth Stage of Paralympic sport, China combined its establishment along with growth for rapid increases in legislation as well as sport achievement for people with disabilities. The transformation followed the death of Chairman Mao and a weakening of power in the Communist party.

From the 1992 Paralympic Games until 2000, the Paralympic Movement was in a Stabilization Stage where governance and classification were reformed. Similarly, China experienced stabilization culturally with regard to disability. Yet, China moved past the 2000 Games by shifting into an Advancement Period and dedicating resources toward accelerating its elite Paralympic performance. Paralympic results confirmed China's dedication, and the emphasis now shifts toward the future and what peer nations can do to catch up with China.

China spent the first 30 years of the Paralympic Movement trailing the world, but has now surpassed the world and is setting the standard for athletic performance in disability sport. The critical eye asks simply: Why? Under Mao, athletic and fit bodies were considered essential because it reflected the body of China as a nation (Brittain, 2006). Disability sport did not fit under this premise. However, in 1984, a shift toward elite sport success—both in the Olympic and Paralympic Games—altered the course of Chinese sport. The country re-emerged in the Olympic Games in Los Angeles after a 32-year absence and won 15 gold medals to place fourth in the medal count (Fan Hong, 2005). It was the same year China elected to compete in the Paralympic Games in New York. Following unanticipated successes in both Games, the nation declared a slogan and dream to "Develop elite sport and make China a superpower in the world" (Fan Hong, 2005, p. 511). While the Great Leap Forward was nearly 50 years in the nation's mirror and considered a miserable failure, dreams and aspirations of establishing China as a global elite power—in anything—remained. It is argued here that residual effects of a failed Great Leap Forward were finally realized through sport, and more specifically disability sport. China attempted to mask its social injustices from the 1950s and 1960s by becoming a global superpower in industry, specifically targeting to surpass Great Britain, and failed. The failure included ignoring a population of people with disabilities due to the emphasis on the strong and fit body, both literally and figuratively. In exploring China's evolution in the Paralympic Games, it becomes evident the nation had a similar goal in leaping forward by embracing and ultimately dominating disability sport, both to display its stronghold on global competition, ironically that has also been traditionally paced by Great Britain, as well as mask its social injustices that continue to prevent people with disabilities from full equality.

Future research and attention must be directed toward communications as the London 2012 Paralympic Games presented a new turn toward Paralympic growth with media as a centralized component. Whether media can be the facilitator for other nations to catch up with China by promoting greater national resources in places like the more traditional Paralympic powers of Australia, Great Britain, Russia, and the United States is left for exploration. With increased media coverage of the Paralympic Games will come greater expectations for performance. Therefore, further examination of the Paralympic Movement and China's performance-based dominance beyond 2012 is essential to continue monitoring China's upward movement and how peer nations are responding.

References

Brittain, I. 2006. "Paralympic success as a measure of national social and economic development". International Journal of Eastern Sports and Physical Education, 10; 38-47.

Brittain, I. 2010. The Paralympic Games explained. New York: Routledge.

China Disabled Persons' Federation. 2008. Statistical communiqué on development of the work for persons with disabilities in 2009. Available at
http://www.cdpf.org.cn/english/statistics/content/2008-04/10/content_84890.htm (Accessed 13th April 2013)

China Disabled Persons' Federation. 2012. Sports. Available at
http://www.cdpf.org.cn/english/sports/content/2012-11/02/content_84857.htm (Accessed 13th April 2013)

China Disabled Persons' Federation. n.d. China Disabled Persons' Federation. Available at
http://www.cdpf.org.cn/english/aboutus/aboutus.htm (Accessed 13th April 2013)

Fan Hong, Ping Wu, & Huan Xiong. 2005. "Beijing ambitions: An analysis of the Chinese elite sports system and its Olympic strategy for the 2008 Olympic Games". International Journal of the History of Sport, 22; 510-529.

Gold, J. R., & Gold, M. M. 2007. "Access for all: The rise of the Paralympic Games". The Journal of the Royal Society for the Promotion of Health, 127(3); 133-141.

Inclusion of People with Disabilities in China. 2009. Fact Sheet. International Labour Organization. Available at http://www.ilo.org/wcmsp5/groups/public/@ed_emp/@ifp_skills/docum ents/publication/wcms_112380.pdf (Accessed 13th April 2013)

Paralympic.org. n.d.a. IPC Historical Results Database. International Paralympic Committee. Available at http://www.paralympic.org/Athletes/Results (Accessed 13th April 2013)

Paralympic.org. n.d.b. Stoke Mandeville & New York 1984. International Paralympic Committee. Available at http://www.paralympic.org/paralympic-games/stoke-mandeville-new-york-1984 (Accessed 13th April 2013)

Peng, X. 1987. "Demographic consequences of the Great Leap Forward in China's provinces". Population and Development Review, 14(4); 639-670.

Prystupa, E., Prystupa, T., & Bolach, E. 2006. "Development trends in sports for the disabled: The case of summer Paralympics". Human Movement, 7(1); 77-83.

Ru, W. 2012. (August 13). We shall overcome. China Daily. Available at http://www.chinadaily.com.cn/china/2012chinaface/2012-08/13/content_15669055.htm (Accessed 13th April 2013)

Zhang, E. 2007. The protection of rights of people with disabilities in China. Disability Word, 28. Available at http://www.disabilityworld.org/01_07/china.shtml (Accessed 13th April 2013)

Chapter 13: Legacy or Fallacy?: Paralympic Stakeholders' Hopes for the London 2012 Paralympic Games' Legacy

David Purdue (Independent Paralympic and Disability Sport Researcher, UK)

Introduction

It has been alleged that London 2012's legacy "offers us a once in a lifetime opportunity to make a meaningful difference for over 10 million disabled people in this country" (ODI, 2011:2). However, legacy is highly complex in terms of conceptualisation and measurable delivery. Moreover, upon closer inspection are perceptions of the London 2012 legacy for disabled people somewhat over-ambitious and as such allowing rhetoric to overtake reality in terms of what an elite disability sport festival can deliver? This chapter seeks to critically reflect upon the London 2012 Paralympic Games' legacy hopes as formulated by Paralympic stakeholders. In doing so, legacy expectations and their feasibility are held up to scrutiny in a bid to demystify legacy ambitions.

To begin, the limited body of pertinent extant social research undertaken into apparent previous Paralympic Games' legacies will be noted. This provides a foundation on which to disseminate and explore empirical data directly relating to the power and scope of influence that Paralympic legacies are perceived to command. This reveals the complexities incumbent within Paralympic legacy.

Previous Paralympic Games' legacies

There exists a rather limited body of Paralympic legacy social research. This can be seen to stem from both the paucity of social research into Paralympic sport as a whole, and the relative lack of attention paid to legacy compared to the more deeply examined topics of classification (Howe and Jones, 2006) and media coverage (Brittain, 2010; Thomas and Smith, 2009) as relating to Paralympic sport. This paper highlights and seeks to begin to address this lacuna.

Legg and Gilbert's (2011) edited collection *Paralympic Legacies* represents a recent concerted effort to address the topic of Paralympic legacy. However, the content and structure of *Paralympic Legacies* is revealing of some fundamental questions at the core of Paralympic legacy research.

When defining the topic of legacy, in regard to the Paralympic Games, Gilbert and Legg (2011a) state 'For the purposes of this book we have chosen…"that which is left behind" [Merriam Webster Dictionary, 2009] as our definitive open ended [Legacy] meaning' (Gilbert and Legg, 2011a:5). However, in doing so, this raises the epistemological concern that anything and everything could be framed as a constituent and/or creator of legacy. The immense range of factors and social constructions that can be collected under the umbrella term 'legacy' as well as its temporal dimension makes legacy difficult to specify and quantify. This is not a criticism of Gilbert and Legg, but instead reflects a considerable issue enveloping Paralympic legacy.

It is debateable whether the ambiguity of 'legacy' serves a purpose for promoters of mega-sporting events as the actual successes of the Games can be talked about in broad, generalised terms, using anecdotal evidence as opposed to being scrutinised by more closely-defined criteria. In part this ambiguity stems from the nature of legacy having a temporal dimension, as how can an event be proven to change the future when there is no way in comparing what society would be like if the event had not occurred? Or if the funds which the event received were used in an alternative manner? It is beyond the remit of this chapter to explore these specific epistemological issues further, needless to say they remain unresolved. As such, the complexities of legacy are hopefully evident. Even though legacy is likely to be a term that we have had significant exposure to, particularly through the media, it remains a concept that lacks considerable clarity of meaning and purpose.

Amongst the limited social research literature relating to Paralympic legacies, there appear to be some emerging areas of interest and concern. On a fundamental basis, previous research has indicated that the creation of a Paralympic legacy has either been alleged, or at least been aspired to, by previous Paralympic Games organizers. The measurable successes of these apparent Paralympic legacies are less clear.

The most obvious and commonly remarked upon legacy of the Paralympic Games has been the changes to the built environment, including and surrounding Paralympic venues (Sainsbury, 2004). Improved attitudes towards individuals with disabilities have also been highlighted as a key legacy output common to all Paralympic Games since at least 1976 up until the 2008 Beijing Paralympic Games (Brittain, 2011; Darcy and Appleby, 2011; Hums, 2011; Jarvis, 2011; Jeon and Legg, 2011; Mushett and Cody, 2011; Shuhan and Le Clair, 2011). A technological legacy has also been alluded to, if not fully articulated. On occasions, previous Paralympic Games have been viewed as showcases for technological improvements which it is hoped will subsequently affect future designs and constructions of wheelchairs and prostheses used for both sporting and non-sporting activities (Cashman, 2006; DePauw and Gavron, 2005; Sherrill, 1989). While these factors are clearly positive, the authenticity of alleged Paralympic legacies has been subject to debate by some scholars. Other areas of extant Paralympic legacies social research expose some concerns surrounding the importance, sustainability and focus of Paralympic legacies.

As research into the Olympic Games far outnumbers the level and quantity of scholarly investigation of the Paralympic Games, so too Paralympic legacy is viewed by some to be at risk of obscurity, hidden by the attention and importance applied to Olympic legacy. The perceived marginalisation of the Paralympic Games by the dominant Olympic Games was remarked upon over ten years ago (Hughes, 1999), and was recently reiterated with the perceived subordination, in terms of the importance and impact, of the London 2012 Paralympic legacy (Weed and Dowse, 2009).

The Sydney 2000 Paralympic Games legacy has been subject to critique. According to Cashman et al (2004) there was apparent short-termism and political expediency on the part of politicians who supported the 2000 Paralympic Games, but were otherwise perceived to be unwilling to engage with debates regarding disability rights. Furthermore, the apparent investment in relatively few elite sportsmen, rather than the broader population engaging in recreational and grassroots sports participation, following the 2000 Paralympic Games was also highlighted (Darcy and Cashman, 2008). As such, Paralympic legacy can be seen to be both value-laden and politically sensitive, hence warranting closer scholarly attention.

This chapter will now share some desires, expectations and value judgements, held by Paralympic stakeholders, relating to the potential legacy of the London 2012 Paralympic Games. These were expressed during 2010 and give an insight into some of the expectations and hopes for the London 2012 Paralympic legacy. Analysis of these comments, which follows a brief account of the methodological procedures which yielded this dataset, provides an insightful critique of the power that Paralympic legacies are perceived to command and the scope of influence they are requested to address.

Method

Semi-structured interviews with Paralympic stakeholders, conducted as part of the author's doctoral research, generated the qualitative data which will be used to critically analyse the anticipated London 2012 Paralympic Games legacy. The key informant technique (Gratton and Jones, 2004), which helped identify some of the key players connected with the Paralympic Movement, was supplemented with some snowball sampling to ensure a rich, qualitative dataset was amassed. Individuals who have operated, continue to operate, and/or had experience of the Paralympic Movement were selected for interview. Hence, interviewees included current and former Paralympians, active and retired disability sport administrators, social researchers of disability and disability sport as well as disability rights advocates.

Comments made during interviews were recorded and transcribed verbatim. Interview transcripts were coded and analysed in accordance with a grounded theory approach (Morse and Richards, 2002). Data collection ceased after the collection of over twenty-one hours of interviewee responses during twenty interviews, at which point it was deemed 'saturation' had been reached as several themes had become apparent within the dataset.

These themes included three a-priori themes namely; 'purpose(s) of the Paralympic Games', 'suitability of impaired bodies as vehicles for elite disability sport' and 'potential future developments of the Paralympic Movement'. One empirical theme emerged from the dataset, entitled the 'impact of the IOC'. Data from the 'potential future developments of the Paralympic Movement' theme are discussed in this paper.

Discussion

It is important to note that, throughout semi-structured interviews held with several Paralympic stakeholders it was essentially the London 2012 Paralympic Games, not the Olympic Games, that was considered the prime vehicle for creating a legacy for disabled people. Broadly speaking interviewees' comments about the London 2012 legacy could be divided into two categories namely, hopes for a sporting legacy and secondly hopes for a legacy which would extend beyond the realm of sport and create wider social change. Both of these types of legacy will now be explored, in turn, using Paralympic stakeholders' insights.

Sporting legacy

A key aspect of the desired sporting legacy expressed was the perception that the London 2012 Paralympic Games legacy should significantly contribute to increasing disability sport participation. Cameron, a disability sport administrator, remarked: "2012 isn't just about those Paralympic teams…it's about using it [2012 Paralympic Games] as a driver to find more athletes across the board to take part in [wheelchair basketball] clubs"(Cameron). Clearly in order to make Paralympic sport sustainable it is important to get more people taking part in Paralympic sport to allow individuals to benefit from the psycho-social and medical benefits that come from being physically active, as well as developing a supply chain of new Paralympians to perform in future Paralympic Games.

Undoubtedly elite athletes with a disability performing at the Paralympic Games is an important stimulus with which to excite and inspire a new generation of individuals to engage in disability sport. However, the practicalities of then finding, and joining, a sports club to begin to participate relies on a raft of other factors, including close proximity of accessible facilities, the availability of necessary disability sports equipment and a conducive social support system to maintain motivation.

With regards to a sporting legacy, there was hope that the London 2012 Paralympic Games would generate greater awareness of disability sport, and subsequently build a greater fan base for Paralympic sport. The media, during the 2012 Paralympic Games, was highlighted as a key facilitator of this. Cameron hoped the awareness generated by the media coverage of the London 2012 Paralympic Games would be maintained and help drive an increase in participation of Paralympic sports, in particular in wheelchair basketball: "hosting it [the Paralympic Games] in Britain you hope that that media coverage [of disability sports] will then continue because people will start to understand [disability] sports" (Cameron).

This aspiration for the London 2012 Paralympic Games remains a possibility. However, this hope is at risk from able-bodied sports post-London 2012 eroding spectatorship of Paralympic sports, to such an extent that the status quo is returned to with able-bodied sport dominating media coverage within the UK.

Some may suggest it is a lack of understanding surrounding Paralympic sports' rules and performances that is hindering the growth of the profile of Paralympic sports. In this regard, there was hope expressed among Paralympic stakeholders that the media can be used to educate individuals about Paralympic sport. This would thereby increase knowledge of Paralympic sports' rules making the sport more accessible and understandable to television audiences. Being equipped with greater knowledge could arguably lead to Paralympians' performance being ascribed greater credibility as their athletic achievements are contextualised in light of their physical abilities. In this regard, Trevor an administrator of Paralympic sport actively involved in preparations for London 2012 Paralympic Games, stated:

> one thing that London [2012] wants to do for the Olympics and Paralympics is to get a more informed spectator group both those who actually physically attend and those who watch through television...One of the pieces that we're trying to do in London [2012], in terms of sports presentation, is to try to ensure that the audience understands what they're seeing and I think that will be a massive help in terms of the promotion of the more severely disabled athletes in the Paralympic Movement and the Paralympic Games, because it will give us an opportunity in sports like boccia and in athletics to explain why this is an elite sport. (Trevor)

Here Trevor hopes the London 2012 Paralympic Games can educate and further build interest amongst spectators about Paralympic sport. The presence of classification systems and the impairment/sport specific demands can arguably be problematic in attempting to market certain Paralympians as credible signifiers of elite sport. It remains to be seen if London 2012 can achieve this objective or instead encounters apathy as spectators' arguably desire excitement, not a detailed insight into the impairments, classification systems and adapted rules which affect Paralympians' performances.

Implicitly, through educating individuals about Paralympic sport and hence identifying and highlighting ability opposed to disability, this may lead to a greater appreciation of the capacity for individuals with a disability to function proficiently within both paid/unpaid employment and roles within voluntary and local organisations. Some Paralympic stakeholders explicit desires for a legacy that extends beyond sport will now be considered.

Wider Social Legacy

Physically accessible environments and athletes acting as disability rights advocates were both elements some Paralympic stakeholders hoped would emanate from a London 2012 Paralympic Games legacy.

Physical Infrastructure

Nathan, a social researcher of disability and disability theory, hoped that London 2012 would create accessible infrastructure around England's capital city, which all disabled people would benefit from. Moreover he hoped London 2012 would inspire a proliferation of accessible environments across the UK. Nathan stated:

> the infrastructure around, and to, the Olympic site...has the potential to have a massive impact upon improving the lot of disabled people in London, because it [accessible infrastructure] will become the norm and it [London] will become an easier place to get around, and that might be its [London 2012's] real long term legacy, to show what modern architecture can achieve...the Olympic facilities will all be accessible, so rather than struggling to the poolside there will be a couple of pools which will be readily accessible for London which is fantastic (Nathan)

Hence, there is an expectation that the ideas and techniques used to create the 'accessible' Olympic and Paralympic environments will proliferate and become standard practice. This hope is very revealing of both the perceived power of the Olympic and Paralympic Games to change society and the perceived lack of existing infrastructure for disabled people.

In terms of critiquing Nathan's assertion, firstly, it is arguably overly simplistic to believe that a particular environment is accessible and ideal for *all* impairment groups. For example, while a gentle slope may be perceived as essential for allowing wheelchair users to move about independently, individuals with cerebral palsy may find shallow steps with a handrail alongside easier to use. In addition, individuals with a visual impairment would benefit from some form of warning, perhaps raised bumps on the pavement, to inform them that a slope/steps is/are being approached. An individual with a hearing impairment may benefit from some form of visual, as opposed to audible, information system while individuals with an intellectual impairment cannot be seen to benefit from the introduction of a modified physical environment. This reiterates the risk of generalisation and indicates how the specificity of impairment should not be overlooked in terms of legacy.

Secondly, Nathan is asserting there is a profound paucity of disability sport provision for disabled people, to the extent that the addition of two swimming pools, accessible to impaired individuals, represents real progress. It is surprising that Nathan has faith in biannual sporting competitions such as the Olympic and Paralympic Games to create significant change in terms of how accessible buildings will be constructed in future, given the perceived lack of accessible infrastructure in London created by a series of disability legislation, including the 1995 disability discrimination act, later updated in April 2005 and the recent 2010 Equality Act[1]. It may be asked why and how a sporting competition lasting a matter of weeks can create the change in infrastructure seemingly needed, when decades of government legislation have seemingly failed to address issues surrounding accessible environments for individuals with an impairment? Ironically here sports competitions are arguably being seen to possess greater power and influence in society than policy makers and legally-binding targeted, specialised legislation[2] seemingly introduced to uphold and safeguard shared moral and societal imperatives, in this instance equality as relating to individuals with a disability.

Nevertheless, creation of accessible physical environments in new and redeveloped Olympic sport venues and related environments, for example the Athletes' village, could arguably improve sporting provision for individuals with a disability and also assist in integrating individuals with a disability into the community, rather than leaving them isolated in their own homes.

Aside from the physical, a potential socio-cultural legacy of the Paralympic Games was desired by Teresa, a former multi-medal winning Paralympic swimmer and current disability rights advocate. In interview, Teresa expressed her hope that a coalition between Paralympians competing at the London 2012 Paralympic Games and disability rights advocates could educate the wider population regarding broader social issues experienced by persons with a disability, including disability discrimination. In doing so, she hoped the Paralympic Games could yield meaningful social change for disabled people including the ways in which this cohort of individuals are perceived and positioned within society. Teresa stated:

> I am determined that London 2012 starts to make this link between Paralympic athletes and the disability rights movement, because they [Paralympians] could be a group who are incredibly influential in shifting the focus away once and for all from 'these are athletes and let's talk about their impairments' to 'these are athletes who are fantastically successful and representing this country'. But there's a job to do for the disability rights community to shift its thinking I think. (Teresa)

In closing here Teresa acknowledges the potential conflict in interests and views that exist between Paralympians and disability rights campaigners. The messages that Paralympians and disability rights groups wish to voice may be contradictory. This issue has been discussed elsewhere (see Huang and Brittain 2006; Purdue & Howe, 2012a,b) as some Paralympic athletes do not identify as being 'disabled' and wish solely to be asked about their sporting performances, not broader social issues, when competing at Paralympic Games. As such, will both Paralympians and disability rights activists wish for the attention given to impairment to be lessened, thereby emphasising that impairment is only one aspect of an individual's identity? The ability of athletes and disability rights advocates to agree on a common message will significantly impact upon the ability of a Paralympic legacy to extend into the realm of disability rights advocacy.

The utilisation of Paralympic athletes at the London 2012 Paralympic Games as role models is arguably implicitly supportive of the generation of social legacies, both sport specific and more broadly. However the politicised mobilisation and use of Paralympic athletes as disability rights advocates inevitably introduces the spectre of negative, critical reflections upon British societal structures. No doubt an unwelcome topic at a high profile global sports event.

Having put the proverbial cart before the horse, it is important to conclude this discussion with the fundamental question which former Paralympian Jack posed. Although believing London 2012 represented a chance to change the social perception of disability within British culture Jack was unsure as to who was going and/or should take responsibility for ensuring this opportunity was not squandered. Jack stated: "we've got a real chance to make a change, but then the question is who are going to be the key drivers moving that forwards...should that be Paralympics GB? Should that be national governing bodies? Should that be media?" In light of previous discussions it is clear that all of the groups named above, and more besides, will be required to facilitate the London 2012 Paralympic Games' legacy.

Conclusion

In accordance with extant Paralympic legacy research, Paralympic stakeholders expressed hopes towards legacies in terms of the built environment (Sainsbury, 2004) and improved social perceptions of individuals with a disability (Brittain, 2011; Darcy and Appleby, 2011; Hums, 2011; Jarvis, 2011; Jeon and Legg, 2011; ; Mushett and Cody, 2011; Shuhan and Le Clair, 2011). Concern about the sustainability of the Paralympic legacy, explicitly expressed by Jack, can be seen to return to issues of short-termism and failure of the Paralympic Games to benefit the majority of individuals with a disability, i.e. not just Paralympians (Cashman et al, 2004; Darcy and Cashman, 2008). Clearly sporting *and* wider social legacies are desirable.

By the time this chapter is published the London 2012 Paralympic Games will have occurred and the legacy, whatever its form, will have begun to take shape. This monograph hopes to provoke future research which takes the pulse of the London 2012 legacy and future Paralympic Games, as well as beginning to address the fundamental epistemological complexities that are incumbent within a concept such as legacy.

Notes

[1] The Equality Act can be accessed via:
http://www.legislation.gov.uk/ukpga/2010/15/contents
[2] Reasons for the perceived failures of disability legislation to date, including relating to the creation of fully accessible environments across the UK, are beyond the remit of this paper.

References

Brittain, I. 2011. The Toronto Olympiad for the Physically Disabled 'A.K.A.' the Fifth Summer Paralympic Games held in 1976. In D. Legg and K. Gilbert (eds.) Paralympic Legacies, Common Ground Publishing; Champaign, Illinois, 35-46.
Brittain, I. 2010. The Paralympic Games Explained. London; Routledge.
Cashman, R. 2006. The Bitter-Sweet Awakening: the legacy of the Sydney 2000 Olympic Games. Sydney; Walla Walla.

Cashman,R.; Toohey,K.; Darcy,S.; Symons,C.; Stewart,B. 2004. "When the carnival is over: evaluating the outcomes of mega sporting events in Australia". Sporting Traditions. 21(1); 1-32.

Darcy, S. and Appleby, L. 2011. Sydney 2000 Moving from Post-Hoc Legacy to Strategic Vision and Operational Partnerships. In D. Legg and K. Gilbert (eds.) Paralympic Legacies. Common Ground Publishing; Champaign, Illinois, 75-98.

Darcy,S. and Cashman,R. 2008. Legacy. In R.Cashman and S.Darcy (eds.) Benchmark Games: the Sydney 2000 Paralympic Games. Sydney; Walla Walla, 218-231.

DePauw, K. and Gavron, S. .2005. Disability Sport. Leeds; Human Kinetics.

Gilbert, K. and Legg, D. 2011a. Conceptualising Legacy. In Gilbert, K. and Legg, D. (eds.) Paralympic Legacies. Champaign, Illinois; Common Ground Publishing, 3-12.

Gratton, C. and Jones, I. 2004. Research methods for sport studies. London: Routledge.

Howe, P. D. and Jones, C. 2006. "Classification of Disabled Athletes: (Dis) Empowering the Paralympic Practice Community". Sociology of Sport Journal. 23; 29-46.

Huang, C. and Brittain, I. 2006. "Negotiating identities through disability sport". Sociology of Sport Journal. 23; 352-375.

Hughes, A. 1999. The Paralympics. In R.Cashman and A.Hughes (eds.) Staging the Olympics: The Event and Its Impact. Sydney; UNSW Press, 170-180.

Hums, M. 2011. Athens 2004 Personal Reflections. In D. Legg and K. Gilbert (eds.) Paralympic Legacies, Champaign, Illinois; Common Ground Publishing, 99-110.

Jarvis, P. 2011. Barcelona 1992 The Coming of Age for the Paralympic Games. In D. Legg and K. Gilbert (eds.) Paralympic Legacies. Champaign, Illinois; Common Ground Publishing, 53-64.

Jeon, J. and Legg, D. 2011. Seoul 1988 The first Modern Paralympic Games. In D. Legg and K. Gilbert (eds.) Paralympic Legacies. Champaign, Illinois; Common Ground Publishing, 47-52.

Legg, D. And Gilbert, K. (eds.) 2011. Paralympic Legacies. Champaign, Illinois; Common Ground Publishing.

Morse, J. and Richards, L. 2002. Readme first: for a user's guide to qualitative methods. London: Sage.

Mushett, T. and Cody, A. 2011. Atlanta 1996 Trials and Triumphs of the Human Spirit. In D. Legg and K. Gilbert (eds.) Paralympic Legacies. Champaign, Illinois; Common Ground Publishing, 65-74.

Office for Disability Issues. 2011. London 2012 a legacy for disabled people. Available at http://odi.dwp.gov.uk/docs/wor/leg/legacy-full.pdf (Accessed 29th June 2011)

Purdue, D.E.J. & Howe, P.D. 2012a. "See the sport, not the disability? – Exploring the Paralympic Paradox". Qualitative Research in Sport, Exercise and Health. 4(2); 189-205.

Purdue, D.E.J. & Howe, P.D. 2012b. "Empower, Inspire, Achieve: (Dis)Empowerment and the Paralympic Games". Disability and Society. 27(7); 903-916.

Sainsbury,T. 2004. Paralympics Past, Present and Future: University lecture on the Olympics. Available at http://olympicstudies.uab.es/lectures/web/pdf/sainsbury.pdf   (Accessed 7th July 2011)

Sherrill, C. 1989. "Yang and Yin of the 1988 Paralympics". Palaestra. 5(4); 53-59, 76.

Shuhan, S. and LeClair, J. 2011. Legacies and Tensions after the 2008 Beijing Paralympic Games. In D. Legg and K. Gilbert (eds.) Paralympic Legacies. Champaign, Illinois; Common Ground Publishing, 111-130.

Thomas, N. and Smith, A. 2009. Disability, Sport and Society. London: Routledge.

Weed, M. and Dowse, S. 2009. "A missed opportunity waiting to happen? The social legacy potential of the London 2012 Paralympic Games". Journal of Policy Research in Tourism, Leisure and Events. 1(2): 170-174.

Chapter 14: Paralympism and Diplomacy: Re-assessing Interest Representation[1]

Aaron Beacom (University of St Mark and John, UK)

Introduction

The emergence of the Paralympic Games is a relatively recent (post war) phenomenon. Given its origins in efforts to engage with sport as a tool to facilitate the rehabilitation of disabled combatants (Stoke Mandeville Games), there are significant historical links between the Games and wider geo-political events. The relatively recent arrival of the Paralympic Games, its smaller scale and political sensitivity towards disability, has meant that they have not featured as prominently in international diplomacy as the Olympic Games. There are however, important caveats to that, namely, since it follows directly after the Olympic Games, the Paralympic Games have been affected by 'overspill' from diplomatic tensions relating to the Olympic Games. In addition, the rapid (though inconsistent) increase in the scale of the event (from 400 hundred athletes from 21 countries competing across 8 sports in 1960, to 4237 athletes from 164 countries competing across 20 sports in 2012) and its links to the wider human rights agenda are, increasingly, drawing the Paralympic Games into mainstream diplomacy.

Diplomacy is increasingly interpreted as constituting much more than the dialogue between states (Barston 2006, Watson 2006). Broadly defined it concerns engagement in a range of mediating and negotiating practices that help regulate relations between collectives - state and non-state (Hocking 2006, Sharp 2009). While collective interest in stability may act as a catalyst for mediation, ultimately organizations (states or other collectives) engage in diplomacy in order to promote their interests within international society. Table 1 outlines one approach to the framing of diplomacy as it relates to the Olympic and Paralympic Games (Beacom 2012)

Table 1. Conceptualizing Olympic and Paralympic diplomacy

Categories	Actors	Activities
State diplomacy relating to the Games	• Foreign Affairs departments, • Trade departments • Diplomatic services	Public policy decisions on engagement (bidding / participation). Medium for development of foreign relations (inc. use of boycott). Soft intelligence gathering.
Support diplomacy relating to the Games	• Foreign embassies, • Consular services, • Passport and immigration services	Wide range of logistical support services and hospitality for athletes, support teams and officials. Close cooperation with Chef de Mission of Olympic / Paralympic teams.
Olympism / Paralympism as diplomacy	• International Olympic Committee / International Paralympic Committee • Olympic / Parasports Federations, • Regional and national Olympic / Paralympic Committees.	Olympic / Paralympic education programmes, development programmes (eg.Olympic Solidarity), cultural programmes initiated at IOC / IPC and host nation levels. IOC / IPC recognition / non-recognition of NOCs / NPCs of newly emerging states
Multi-Stakeholder Diplomacy relating to the Games	• Governmental organizations at international, supranational, national and sub-national level. • Civic society organizations, sports federations, • Business and commercial organizations at local, national regional and international level (eg, Sainsbury as key sponsor of 2012 Paralympic Games).	All of the above. Also- Sub-state lobbying relating to bid and when providing services as host, range of business promotional activities at local, national, regional and international level. Interest and pressure groups engaged in lobbying concerning related activities.

This paper is concerned in part, with state diplomacy where it relates to domestic and foreign policy decisions and also where it concerns the development of diplomatic and consular support for Paralympic teams. The particular challenges in relation to the constitution and accreditation of support personnel and the logistics of securing specialist equipment and venues feature prominently in interviews with officers working in the field. As in the case of the Olympic Games, diplomacy beyond the parameters of state based activity, also plays a significant role in diplomatic discourse relating to the Paralympic Movement. One catalyst for this is the way in which institutions that constitute the Paralympic Movement have engaged in wider concerns with the rights of people with disabilities. In this respect, links between the International Olympic Committee (IOC), International Paralympic Committee (IPC) and the United Nations (UN) on international conventions for people with a disability have a particular significance[2]. The idea of the IPC as an advocacy body engaged diplomatically within international society to promote disability rights is considered within the wider context of debate concerning the capacity of international sports NGOs to influence international affairs.

The rapid increase in the scale of the Paralympic Games over recent years and the increased media interest in the Games helps foster the view that the Paralympic Games have been 'mainstreamed'. It would follow that the Paralympic Games should attract the attention of those organizations seeking to use international sport as a conduit for diplomatic discourse. A combination of the politicization of disability and relationships between organizations representing able bodied and disabled sport has however set a specific frame of reference for the development of Paralympism and the extent to which Paralympism can be drawn into the wider political and diplomatic debate.

The interface between Olympic and Paralympic sport is a complex issue. The IPC have demonstrated their determination to protect the integrity of Paralympism as a distinct and separate entity, while at the same time, benefiting from a close association with the wider Olympic Movement. The Olympic Movement is formally recognized as constituting the IOC, the National Olympic Committees (NOCs) and the international Olympic sports federations. It is noteworthy, however, that promotional material supporting Olympic and Paralympic bids frequently presents the Paralympics as part of that 'Movement'. For example, under the banner of 'The Olympic Movement' the Chicago bid committee for the 2016 Games referred to the Olympic and Paralympic Games as together celebrating 'unity and excellence through the universal language of sport. This communal, joyful conversation creates the Olympic Movement'.[3] In some respects this linkage is evident in diplomatic discourse that frames both Games. For example, in terms of state diplomacy relating to the Games, diplomatic services incorporate their support networks for both their national Olympic and Paralympic teams. Organizationally, the two Games have been drawn together through the revised bidding and evaluation processes and there appears to be a clear commitment by the IOC and IPC to develop closer ties across a range of issues.[4] At the same time, the IPC is an influential autonomous international organization with its own agenda that includes its commitment to advocacy for people with disabilities internationally. It is unlikely that it would wish to risk that influence being diluted through formal integration into the Olympic Movement.

Diplomacy and the Paralympic Movement

As an international sporting event closely linked to the Olympic Games and engaged directly in advocating disability rights, the Paralympic Games are increasingly being drawn into international debate concerning the politics of disability. This process is complicated by the maturing of the Games which, according to Horton and Toohey (2008), has led to loss of their sporting innocence. They cite Craft's (2001) comment that as Paralympic sport has matured, it has appropriated some of the most desirable aspects of mainstream Olympic sport. At the same time however, 'there were the less desirable signs of maturation - evidence of banned drug use, increased security precautions, and the shake out of less glamorous sports in favour of the flashy ones that sell well'. As the Games have worked to enhance their profile, they have increased their political currency. States, most notably China, have invested heavily in improving their performance in the medals tally. The perception that improved performance will promote international prestige and that states supporting disability in such a visible way, will be viewed in a more positive light regarding their social and cultural policies, is implicit in such increased investment. At the same time, the IPC and other disability sports actors (as well as international Disabled Persons Organisations - DPOs - generally) are availing themselves of the opportunity to promote their own interests in an environment in which states vie with one another to enhance their reputation regarding civil liberty and inclusion.

Diplomacy, the State and the Paralympic Games

The idea that the Olympic Games can become a conduit for the pursuit of state foreign policy objectives is a consistent theme in literature on sport and international relations. The extent to which the Paralympics is drawn into this policy frame is less clear. The proximity of the Paralympic Games to the Olympic Games, particularly since 1988, has resulted in spill-over of diplomatic activity. In relation to British support diplomacy Olympic Attachés are for example, responsible for providing support for both the Olympic and Paralympic teams (see table 1 – 'support diplomacy'). As the scale of the Paralympic Games has increased, this has significantly increased the responsibility of diplomatic services in the build-up to the Games, a point readily acknowledged by operatives working in the field.

The potential of the Paralympic Games to provide a conduit for traditional state diplomacy is noteworthy on a number of levels. At a most fundamental level, the capacity of the Paralympics to provide a platform for senior politicians and Heads of State to enhance their visibility against the backdrop of such an ostensibly positive activity likely to engender public empathy as sport and disability, should not be under-rated. It is noteworthy that at a time of increasing tension between Western powers and Iran, the Iranian President Mahmoud Ahmadinejad took the opportunity of the opening ceremony of the 2008

Paralympics in Beijing, to travel to China and meet a number of senior diplomatic and government figures. The official press commented that the Iranian entourage included the Foreign Minister Manuchehr Mottaki, Vice President Esfandiar Rahim Mashaii, Physical Education Organization head Mohammad Aliabadi and senior advisor to the government Mojtaba Samareh Hashemi. The high profile visit contributed to attempts to develop a more progressive perspective of the regime regarding the rights of minority groups. Coinciding with the visit, the official Iranian news agency IRNA issued a press release noting that Iranian female athletes with physical disabilities would for the first time participate in the Paralympic Games, competing in track and field, shooting and table tennis. Prior to the visit, an Iranian Foreign Ministry spokesman Hassan Qashqavi made the unfortunate remark when, in releasing a statement noting that Ahmadinejad's visit was 'aimed at highlighting the great ability of the [Paralympic] athletes', he referred to Paralympians as 'suffering' from disability.[5] At the same time he commented that the visit would provide the opportunity for senior officials of the two countries to hold talks on 'issues of mutual interest'.[6]

Attempts to enhance international perceptions of a state through hosting Paralympic events are evident when reading accounts of journalists, spectators and participants who have travelled abroad for events. This certainly formed the backdrop for the Paralympics in Beijing in 2008. Prior to the Beijing Games of 2008, there was intense speculation concerning how the Chinese government would respond to the challenge of hosting an event for disabled athletes, given the negative publicity China had received in the past, regarding disability rights. Prior to the Games the Chinese government engaged in a number of high profile initiatives that helped to enhance the perception of respect for disability rights within Chinese society. This included China as a signatory to the UN Convention in the Rights of Persons with Disabilities in March 2007.[7] Other national initiatives included the heightened profile given to the long-standing national Help-the-Disabled-Day, held in China on the third Sunday of every May, in the form of widely publicised free medical checkups, job fairs and a series of consultations on inclusive building design.[8]

Beyond the Paralympic Games, hosting of world Championships in a range of para-sports has provided the opportunity for Municipal Authorities and states to develop their human rights profile in the international arena. The Paralympic shooting world championships held in Zagreb, Croatia, in July 2010 is one example. This was a significant event for the host country, which is still engaged in developing its international profile in the wake of the Balkan conflict of the 1990s. Organized by the Croatian NPC, this was the first world championship in a sport for athletes with a disability, to be held in the country.[9] It is noteworthy that the Prime Minister of Croatia attended the event and, along with the Mayor of Zagreb and the IPC President were engaged in the ceremonies and welcoming speeches that accompanied the competition.

Beyond providing a forum for developing the profile of senior politicians domestically and internationally, the Paralympics (and their forerunner the International Stoke Mandeville Games) are from time to time drawn into wider foreign policy developments. Most notably, the Movement was caught up in the unfolding debate about how to respond to sporting links with South Africa. While some commentators argued that disability was a levelling experience and that disability sport should not be drawn into international politics (hence the admittance of the South African team to the 1968 Stoke Mandeville Games), the government of the Netherlands succeeded in getting the South African team excluded from the 1980 Games (Little, 2008).

In the context of public policy, interest groups (for example disability rights groups who may attract the support of sympathetic Paralympic athletes) have the capacity to use the Games to express their opposition to particular policy developments perceived to have a negative effect on the quality of life of people with disabilities. Of particular note here, was the concerted campaign to highlight the impact of proposed cuts by the British government, to the Disability Living Allowance in advance of the Paralympic Games of 2012.[10]

Diplomatic Discourse and the Paralympic Games: Beyond the State

The capacity of organizations responsible for the governance of disability sports, to engage in interest representation as part of wider diplomatic discourse, is evident at a number of levels. As outlined in the introduction to the chapter, the politicization of disability rights and the perception that disability sports organizations, primarily the IPC, could effectively lobby to promote disability awareness, has drawn the IPC into international political discourse. This has not always worked to the favour of the international sports vested interests. For example, when China won the bid to host the 2008 Olympic and Paralympic Games, a number of influential stakeholders highlighted their concerns given China's poor track record concerning disability rights.[11] This initially included comments made by Tanni-Grey Thompson, highlighting concerns about disability rights in China and suggesting the danger of using the Paralympics to mask underlying issues with their human rights record.

The staging of the Paralympic Games provided the opportunity for a number of DPOs to monitor disability rights in an unprecedented way. The campaigning journal *Disability Now* dispatched four individuals with disabilities to monitor the level and quality of provision for the disabled. This included Zara Todd, campaigns officer at the charity Scope and the BBCs disability affairs correspondent. Todd reported that although volunteers were enthusiastic, adaptive measures did not generally appear to have been developed in consultation with people with disabilities. Todd suggested that, while exposure to coverage of disability sport could help promote disability awareness, China was indeed only beginning to find its way when it came to disability rights. At the same time, the *Disability Now* journalist White reported his shock at the apparent lack of disability awareness within much of the population.[12] Such a perspective is tempered by reports from other commentators that three years before the Games, a disabled person would be pointed out in the street. However, the Paralympics, despite widely reported limitations, had resulted in people with disabilities in China 'coming out of the shadows'.

Beyond such campaigning organizations and individuals, the IPC emerges as a key sports INGO with the capacity to engage directly in international diplomatic discourse. Since its inception, the IPC as the most influential of the disability sports organizations has taken increasing control over the classification and administration of international disability sport (Howe and Jones, 2006). From a wider perspective, they have engaged in a number of disability sport and development initiatives in partnership with a range of stakeholders (some examples outlined in Table 2) that are illustrative of efforts to enhance their profile as an international disability rights advocacy body.

Table 2: IPC Development Partnerships[14]

International Paralympic Committee (IPC)	Disability rights toolkit	To heighten awareness of the rights of the disabled and advocate creation of UN Convention
IPC	Paralympic School Day Programme	educational programme initiated by the IPC which aims to create awareness and understanding in schools about persons with a disability
IPC / Care International Deutschland	Partnership Initiative	supported the Rehabilitation Through Sport initiative in the Tsunami Areas (ReSTA) project in Sri Lanka in 2005-2006
IPC / Handicap International	Partnership initiative	To share expertise and promote the rights and opportunities for persons with a disability in sport.
IPC / UNESCO	Partnership initiative	To promote the Convention Against Doping in Sport, increase awareness about persons with a disability in formal education systems through the IPC's Paralympic School Day programme and promote girls and women as leaders within sport.
IPC / International Association for Sports and Leisure Facilities	Partnership initiative	To award the IPC/IAKS Distinction for sports facilities suitable for persons with a disability (promoting accessibility and inclusion).

Whilst the perception that disability rights are less respected in states located in resource poor regions, is not necessarily based on empirical evidence, challenges concerning disability rights which are common to a number of these states can be identified. This relates to relatively low GDP, under-provision in basic health care, transport and communication problems and political instability (leading to increased risk of conflict with corresponding disabling injuries). In this context the IPC has a particular interest, using a range of sporting events, for example the All African Games, as a conduit for exercising its advocacy role to address a range of issues relating to disability rights across Africa. Rather ambitious statements made by the President of the African Paralympic Committee after the Joint Planning Meeting (October 2010) for the tenth All African Games in September 2011, reflect the heightened expectations that such events can make an impact on the priorities of policy makers and perceptions of wider society, toward disability.[13]

The influence of the Paralympic Movement as an advocacy organization engaged in the promotion of disability rights is not limited to the IPC but also relates to the activities of NPCs - often in partnership with other stakeholders - and regional Paralympic Committees. International Disability Day, co-ordinated by UNICEF provides one such opportunity for NPCs with limited resources, to engage in wider promotional work to enhance their profile. The Rwandan NPC for example, in partnership with UNICEF and Right to Play Rwanda, were able in 2011, to introduce Boccia, Goalball and Sitting Volleyball, through inter-school competitions as part of International Disability Day celebrations.[15] Notwithstanding the very limited scale of the programme and the embryonic state of the NPC, this provided the opportunity to develop links with the Ministry of education, as well as wider social networking. Such examples highlight the relationship between the domestic and international political agenda in the context of disability sport. The shared interests of the Rwandan NPC and Right To Play (an international development organization) as advocates for disability rights and promoters of sport as a conduit for development creates a platform to engage with political interests, particularly in a situation where the local infrastructure is resource limited and under severe pressure as a result of regional political instability.

Beyond the IPC and NPCs, other non-state organizations engage in activities to promote disability rights through paralympic sport. The *Whole Wide World* initiative for example, developed by the UK based private consultancy organization *Smaller World* responded to the issue of the number of states who were not represented within the Paralympic Movement. The programme was based on research of existing small teams who were already successfully engaged in Para-sport. It aimed to identify key aspects of their infrastructure and delivery which facilitated this engagement (the role of the education system, lobbying by government ministers, alternative funding streams *etceteras*). This formed the basis of a general strategy aimed at facilitating the development of Paralympic teams in other states currently not participating in Paralympic competition. Alongside presentation of the strategy, the organization impressed on states not represented within the Paralympic Movement, the positive benefits of engagement on the basis of promoting a more progressive and inclusive image of their societies, within the international community.[16] Generally then, a systemic relationship has evolved between the Paralympic Games and the issue of diversity and inclusion of people with disabilities in society. In turn, this is related to concerns with how states are perceived in the context of disability rights internationally and in this sense, engagement in Paralympism bridges the interests of state and non-state organizations.

Significant in the context of Multi-Stakeholder Diplomacy (the engagement of a range of stakeholders in diplomatic discourse – see table 1), the convergence of state and non-state interests is evident at a number of levels. At a symbolic level, the ceremony to launch the new Paralympic logo for the Sochi 2014 Paralympic Games drew together the IPC president Philip Craven, the Russian Deputy Prime Minister Aleksandr Zhukoc and the UN Special Advisor on Sport for Development and Peace, Wilfried Lemke, along with a range of senior sports officials and event organizers.[17] Notwithstanding anxieties with the organization of the 2014 Games, as well as lingering concerns over the human rights record of the Russian regime, there is a shared interest among stakeholders to ensure that the event is successful. Engagement with the machinery of international diplomacy forms an increasingly important part of that process.

Diplomatic Discourse Relating to the 2012 Paralympic Games: A British perspective

It is difficult to unravel diplomatic discourse relating to the build-up to the 2012 Paralympic Games, as distinct from wider discourse concerning London 2012. Specific reference to the Paralympic Games does however, emerge from time to time. (For example, key sponsors Sainsburys are the first to sponsor specifically the Paralympic Games). Focusing on state bodies, the activities of the Foreign and Commonwealth Office (FCO) and the British Council, are noteworthy.

In relation to the FCO written evidence given by Prof. Nick Cull to the Foreign Affairs Select Committee on FCO Public Diplomacy made particular reference to the prominence given to the Paralympic Games within the FCO 2012 plan. Cull argues the point that;

> There are many countries around the world in which differently-abled people do not have the opportunities they enjoy in Britain, and by increasing international exposure to the Paralympics emphasis on what people can do the FCO is performing a significant act of ethical leadership and associating the UK with some truly inspirational people.[18]

The Foreign Affairs Select Committee concluded its inquiry into FCO Public Diplomacy relating to the Olympic and Paralympic Games and published its findings on 6 February 2011. Noteworthy, beyond Cull's commentary, was the lack of specific reference to the Paralympic Games (as opposed to reference in conjunction with the Olympic Games). Oral evidence given by Conrad Bird, Head of Public Diplomacy at the FCO in response to a question (question fifty two) by MP David Watts concerned the use of the Paralympic Games to promote the image of Britain as an open and inclusive society. In this he drew attention to the engagement of Tanni-Grey Thompson as an Olympic Ambassador and her visit to Palestine. Bird suggested 'We felt that the Paralympics was a good opportunity to demonstrate British attitudes toward disability. We felt that could be an example of promoting the British way of doing things and our values'.

Beyond the Foreign Office, the British Council has also been engaged in developing initiatives relating to disability rights in the context of the Paralympic Games. The Young Advocates programme was launched in Beijing in 2008 as a joint initiative with the Chinese Disabled People's Federation, to promote leadership within the disability community and inclusive practices across wider society. While rather modest in its scope, the project did provide a vehicle for promoting cross-cultural appreciation of issues relating to disability and inclusion, as well as opening up dialogue with a range of international and national partners.[19] It again demonstrated the central role of the British Council in the developing portfolio of sports based diplomatic initiatives (for example, involvement with the *International Inspiration* programme, which also encapsulates disability sports based projects – Beacom 2012a and b).

Beyond state diplomacy, the capacity of the Paralympics to provide the opportunity for a range of interest groups and non-state bodies to engage in interest representation (bearing in mind the legacy objectives of the Games) is a significant consideration. Domestically, there are growing concerns regarding the impact of reductions in public expenditure, on state support for people with disabilities. This relates in particular to potential reductions in housing allowance and the phasing out of the Independent Living Allowance which could mean the institutionalization of large numbers of people with disabilities (estimates vary dependent on source), who depend on this to finance adaptive devices and support to enable them to retain their independence. The publicity surrounding the Paralympics provided an opportunity for organizations such as SCOPE to lobby against existing policy objectives. Despite such concerns, the FCO clearly identified the capacity for discourse relating to the 2012 Games to make a positive contribution to the public diplomacy portfolio, with the opportunity to present itself on the international stage as an advocate for diversity and inclusion promoted through the Paralympic Movement.[20]

Conclusion

A consideration of diplomatic discourse relating to the Paralympic Games in the context of this chapter, pre-supposes a close relationship between the IOC and IPC reflected in a number of protocols concerning bidding for and hosting the Olympic and Paralympic Games. The geographical and chronological proximity of two events whose administrative and logistical frameworks are increasingly integrated from the bidding stages, through to issues relating to transport, accommodation and security, and who both represent the pinnacle of sporting excellence, means it is inevitable that discourse relating to the Paralympic Games, is considered as part of the wider assessment of 'Olympic diplomacy'. While organizationally, legally and philosophically, the Olympic and Paralympic Movements can still be considered as separate entities, at a practical level this is increasingly difficult to do. Much of the diplomatic discourse investigated by this author, cuts across the Olympic and Paralympic Movements. This relates to practices concerning state diplomacy, support diplomacy and multi-stakeholder activity for example, interest group representation by sub-state and commercial organizations. Nevertheless there are a number of issues specific to the Paralympic Games and, more generally, the Paralympic Movement, that generate distinctive forms of diplomatic discourse.

The central theme of the chapter related to the linkage between disability rights and the mainstreaming of disability sport. As disability rights (forming part of the wider human rights agenda) has been elevated within domestic and international political discourse, this has acted as a catalyst for the mainstreaming of disability sport. At the same time, disability sports organizations, in particular the IPC and NPCs have demonstrated that they have (varying degrees of) agency in promoting these wider political changes. While primarily lobbying to promote their respective sporting agendas, they are also advocacy bodies, actively engaged with the disability rights agenda at domestic, regional and international level.

The rapid development of the Paralympic Games, in scale and complexity, has created a number of challenges for the Paralympic Movement and in some respects these have implications for related diplomatic discourse. The re-introduction of athletes with an intellectual disability in three sports in 2012 changes the dynamics of the Games. The right of people with intellectual disabilities to compete is likely to feature in debate concerning the future contours of the Games. This is particularly the case since attempts by the IPC to develop its status as a disability advocacy organization, is dependent upon its capacity to provide an inclusive competitive experience. By including intellectually disabled athletes, this enhances the capacity of the Paralympic Movement to develop its advocacy role. Nevertheless, the complexity of classifying intellectual disability remains a major challenge for Paralympic sports who ultimately have responsibility for the development of relevant classification systems.

As the wider Olympic family continues to develop and to formalize its relationships, recognition of organizations beyond the IOC and IPC will increasingly form part of the international sporting agenda and by extension, will feature within diplomatic discourse. In the context of disability the Special Olympics has evolved since 1968 quite separately, into an extensive international grass roots organization with the clear objective of enhancing quality of life for people with intellectual disabilities, through engagement with organized physical activity and competitive sport.[21] While its origins as a community based voluntary organization and its participatory objectives, identify it as clearly distinctive from the Paralympic Movement (with its focus on elite performance), it is recognized as part of the Olympic family and its international advocacy work, for example in partnership with UNICEF, locates it as an actor in the sport diplomacy frame.[22] Recognition of the Special Olympics by the IPC, forms part of its strategy of developing relationships with an increasing number of stakeholders (sport and non-sport) as Paralympism moves toward the centre of the world sporting stage.

Ultimately the scale of the modern Paralympic Games and the linkage of Paralympic sport with wider debate on the rights of people with disabilities (reflected in national legislation and international conventions) have elevated the influence of the IPC on the international stage. Ongoing debate concerning the appropriateness of bringing together Olympic and Paralympic sport in the longer term would do well be bear in mind the likelihood of any organization which is in the ascendancy (and relatively untainted by corruption and political intrigue), being party to its own demise.

Notes

[1] This chapter draws from material included in Beacom A. (2012) *International Diplomacy and the Olympic Movement: The New Mediators.* Basingstoke: Palgrave.
[2] *IPC News Release* (21 October 2009) 'UN General Assembly Adopts Truce Resolution'
http://www.paralympic.org/Media_Centre/News/General_News/2009_10_21_a.h tml (accessed 25 February 2011)
[3] Chicago Bid Committee for the 2016 Olympic and Paralympic Games (May 2009)
http://www.chicago2016.org/the-olympic-movement.aspx (accessed 27 July 2010)
[4] *IPC Press Release* (25 June 2006) 'IPC and IOC extend Games co-operation until 2016' http://www.sportbusiness.com/news/159972/ioc-and-ipc-extend-games-co-operation-until-2016 (accessed 25 February 2011).
[5] *People's Daily* (2 September 2008) 'Iranian President to Attend Paralympics Opening Ceremony'. Use of the term 'suffering' was considered entirely inappropriate given efforts by the movement to focus on the abilities rather than the disabilities of athletes.
[6] *Xinhua* (6 September 2009) 'Chinese President meets Iranian Counterpart' http://news.xinhuanet.com/english/2008-09/06/content_9806940.htm (accessed 20 October 2011)
[7] *China Daily* (31March 2007) 'China Signs UN Accord on Disability Rights', http://www.chinadaily.com.cn/china/2007-03/31/content_840971.htm (accessed 17 March 2011)
[8] *Cri* (31 March 2007) 'China Marks Help-The Disabled Day', http://english.cri.cn/2946/2007/05/20/65@229167.htm (accessed 17 March 2011)
[9] *IPC* (14 July 2010) 'Opening Ceremony to kick-off the Shooting World Championships',
http://www.paralympic.org/Media_Centre/News/Sport_News/2010_07_14_a.htm l (accessed 4 October 2011)
[10] *DisabledGoNews* (October 2011) 'Minister and Mayor face angry hecklers over cuts and Atos', http://www.disabledgo.com/blog/2011/10/minister-and-mayor-face-angry-hecklers-over-cuts-and-atos/, (accessed 6 December 2011)
[11] *The Telegraph* (16 July 2001) 'Paralympic Games: Disabled threaten boycott over 'human Wrongs', http://www.telegraph.co.uk/sport/3009026/Paralympic-Games-Disabled-threaten-boycott-over-human-wrongs.html (accessed 11 March 2011)
[12] *Disability Now* (October 2008) http://www.disabiltynow.org.uk/latest-news2/world_view/beijing_the_paralympic_legacy (accessed 23 August 2011)

[13] *IPC Press Release* (21 October 2010) 'All African Games Has the Potential to Create Significant Change', *http://www.paralympic.org/press-release/all-african-games-have-potential-create-significant-change*(accessed 14 December 2010)

[14] Information relating to partnership initiatives was sourced with the assistance of 'IPC Development Partnerships' (undated) http://www.paralympic.org/IPC/Development/Development_Partnerships/ (accessed 7 December 2012) A range of additional partnership initiatives are currently being developed with Commonwealth Games International, the Global Sports Development Foundation, the Christopher Reeve Paralysis Foundation and the Swiss Agency for Development and Co-operation.

[15] *IPC News Bulletin* (2 March 2011) 'NPC Rwanda Celebrates International Disability Day',. http://www.paralymic.org/Media_Centre/News/General_News/2011_03_02_b.html (accessed 21 March 2011)

[16] A representative from *Smaller World commented that* the IPC, while receiving the proposal positively, did however, indicate some concern about the implications for resourcing. Nevertheless, there are some indications that the initiative did make some contribution to expanding the influence of the Paralympics. For example, it was instrumental in facilitating the participation of Andorra in Summer Paralympics for first time in 2012.

[17] *Wordpress.com* (12 December 2009) 'Ceremony for Launch of Sochi Paralympic Logo', http://02varvara.wordpress.com/2009/12/12/sochi-2014-launches-new -paralympic-games-emblem-on-russias-first-ever-international-paralympic-winter-day/ (accessed 27 August 2011)

[18] *Written evidence to House of Commons Select Committee* (10 November 2010) 'FCO Public Diplomacy: 2012 Olympics' (response by Cull), http://www.publications.parliament.uk/pa/cm201011/cmselect/cmfaff/writev/oly mpics/oly03.htm (accessed 21 December 2010)

[19] *Flintshire Youth Service* (2008) 'Young Advocates at the Beijing Olympics', http://www.cyfanfyd.org.uk/resources/global-toolkit/Case-Studies/Young-Advocates-at-the-Beijing-Paralympics.pdf (accessed 8 September 2011) Also outlining this programme; *British Council Press Release* (30 May 2008) 'British Council Launches Para-leadership Sports Programme in Hong Kong Today to Address Diversity Issues and to Spread the Paralympic Spirit', http://www.britishcouncil.org/yap_press_release_e_post_event-2.pdf (accessed 8 September 2008)

[20] *FCO* (undated) 'Digital Diplomacy Case Studies', http://digitaldiplomacy.fco.gov.uk/en/about/case-studies/post/110-paralympic-quiz (accessed 27 January 2011)

[21] *Special Olympics Mission Statement* (undated) 'Through the power of sport, Special Olympics strives to create a better world by fostering the acceptance and inclusion of all people', http://www.specialolympics.org/mission.aspx (accessed 21 March 2011)

[22] *Special Olympics* (3 October 2007) 'UNICEF and Special Olympics partner in China to raise disability awareness', http://www.unicef.org/ sports/ china_41109.html , One day global summit to mark beginning of UNICEF / Special Olympics International partnership to promote the cause of children with disabilities. Objective to raise public awareness, promote participation and

empowerment of young people with disabilities and improve research and data-gathering efforts. (accessed 12 March 2011)

References

Barston, R. 2006. Modern Diplomacy (3rd ed), London: Longman.

Beacom, A. 2012a "Disability Sport and the Politics of Development", In Levermore, R. and Beacom, A. (eds) Sport and International Development. Basingstoke: Palgrave, 98-123.

Beacom, A. 2012b. International Diplomacy and the Olympic Movement: The New Mediators, Basingstoke: Palgrave.

Hocking, B. 2006. "Multistakeholder diplomacy: Foundations, forms, functions and frustrations", In Kurbalija, J. and Katrandjiev, V. (eds) Multistakeholder diplomacy: Challenges and opportunities. Malta/ Geneva: Diplofoundation, 13–29.

Horton, P and Toohey, K. 2008. "It comes with the Territory: terrorism and the Paralympics", In Gilbert, K. and Schantz, O. (eds) The Paralympic Games: Empowerment or sideshow? Maidenhead: Meyer and Meyer, 190-198.

Howe, D. and Jones, C. 2005. "The Conceptual Boundaries of Sports for the Disabled: Classification and athletic performance", Journal of the Philosophy of Sport, 32: 133-146.

Howe, D. and Jones, C. 2006. "Classification of Disabled Athletes: (Dis)empowering the Paralympic Practice Community", Sociology of Sport Journal, 23: 29-46.

Kell, P. Kell, M. and Price, N. 2008. "Two Games and One Movement? The Paralympics and the Olympic Movement", In Kell, P. Vialle, W. Konza, D. and Vogl, G. (eds). Learning and the Learner: Exploring Learning for New Times, Wollongong: University of Wollongong Faculty of Education Papers, 65-78.

Little, C. 2008. The Paralympic Protest Paradox: The Politics of Rhodesian Participation in the Paralympic Games 1960 – 1980, Available at http://www.la84foundation.org/SportsLibrary/ISOR/isor2008p.pdf (Accessed 6th December 2011)

Sharp, P. 2009. Diplomatic Theory of International Relations, Cambridge: Cambridge University Press.

Stone, E. 2009. "Disability, Sport and the Body in China", Sociology of Sport Journal, 18: 57-68.

Thomas, N. and Smith, A. 2009. Disability Sport and Society: An Introduction. London: Routledge.

Watson, A. 2006. Diplomacy: The Dialogue Between States (second edition), NY: New Press.

Chapter 15: Athletes' and Coaches' Perceptions of Service Quality at a U.S. Paralympic Training Site

Joshua R. Pate (James Madison University, USA) and
Robin Hardin (University of Tennessee, USA)

Introduction

The United States sent 227 athletes to compete at the 2012 Paralympic Games in London and countless more trained as Paralympic hopefuls at various training locations across the United States. A training environment that is accessible and conducive to the athletes' physical needs may yield a more positive training experience and potentially create brand-loyal consumers. Therefore, exploration of the athletes' and coaches' experiences is merited.

The United States finished first in the medal count in each summer Paralympic Games from 1976 in Toronto until 1996 in Atlanta. However, the nation finished fifth in the medal count at the 2000 Sydney Games, fourth at the 2004 Athens Games, and third at the 2008 Beijing Games (International Paralympic Committee, n.d.). Other national teams are increasing their level of competition, and therefore the United States is required to increase its level of competition as well if it is to keep pace with the competition. One way to increase the level of competition is by enhancing the training environment.

U.S. Paralympic Training

Research is lacking in the area of the Paralympic Games in general (Gilbert & Schantz, 2008) and sport and disability as a whole (Prystupa et al., 2006). More specifically, Paralympic sport is understudied in the areas of access (Gold & Gold, 2007), athletes (Banack, 2009), and governance and structure (Hums & MacLean, 2008; Hums et al., 2003). Pate and Hardin (2012) examined the importance of U.S. Paralympic training sites and the service provided to athletes with disabilities. The current study sought to add to that body of work by focusing on athlete perceptions of service quality within a U.S. Paralympic training site. More specifically, the purpose of this study was to explore the service quality experiences of elite athletes and coaches at Lakeshore Foundation's Paralympic training site.

Figure 1. U.S. Olympic and Paralympic Training Site (USOC)

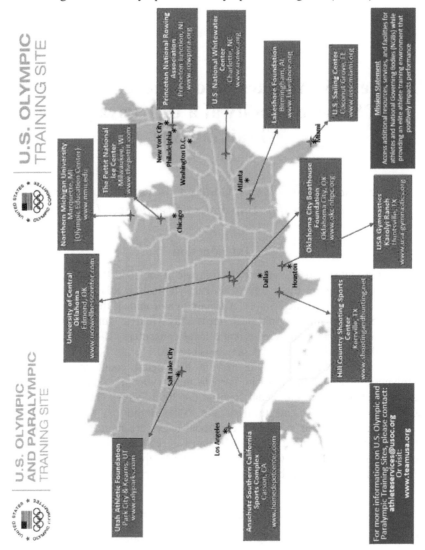

The United States has two primary levels of training facilities for Olympic and Paralympic athletes. There are three U.S. Olympic Training Centers, which offer lodging, dining, sport science research support, and athletic facilities. Additionally, there are 12 designated U.S. Olympic Training Sites that offer facilities for teams and athletes, three of which also support Paralympic training. Lakeshore Foundation, one of the three sites that support Paralympic training, is considered unique because it offers services much like the training centers (see Figure 1). Lakeshore presents itself as a reputational case study due to its longstanding position with regard to Paralympic sport and training (Merriam, 2009).

Lakeshore Foundation is a private, not-for-profit 501(c)3 foundation near Birmingham, AL, in the Southern region of the United States. It operates daily as a fitness center focused primarily on serving people with disabilities and, as of 2012, was the only training center of its kind in the Southeastern United States with accessible facilities (Lakeshore Foundation, n.d.). Lakeshore Foundation was designated as the first U.S. Olympic and Paralympic Training Site in 2003 and is the training location for at least three U.S. Paralympic teams: men's wheelchair rugby, women's wheelchair basketball, and women's goalball. Lakeshore has garnered a reputation in Paralympic sport as coaches and athletes who train there return and often do so despite living closer to other U.S. training sites and centers. Therefore, it is essential to examine the service quality dimensions offered by Lakeshore as a premier training facility for Paralympic hopefuls, particularly focusing on the athletes' perceptions.

Service Quality

Service quality is a concept that explores the nature of the experience someone has with a venue, person, or product (Rust & Oliver, 1994). Service quality is comprised of three dimensions: environmental, functional, and technical. This study focused solely on the environmental and functional dimensions. The environmental dimension is a consumer's perceptions of facilities and surroundings. Especially in the sports context, the service environment makes important contributions to satisfaction levels since the consumer spends an extended period of time observing and experiencing the environment (Baker, 1986; Bitner, 1990; Wakefield et al., 1996). The functional dimension is how a service is delivered to consumers. For example, the functional dimension offered at a fitness facility includes the staff's education of disabilities, preferences, and disability sport overall. Employees are important because they are the first point of contact with consumers during the service delivery. The technical dimension is a product delivered to the consumer. The technical dimension was not explored in this study because of a focus on the training atmosphere provided by the facility and employees.

Pate and Hardin's (2012) study of U.S. Paralympic training site importance focused solely on the functional dimension of service quality. The current study builds upon that work by using the voices of the consumers (e.g., athletes and coaches) to explore their perceptions of the environmental and functional dimensions of service quality. This study set out to examine those services by asking the following research question:

> RQ: How were team training camp experiences shaped by Lakeshore Foundation's service quality dimensions?

Methodology

Case study methodology was used with semi-structured interviews, observations, and document analysis for data collection methods (Merriam, 2009). Convenience sampling was used to identify teams training at Lakeshore and willing to participate in the study. Coaches from the U.S. women's goalball team and the U.S. women's wheelchair basketball team agreed to participate in the study. Snowball sampling was used to seek athletes as the coaches suggested which athletes should be invited to participate (Merriam, 2009). Saturation was reached after interviews with five athletes and four coaches as participants were making similar statements in response to questioning. This study had a total of nine participants, which is an acceptable number (Merriam, 2009).

Data were collected through interviews, observations, and document analysis (Creswell, 2007; Yin, 2009) and took place between November 2011 and January 2012. Interviews were based upon SERVQUAL interview questions developed by Landrum et al. (2009). Observations took place on two site visits during the training camps. Document analysis was conducted using Lakeshore's application for training site designation, the U.S. Olympic and Paralympic Training Site Designation Plan from the USOC, and the Lakeshore website.

Meaning condensation was the type of narrative analysis used with the transcripts and field notes as long passages were analyzed and shortened to meaning statements (Kvale & Brinkmann, 2009). Ethnographic content analysis was used during document analysis to "document and understand the communication of meaning" with the aim to be systematic in evaluating the information (Altheide, 1987, p. 68).

Findings

Competitive teams trained at Lakeshore because they were "drawn here by the Foundation's barrier-free athletic complex, experienced staff, and by our long-standing commitment to expand opportunities for those who have experienced a physical disability" (Lakeshore Foundation, n.d.b, para. 2). Data revealed that elite athletes with disabilities and elite teams experienced a mix of environmental and functional dimensions of service quality. Findings were informed by interviews, observations, and document analysis, with the narrative blending the data.

Environmental Dimension

It was important to note how Lakeshore positioned itself with regard to the environmental dimension of service quality. Athletes and coaches recognized a focus on service quality, citing how Lakeshore's environment made them feel comfortable. "It's a comfortable environment, and it's comfortable because you can rely on it. You know what you're going to get out of it," said Coach 2. Athletes recognized the sacrifices of bypassing training centers like Colorado Springs to seek the advantages Lakeshore offered. "I would say it feels a little bit more that you're being acknowledged by the USOC when you go to those training sites, but here is where we're most comfortable. We can do the things that our team does," said Athlete 5. That reliability offered by Lakeshore employees built upon the consistent environment athletes and coaches noted with regard to accessible facilities and the teams' ability to achieve success without distraction.

Consistency and comfort were two qualities that athletes and coaches cited as influences on their Paralympic success. "… [F]or us having a place where we're comfortable, where we can go and build ourselves as players, build ourselves as a team, get in, get out, do our business, I think it contributes greatly to our success," said Athlete 5. Athletes and coaches credited that consistency in environment and treatment as a reason for improving performance in competition.

Athletes mentioned crowded gym space at other locations as being a difference between those environments and that at Lakeshore. Much of the contention toward other locations stemmed from an uncomfortable environment due to crowded space and space that was not designed with Paralympic sport in mind.

> Lakeshore has always been very accommodating for our team. From everything from testing to gym time we're treated first priority here as opposed to other bigger training sites where we won't get testing we need, we won't get this or that we need. We're very much, you know, the stepchild of it. So we've always come here because they've always given us basically what we want and what we needed to get done as a team. (Athlete 1)

Additionally, Lakeshore's environmental dimension was impacted by facility accessibility, which was set forth by designers and the administrative team well before it was designated a training site. Athletes said the accessible facilities were among the reasons they chose to regularly train at Lakeshore Foundation. Lakeshore's fieldhouse, for example, has automatic door entrances at two locations and the floor to enter the fieldhouse has no door lip that would result in a bump for wheelchairs. The hardwood basketball courts are flat with the surrounding track surface, which is also the same grade as the rubber-like flooring surrounding the track (see Figure 2).

Figure 2. Lakeshore Track and Basketball Surface

Accessible facilities, in fact, resulted in Lakeshore hosting major competitions for athletes with disabilities and becoming the home base for U.S. women's goalball, U.S. women's wheelchair basketball, and U.S. men's wheelchair rugby, thus filling a void that athletes and coaches said was present with training facilities beyond Lakeshore.

> Yeah, we really couldn't ask for much more because everything is so close and with tryouts, especially, we go and have a three-hour training session and then we have a limited amount of down time. And in that time we have to get treatment and eat and try to get some rest. Having everything close together is just a huge benefit for us. (Athlete 4)

The Lakeshore dormitory was designed for accessibility, and people with disabilities were consulted in the design, which included visual contrasts in lighting and spatial concerns within the floor plan. As an example, dim lighting in the hallways, controlled lighting inside the dorm rooms, and colored tile marking each doorway addressed many accessibility needs for people with visual impairments.

Other accessibility components built into the design included wider doorways beyond the ADA-mandated 36-inch opening. The facility design team installed 40-inch wide doorways to accommodate for sport wheelchairs which typically have negative-cambered wheels that are wider than traditional wheelchairs. Additionally, the tables in the dining area offered the ability to reconfigure the layout, and the food service line was constructed low to give wheelchair users the opportunity to better evaluate menu choices. Athletes and coaches noted the attention to detail with regard to Lakeshore's service through its facility design.

> We carry tape measures with us when we go on these site visits (prior to training camps). Can we get in the doors? Are we going to be able to get in the showers? Are we going to be able to go in the door to go to the bathroom? Is there enough turn space in there? Those are a lot of things that an able-bodied person doesn't think about or even have the care to think about. In our sport, that's a significant thing for our team. (Coach 3)

Facility accessibility, as noted by the athletes and coaches, was an essential component not for a better choice of training facility but to provide manageable activities of daily living. Accessibility components, however, were not accentuated but rather integrated within the design. "They have complete accessibility for all disabilities here, and I think all training centers should, across the board. Not just, hey, there's a special room or a special wing, you know?" said Athlete 2, noting the universal design.

Universal design qualities hearken back to the reasons athletes and coaches said they return to Lakeshore with regard to its environmental dimension of service quality: comfort and consistency. The accessible features ensure the athletes and coaches with physical disabilities can move comfortably about the facility, and they noted the Lakeshore staff offered consistent support with regard to preparing the facility for training camp use.

Functional Dimension

Lakeshore's focus on personal attention for athletes with physical disabilities was outlined in its application to be designated a U.S. Olympic and Paralympic Training Site.

> If our country is to truly excel in the International Paralympic Games, as well as in other world championships, we must offer complete, consistent, and ongoing training opportunities. We must also continue to develop new Paralympians. We must increase our understanding of sports science for athletes with disabilities, so that we can combine practical training experience with sound scientific principals [*sic*]. (Application, 2000, p. 4)

The Lakeshore application reinforced its history of providing coaches, trainers, and experienced staff to offer full-service care for athletes with disabilities. The organization highlighted its commitment to research and education for athletes with disabilities "on a scale unlike other efforts," further stating that "[s]cientists around the world have confirmed that this component of our program is an essential element missing in current training for these athletes" (Application, 2000, p. 4).

Athletes and coaches said Lakeshore demonstrates the functional dimension of service quality through offering personal attention and maintaining an interest in Paralympic sport. Examples of both qualities were observed during the women's wheelchair basketball training camp. Lakeshore Foundation's president slowly walked onto the sideline sipping from a cup of coffee in his left hand and clasping a white paper in his right hand. He wore khaki dress pants, dress shoes, a pressed white collared shirt and a necktie, making him noticeably different from the rest of the fieldhouse personnel in gym clothes. He watched the court intently, following the action as if he were evaluating the play. One of the basketball players came off the court for a rest, and he talked with her briefly as she drank water. They both continued to watch the scrimmage.

The athletes and coaches knew the president and were aware that he came to watch them scrimmage. His presence, according to them, was not unusual during training camps. "(He) usually comes out almost all the time. You're not going to see that at most of the training centers. The CEO is not going to come out and say, 'Hey, what's up,'" said Athlete 3. Coaches agreed that was one example of how Lakeshore displays personal attention to the teams while maintaining a focus on Paralympic sport. "Just overall, we know that we're going to be treated very, very well here. Lakeshore has made a commitment to this team, and we've been told we're one of their priority groups," said Coach 3. Athletes and coaches, in fact, said the personalization was what made the training site unique in addition to accessibility.

The functional dimension of service quality offered by the Lakeshore employees made a difference in overall experience for the athletes and coaches. "There are certain staff members here who would do anything for the athletes. It really shows," said Athlete 1. That dedication was displayed by employees who said they followed the teams in international competition, even setting a 2 a.m. alarm to watch one of the team's competitions on the Internet.

Athletes and coaches noted Lakeshore employees' passion for Paralympic sport, and acknowledged that as a missing quality at other locations.

> The people who work here have a passion for, at least most of them, have a passion for working with people with disabilities and that's why it does so well. Other gyms and other training centers don't; they don't have that passion. So that's why you don't have that close personal relationship and things. (Athlete 1)

Incorporating a greater focus on Paralympic sport was rewarding to athletes with regard to Lakeshore's service mentality. An example of how Lakeshore employees focused on Paralympic sport, specifically, was the education of the athletic training staff and the other Lakeshore employees with regard to sport-specific injuries, according to the athletes. The athletes said Lakeshore employees were prepared to address injuries that come from wheelchair sports more than other locations at which they trained. Injuries for wheelchair sports were identified as primarily occurring in the shoulders, elbows, and wrists as well as blisters on the hands, a contrast to lower-body injuries that trainers may address in able-bodied athletes. Having trainers who were familiar with those risks added to the attention shown by the staff, said the athletes

Ultimately, the athletes and coaches who trained at Lakeshore said the organization's focus on sport for people with disabilities was a factor in having a positive experience and returning to Lakeshore. Athletes said that Lakeshore proved Paralympic sport was among its top priorities even through imagery. For example, Lakeshore had other people of all ages and different abilities using the facility, ranging from senior adults to youth and from amputees to spinal cord injuries. The fieldhouse was equipped with goalball nets (see Figure 3) and the floor could be lined with raised and textured tape so the athletes could feel the lines (see Figure 4).

Figure 3. Goalball Nets at Lakeshore

Figure 4. Goalball Taped and Textured Lines

Additionally, Lakeshore had four banners hanging from the fieldhouse rafters honoring Paralympic teams that trained there and earned medals at the Paralympic Games (see Figure 5).

Figure 5. U.S. Paralympic Imagery in Lakeshore

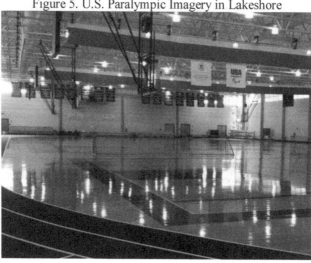

You're not going to go anywhere else where you see banners hanging up for Paralympic teams for gold medals. You're just not going to see that anywhere else where that pride is there for disabled sports. I'm not sure you see it at the other training sites. (Athlete 3)

The lack of imagery at other training locations offered a reminder to athletes that other locations had an Olympic focus. Lakeshore, according to participants, was just the opposite by providing personal attention and a focus on Paralympic sport while also ensuring the environment was conducive to the athletes' success.

Conclusion

Findings revealed that U.S. Paralympic teams had positive training experiences at Lakeshore due to a combination of the environmental and functional dimensions of service quality. Accessible facilities not only made training camp logistics convenient, but also assisted with daily living and athletic challenges faced by the athletes with regard to physical spaces. Lakeshore's facilities were designed with the forethought of disability in mind, constructing the athletic grounds, the dormitory, and the dining hall accessible to people with different types of disabilities. These accessible facilities show Lakeshore administration was aware of the needs of its consumers while also savvy enough to position itself as a leader in U.S. Paralympic sport training. Consumer satisfaction with regard to the environmental dimension of service quality is essential due to the amount of time the consumer spends within that environment (Baker, 1986; Bitner, 1990; Wakefield et al., 1996). Lakeshore recognized the significance of the environmental dimension, particularly with its target population, and used its accessible facilities to attract Paralympic athletes and teams. In turn, athletes and coaches repeatedly noted that the environmental dimension reinforced comfort and consistency with regard to their training.

Athletes and coaches also recognized that Lakeshore's functional dimension of service quality was essential in delivering the service for teams choosing to train there. Athletes identified the passion and knowledge for disability sport displayed by the Lakeshore staff as an attractive quality for training there. Additionally, imagery throughout the facility, which included banners and other people with disabilities, offered evidence of both environmental and functional dimensions of service quality.

This study explored athlete and coach perceptions of service quality dimensions. Therefore, the practical implications from this study suggest that organizations seeking to maximize service quality with consumers should explore the perceptions those very consumers hold to ensure their needs and preferences are being met. Additionally, this study sheds light on the fact that organizations offering services to people with disabilities should be aware of the environmental dimension of their facilities with regard to comfort and consistency while also focusing on the functional dimension offered through service delivery to develop a brand-loyal consumer. Athletes and coaches in this study said they had positive experiences at Lakeshore due to the organization focusing its efforts on both environmental and functional dimensions of service quality.

References

Altheide, D. L. 1987. "Ethnographic content analysis". Qualitative Sociology, 10(1): 65-77.

Application to the United States Olympic Committee for Paralympic Training Site designation for basketball, tennis, rugby, shooting sports, swimming and weightlifting. 2000. (February). [Training site application]. Lakeshore Foundation. Birmingham, AL.

Baker, J. 1986. The role of the environment in marketing services: The consumer perspective. In C. Congram, J. Cepeil, & J. Shanahan (eds.), The services challenge: Integrating for competitive advantage, Chicago, IL: American Marketing Association, 79-84.

Banack, H. 2009. Coaching behaviours and the motivation of Paralympic athletes (Master's thesis). Available at http://digitool.library.mcgill.ca/webclient/StreamGate?folder_id=0&dvs =1305430514823~438 (Accessed 13th April 2013)

Bitner, M. 1990. "Evaluating service encounters: The effects of physical surrounding on employee responses". Journal of Marketing, 54(2); 69-82.

Creswell, J. W. 2007. Qualitative inquiry and research design: Choosing among five approaches (2nd ed.). Thousand Oaks, CA: Sage Publications.

Gilbert, K., & Schantz, O. J. 2008. The Paralympic Games: Empowerment or side show? Maidenhead: Meyer & Meyer Ltd.

Gold, J., & Gold, M. 2007. "Access for all: The rise of the Paralympic Games". The Journal of the Royal Society for the Promotion of Health, 127; 133-141.

Hums, M. A., & MacLean, J. 2008. Governance and policy development in sport organizations. Scottsdale, AR: Holcomb Hathaway Publishers.

Hums, M. A., Moorman, A. M., & Wolff, E. A. 2003. "The inclusion of the Paralympics in the Olympic and Amateur Sports Act: Legal and policy implications for integration of athletes with disabilities into the United States Olympic Committee and National Governing Bodies". Journal of Sport and Social Issues, 27; 261-275.

International Paralympic Committee. (n.d.). Athletes: IPC Historical Results Database. Available at http://www.paralympic.org/Athletes/Results (Accessed 13th April 2013)

Kvale, S., & Brinkmann, S. 2009. InterViews: Learning the craft of qualitative research interviewing (2nd ed.). Thousand Oaks, CA: Sage.

Lakeshore Foundation. n.d. Competitive athletics. Available from http://www.lakeshore.org/index.php?src=gendocs&link=Competitive_At hletics&category=Main (Accessed 13th April 2013)

Landrum, H., Prybutok, V., Zhang, X., & Peak, D. 2009. "Measuring IS system service quality with SERVQUAL: Users' perceptions of relative importance of the five SERVPERF dimensions". Informing Science, 12; 17-35.

Merriam, S. B. 2009. Qualitative research: A guide to design and implementation (3rd ed.). San Francisco, CA: Jossey-Bass.

Pate, J. R., & Hardin, R. 2012. "Importance of training sites dedicated to Paralympic sport". Global Sport Management News: Olympic Special Edition, 3; 12-14.

Prystupa, E., Prystupa, T., & Bolach, E. 2006. "Developmental trends in sports for the disabled: The case of summer Paralympics". Human Movement, 7; 77-83.

Rust, R. T., & Oliver, R. L. 1994. Service quality: New directions in theory and practice. Thousand Oaks, CA: Sage Publications.

Wakefield, K. L., Blodgett, J. G., & Sloan, H. J. 1996. "Measurement and management of the sportscape". Journal of Sport Management, 10; 15-31.

Yin, R. K. 2009. Case study research: Design and methods (4th ed.). Thousand Oaks, CA: Sage Publications, Inc.

Chapter 16: The Influence of Team Composition on Paralympic Success

Jennifer Wong (ICSPPE), Joeri Verellen, and Yves Vandlandewijck (Katholieke Universiteit Leuven, Belgium)

Introduction

This article was written based on research that was carried out towards the completion of the Erasmus Mundus Masters in Adapted Physical Education (2010-12) at Katholieke Universiteit Leuven in Belgium. With competition and participation continuing to increase in Paralympic sport, this study explores team composition variables and their relationship to Paralympic success. The objective was to find patterns in team composition, which lead to higher medal success, particularly in countries with moderate to low incomes and/or with small populations. Using data from the 2008 Paralympic Games, countries were categorized by population and wealth to highlight trends in team size, number of sports/team sports and type of sports in medal and non-medal winning countries. Although findings confirmed team size as the strongest predictor of Paralympic success, further analysis drew findings strategically useful to countries unable to support large teams due to limited finances and/or small populations. In this regard, it was shown that some developing countries were able to attain medal success when resources were concentrated on a small number of sports with multi-medal potential; that there was a wealth/population threshold for nations to compete in team sports; and that government commitment and financial investment was critical to success. It is hoped that these findings will be a useful starting point for strategic Paralympic development and lead to further research surrounding disability sport policy.

The Influence of Team Composition on Paralympic Success

As participation and competition increase in Paralympic sport, countries are seeking strategies and scientific evidence to support financial investment and resource allocation to increase their chances of success. Previous literature has shown that a country's population and wealth (Gross Domestic Product per capita) are key factors in achieving success at the Paralympic Games (Heyndels, Jegers, & Buts, 2011;Vanlandewijck, Van Biesen, Verellen, Reynders, Meyer, & Van de Vliet, 2007). As a country cannot readily change its population or economic situation, it seems essential to investigate factors influential at a policy level. In an Olympic context, the SPLISS Group (Sport Policies Leading to International Sporting Success) has been examining explanations of Olympic Success from a policy perspective. The SPLISS model outlines 9 pillars contributing to Olympic success, including a country's *inputs* - financial support and sport policies; *throughputs* - foundation/participation, talent identification/development, facilities, athlete support, coach development, national/ international competition and scientific research; and *outputs* - medal success (De Bosscher, De Knop, & Heyndels, (2003); De Bosscher, De Knop, Van Bottenburg, Shilbli, (2007); De Bosscher, De Knop, van Bottenburg, Shibli, & Bingham, 2009). This research is currently being completed in a cross-national context with 15 countries.

Although in the long run, developing a comprehensive project of this magnitude for the Paralympic Movement would be immensely informative, this current study is limited by resources, and set out to investigate variables potentially influencing success that were both consistent and readily available across all countries participating in the Paralympic Games. For this reason, team composition variables including team size, number of sports, number of team sports and type of sports were selected as the data was publically available on the International Paralympic Committee (IPC) website and these variables are managed by each individual competing nation. While the variable, team size (often called participation) is often used as an output measure interchangeably with medal success, the variables that makeup a nation's team can arguably be identified as inputs evolving from sport policy decisions. A recent study by Vagenas and Vlachokyriakou (2012) concluded team size was the single best predictor of Olympic medals. A literature search did not reveal studies specifically examining the makeup of teams competing in the Paralympic Games.

Method

Medal totals and team composition variables (team size, number of sports, number of team sports and types of sports) were sourced from the IPC website (www.paralympic.org) for the 2008 Beijing Paralympic Games (n=145)[1], while population and GDP per capita values were sourced from the 2008 World Fact Book (www.cia.org). Medal success was calculated as the total of weighted medals achieved (gold =3, silver=2, bronze=1). All countries were categorized into groups first by income. The three (3) groups were: *high income,* USD20-55,000 GDP per capita; *middle income*, USD5-20,000 GDP per capita, and *low income*, <USD5,000 GDP per capita. Secondly, countries were separated into medal winning and non-medal winning countries. Finally each group was divided into 3 population categories, (*small populations*, 1-10M; *medium populations*, 10-40M; and *large populations*, 40+M). Maximum, minimum and average scores and frequency of sport types were computed for each group.

Results

When team composition characteristics were examined for patterns, it was found that the number of medals, athletes, sports, and team sports were not evenly distributed across all nations participating in the 2008 Paralympic Games. While a total of 145 countries took part in this competition, the average team size was 28 athletes with 71 countries (49%) sending 3 athletes or less. An examination of the top 10 medal winners (*Table 1A*) showed that these countries had the largest teams, competed in the highest number of sports, and the highest number of team sports. The bottom 10 medal winners (*Table 1B*) had very small teams (<5 participants), with the exception of Belgium and Lebanon who sent 21 and 11 athletes respectively and subsequently participated in a higher number of sports.

Table 1. A summary of team composition variables for top and bottom medal winning countries.

A. Top 10 Medal Winning Countries

Country	Weighted Medals	Team Size	# Sports	# Team Sports
China	459	334	20	6
Great Britain	215	210	18	4
USA	206	209	18	4
Australia	154	161	13	2
Ukraine	140	123	11	2
Russia	122	145	13	2
Germany	112	172	16	3
Spain	109	138	15	2
Canada	98	146	15	3
France	97	120	13	0

B. Bottom 10 Medal Winning Countries

Country	Weighted Medals	Team Size	# Sports	# Team Sports
Papua New Guinea	2	2	1	0
Lebanon	2	1	1	0
Belgium	1	21	7	1
Malaysia	1	11	5	0
Syria	1	5	2	0
Jamaica	1	4	1	0
Estonia	1	3	2	0
Puerto Rico	1	3	3	0
Laos	1	1	1	0
Namibia	1	1	1	0

An examination of income, population, and medal success divide participating countries into groups (See Appendix 1). The most successful grouping had a combination of high income (between US$20,000 and US$55,000 GDP per capita) and populations larger than 40 million inhabitants; examples included Great Britain, USA and Germany. The next most successful grouping had middle incomes (between US$5,000 and US$20,000 GDP per capita) with large populations, for example China, Brazil, Russia. When low income countries were examined, only 11 countries (22%) had successfully won medals and these countries had medium to large populations. Countries with incomes lower than US$2,000 GDP per capita were not medal successful.

All non-medal winning countries, regardless of population and/or GDP per capita, shared similar characteristics including: average team size of two athletes, participation in an average of two sports, and no participation in team sports. Latin American countries (with the exception of Mexico, Brazil and Argentina) were not medal successful although their GDP per capita and populations showed potential to support success.

When examining participation, countries with the largest teams were the most successful. The largest teams were found in the middle income group with the highest population, (including China, Brazil and Russia), but on average the high income group with large populations had the largest teams. The majority of low income countries sent small teams, typically between 1-3 athletes. While the most successful low income countries (medal winning countries) sent larger teams (up to 23 athletes) and participated in a maximum of four sports.

Participation in team sports was limited to the top income group, with the exception of middle income countries with large populations. Countries with larger populations in both the high and middle income groups were able to support larger teams and a higher number of sports. Iraq was the only low income country to compete in a team sport (seated volleyball).

The program for the 2008 Paralympic Games included 20 sports, six of which were team sports. Athletics and swimming had the most participation opportunities: athletics, 1028 slots and 480 available medals; swimming, 547 slots and 422 available medals. Athletics, swimming and powerlifting were the sports with the highest participation rates. Smaller countries in both the high and moderate income groups participated in a higher number of non-equipment team sports (eg. seated volleyball, goalball), rather than wheelchair based sports which were limited to high income countries and countries with large populations.

Discussion

As approximately half of participating nations did not win medals and sent 3 athletes or less, it is evident that Paralympic sport is not equally developed globally. An explanation for this wide gap could be that disability sport in general remains under-developed globally, with the exception of Europe, North America and parts of Asia (Lauff, 2011). Perhaps some of this can be attributed to the fact that the Paralympic movement is a western concept with its roots at the Stoke Mandeville Hospital in the UK. Study results show that highly populated, wealthier countries were clearly more successful in the 2008 Paralympic Games. These countries were able to send the most athletes and compete in a variety of individual and team sports, including those with technically demanding equipment. It can be supposed that in order to achieve high levels of Paralympic success, these countries must be supported by a broader sport and physical education system, inclusive strong awareness of the rights and abilities of people with disabilities, quality health care and educational opportunities, and higher levels of dispensable income for investment in leisure activities. Further research would be needed to understand these influences and their relationships.

Further analysis of middle to low income countries found three useful findings. To begin, countries with the most medal success in each population/wealth grouping were not necessarily the richest or most populated countries. This suggests that a country's investment and commitment plays a major role in achieving success. An interesting observation was the success of Ukraine, Tunisia and Australia who were all successful beyond their socio-economic expectations. In part, research on Games hosting (Hoffman et al., 2002; Balmer et al., 2001; Johnson & Ali, 2004, Bernard & Brusse, 2004) and political orientation (Bernard & Brusse, 2004; Ball, 1972) provides rationale for the successful achievements of these countries. These studies, the majority in an Olympic context, suggest that increased financial investment by national governments consequently leads to better sport programmes and facilities as well as higher investment in elite training and competition.

To continue, some low and middle income countries with small populations achieved medal success, notably, Kenya, Morocco, Iraq, and Tunisia despite limited economic resources. Tunisia, as an example, sent 33 athletes and brought home a total of 23 medals. All of Tunisia's athletes competed in athletics. Although, studies by Maharaj, (2011) and Crawford & Stodolska, (2008), suggest that low-income countries may not be able to find the necessary resources to support and sustain successful Paralympic sport programmes, the example of Tunisia highlights the positive outcome of what appears to be focused resources on a single sport. Also contributing to the high number of nations competing with 3 or fewer athletes is the IPC implemented Universality Wild Card system which allows National Paralympic Committees with no qualifying athletes to apply and send 1 female and 1 male competitor in the eligible sports, traditionally these have been athletics, powerlifing and swimming. These efforts have helped to ensure a wider participation in the Games but does not ensure the development of national disability sport systems to support these athletes.

Finally, a clear population/wealth threshold for countries competing in team sports was evident. Low income countries did not take part in team sports (with the exception of Iraq's participation in seated volleyball) and middle-income countries did not participate in wheelchair team sports unless they had large populations. Typically, a slightly wider range of countries participated in team sports that require less expensive equipment (eg. goalball, football and seated volleyball). These included more middle-income countries (specifically in the Eastern European and West Asian nations). A number of factors contribute to a country's decision to invest in team sports. While the prestige of winning a wheelchair basketball final is unmatched, there is a much greater investment need to activate the necessary resources to develop, select, train and travel with a team. Qualification requires the formation of a national league, travel to regional and international qualification events and top of the line equipment. In combination, competition is high, as the number of qualifying spots at the Paralympic level is limited 6 to 8 teams. It could also be the case that middle and low income countries compete in team sports, at a national or regional level, but do not qualify for international competition such as the Paralympic Games.

Although these conclusions have useful implications, it should be recognized that the findings from this study are limited with regards to general applicability, as it only examined one variable over the course of a single Games.

Conclusion

To summarize, all nations participating in Paralympic sport have finite human and financial resources. Previous literature concludes that a country's income per capita and total population have major impacts upon its success at the Paralympic Games. Having adequate resources to develop and sustain disability sport and a large enough pool of talented athletes with disabilities are critical factors. This study set out to investigate patterns in team composition to gather useful policy information for middle and low income countries and those countries with small populations. It was evident that some countries were able to achieve high levels of success by focusing their efforts into a limited number of sports with multi medal potential and that team sports especially those with technical equipment needs were difficult for low and middle income countries to qualify for, let alone win medals. Finally and most importantly, national investment and government commitment is critical to national Paralympic development and success.

Scientific evidence to support Paralympic and disability sport development at a policy level is very limited. In order to justify investment and make critical policy decisions towards its allocation, more research evidence is needed at national, regional and international levels. As disability and Paralympic sport continues to grow, it is hoped that this study can be used as a starting point to encourage further examination of sport policy variables leading to wider understanding and development of disability sport globally

Notes

[1] Palestine was excluded as it was not clearly defined in World Fact Book data

References

Ball, D. W. 1972. Olympic Games competition. "Structural correlates of national success". International Journal of Comparative Sociology, 13: 186-200.

Balmer, N. J., Nevill, A. M., & Williams, A. M. 2001. "Home advantage in the Winter Olympics (1908_1998)". Journal of Sports Sciences, 19: 129-139.

Bernard, A. B., & Busse, M. R. 2004. "Who wins the Olympic Games: Economic resources and medal totals". The Review of Economics and Statistics, 86: 413-417.

Buts, C., Du Bois, C., & Heyndels, B. 2011." Socio-economic determinants of success at the Summer Paralympics". Journal of Sport Economics. 14: 133-147.

Crawford, J. L., & Stodolska, M. 2008. "Constraints Experienced by Elite Athletes with Disabilities in Kenya, with Implications for the

Development of a New Hierarchical Model of Constraints at the Societal Level". Journal of Leisure Research, 40: 128-155.

De Bosscher, V. De Knop, P., Van Bottenburg, M., Shilbli, S. 2007. "A Conceptual Framework for Analysis of Sport Policy Factors Leading to International Sporting Success". European Sport Management Quarterly, 6: 185-215.

De Bosscher, V., De Knop, P., & Heyndels, B. 2003. "Comparing Relative Sporting Success Among Countries: Creating Equal Opportunities in Sport". International Journal of Physical Education, 3: 109-119.

De Bosscher, V., Heyndels, B., & De Knop, P. 2008. "The Paradox of Measuring Success of Nations in Elite Sport". Belgeo, 2: 1-18.

De Bosscher, V., De Knop,P., van Bottenburg, M., Shibli, S., Bingham, J. 2009. "Explaining international sporting success. An International comparison of elite sport systems and policies in six nations". Sport Management Review, 12: 113-136

Hoffmann, R., Chew Ging, L., & Ramasamy, B. 2002. "Public policy and Olympic success". Applied Economics Letters, 9: 545-548.

Johnson, D. & Ali, A. 2004. "A tale of two seasons: Participation and medal counts at the summer and winter Olympic Games". Social Science Quarterly, 85: 974-993.

Lauff, J. 2011. "Participation rates of developing countries in international disability sport: a summary and the importance of statistics for understanding and planning". Sport and Society, 14: 1280-1284.

Maharaj, J. 2011. "Living disability and restructuring International Paralympic Sport in Oceania: the challenge of perceptions, spatial dispersal and limited resources". Sport in Society. 14(9): 1211-1226.

SPSS Inc. 2011. SPSS Base 18.0 for Macintosh User Guide. SPSS Inc. Chicago IL.

Vagenas, G. & Vlachokyriakou, E. 2012. "Olympic Medals and Demo-economic Factors: the ex-host effect, the exact role of team size and the "population-GDP" model revisited". Sport Management Review, 15: 211-217.

Vanlandewijck, Y.C., Van Biesen, D., Verellen, J., Reynders, S., Meyer, C. & Van de Vliet, P. 2007. "Socio economic Determinants of Paralympic Success. Book of Proceedings 16th International Symposium of Adapted Physical Activity". Journal of the Brazilian Society of Adapted Motor Activity, 12: 16-22.

Appendix 1

Countries participating in the 2008 Paralympic Games, grouped by income using GDP per capita (high, middle, low); medal success (medal winning, non-medal winning); population (large, medium, small). Main findings are highlighted in **bold**.

	High Income $20-55,000 USD$ ^{GDP} per Capita	Middle Income $5-20,000 USD$ $^{GDP per}$ Capita	Low Income $<5,000 USD$ $^{GDP per}$ Capita
Medal winners	Large populations - *40+ million people*		
	eg. Great Britain, USA, Germany • Avg. teams size 147 • Avg. # sports 15 • Avg. # teams sport 2 **Highest # of medals**	*eg. China, Brazil, Russia* • Avg. team size 95 • Avg. # sports 10 • Avg. # teams sports 2 **Largest team (China)** **Highest # team sports (China, Brazil)** **Second # highest medals**	*eg. Indonesia, Pakistan, Nigeria* • Avg. team size 10 • Avg. # sports 3 • Avg. # teams sports 0 **Most successful countries sent larger teams (up to 23 athlete)** **No team sports**
	Medium population *10-40 million people*		
	Eg. Australia, Canada, Greece • Avg. team size 73 • Avg. # sports 10 • Avg. # team sports 1 **Third highest # of medals**	*Eg. Poland, Cuba, Algeria* • Avg. team size 26 • Avg. # sports 4 • Avg. # team sports 0 **No team sports**	*eg. Kenya, Morocco, Iraq* • Avg. team size 9 • Avg. # sports 2 • Avg. # teams sports 0 **No team sports**
	Small populations 1-10 million people		
	Eg. Sweden, New Zealand, Cyprus • Avg. team size 28 • Avg. # sports 8 • Avg. # team sports 1	*Eg. Tunisia, Belarus, Azerbaijan* • Avg. team size 17 • Avg. # sports 3 • Avg. # team sports 0 **No team sports**	**No medals**
Non Medal Winners **48% of participating countries**	All populations		
	Eg. Kuwait, Qatar, Bahrain	*Eg. Tonga, Samoa, Barbados*	*Eg. Georgia, Honduras, Sri Lanka*
	Team size typically 1-3 athletes **No team sports**		**<$2000USD did not win medals**

Chapter 17: Climbing and Impairment

Knut Magne Aanestad (Sogn og Fjordane Univerity College, Norway)

Introduction

This presentation is grounded in the empirical material of an on-going sociological study[1] of a group of sport climbers in Norway, RettOpp ("StraightUp"). Compared to other climbing groups, the special characteristic of RettOpp is that all of its members have some kind of acquired physical impairment.

The purpose of the presentation is twofold. First, it gives an introduction to climbing as a sport for persons with impairments[2]. The outlines will be in a general form, as the existing variety of physiological capabilities among persons with impairments could not possibly be dealt with in our context. Secondly, the RettOpp climbing group is presented, accompanied by some reflections on the processes of empowerment involved in and around the climbing activities of the group. Towards the end some theoretical analyses are made regarding dimensions of meaning in connection to impairment and physical activity.

The reflections on climbing and impairment in general, and RettOpp in particular, are mainly based on findings from depth interviews with the members of the group (2011), and from participant observation at a number of their climbing sessions (2010 and 2011)[3]. Some insights stem from seminars and climbing gatherings held by the Norwegian Climbing Federation (NKF) in relation to their integration programme.

Climbing

Climbing is an outdoor and indoor activity alike. The overall principle in climbing is to manage your way up a route by use of hands and feet, secured by a rope (so-called free climbing). There is one climber and one belayer. In traditional outdoor rock climbing, the climber places belay devices along the route. In sport climbing, however – and which is the focus in our context – the belay system in the wall consists of permanent bolts which are placed regularly along the route, and an abseil anchor to rappel from when the route has been topped out.

The climber and the belayer constitute a team. The belayer is in control of the rope, and uses a belay device for effectively breaking it in case of a fall. The climber has the rope tied to his/her climbing harness. During ascent, the climber clips the rope onto the bolts – this is called lead climbing (one "leads" the route). Another possibility is having the rope fixed in the top anchor, which is called top roping. In top roping, every kind of fall can be effectively prevented by the belayer, in that the last attach point is never below the climber (which is frequently the case in lead climbing). For many climbers with impairments, top roping is the more convenient way of climbing.

Challenging Physical Activity

In recent years, there has been an overall increase in interest in various kinds of challenging physical activity – e.g. rafting, paragliding and climbing[4]. Traditionally, these kinds of sports have to a large extent been regarded as off-limit to persons with impairments. There has been a tendency to considering the few persons with impairments engaging into such activities as being individual "exceptions" (Engelstad 2010).

During the last few years, this view seems to have changed to some extent. Today, an increased number of persons with impairments are engaging in challenging sports - as is exemplified by the RettOpp climbing group. This offers new possibilities to disciplines such as disability studies and sociology of impairment regarding various social dimensions involving combinations of impairment and challenging physical activity.

Physical and Psychological Benefits of Climbing

Some gains acquired through climbing, physiological as well as psychological, are much the same for nearly all persons involved in the sport.

Physically, a quite obvious gain is that one acquires strength in fingers, arms and shoulders. More characteristic of climbing, however, is the improvement one might experience in stabilization musculature and in the overall corporal balance.

Psychologically, one could mention the sense of mastery through improving one's physical climbing skills in combination with conquering of fear (most climbers experience anxiety or fear regarding height to some extent, even if it is not strong enough to qualify for the term *acrophobia)* (Gangdal 2008).

Some gains might be extra prominent to persons with different kinds of impairments or temporary corporal damages. For example, the rehabilitating of basic muscular and motor skills after an accident might be a long-lasting, repetitive, and even boring endeavour. To many persons with such conditions, climbing might be an especially good tool in the recovery process. To a great extent, climbing is in nature a sport where one can very easily "forget" about the corporal work because one is mentally focused on how to solve a certain problem in the wall, in combination with an explicit recognition and maybe slight fear of the height. Simply put, one may experience that much of the recovery training just comes along while one is focused on other things. (In the same context it should be mentioned, however, that for the same reason there is also the possible danger of overloading corporal mechanisms.)

Climbing contributes in the increase of muscular and tendon strength alike, but it is also good for motor precision. Persons with multiple sclerosis, for example, might experience an improvement of motor precision through the mere endeavour of reaching out to the holds and in the positioning of hands and feet on different kinds of holds.

Climbing with Impairment

So, what is it like to climb with an impairment? Obviously, that depends on the person, impairment and context. The departure point here, however, is the general assumption that climbing is a sport suitable for a wide range of personality types and capabilities – and possibly to a far greater extent than people may expect. In spite of the sport's considerable increase in popularity during the last decade, there are still some prevalent, and not very accurate, general assumptions about climbing to be found amongst people; e.g. that it is difficult, that it is dangerous, that it is only for "brave" people, that it is a sport for exhibitionists, and that it is a sport worshiping individualism (Gangdal 2008). This is not the place for discussing these assumptions one by one. Suffice it to say that none of them are unequivocally true and I will exemplify by commenting upon two of them.

First: Is climbing difficult? There are all kinds of climbing grades, from very easy to very difficult. It depends on the combination of how good the holds are and the distance between them, and the steepness of the wall (slope - vertical - overhang). Taking into account the possibility to pause using the rope or even getting some lifting assistance from the belayer in top roping, the possibilities of adapting the sport to very different individual capabilities are very good from the outset. There are persons with absolutely no mobility in their legs enjoying climbing. There are blind persons with quite above average body mass enjoying climbing. And even regarding "the climbing limb *per se*", the hand: At present, there are technical devices for prosthetic arms being developed especially for climbers.

Secondly: Is climbing dangerous? Not necessarily, if one takes precautions regarding the type of climbing in relation to one's own capabilities and condition, and follows the general security rules in climbing (amongst others that climber and belayer check each other's harnesses, knots and belay devices before every climb, without any exceptions)[5]. Regarding the bolts along the route and in the top anchor, it is quite unlikely that a component should break and in the extremely unlikely event that this should happen, one will always have a backup (e.g. the top anchor is always connected to the wall through at least two separate bolts).

With regards to existing climbing facilities, indoor and outdoor alike, the biggest challenge for persons with impairments might seem to be that the local indoor climbing walls often have steep sections exclusively, and/or that the outdoor climbing routes (on cliffs/rock) in the area are all too difficult due to nature's own hand. From time to time, one can also experience the slightly paradoxical fact that the mere approaching of the outdoor climbing area (the "crag") is harder than the climbing itself. This highlights the need for some adaptation for persons with impairments, when it comes to making climbing sport accessible to as many people as possible.

Some rehabilitation centres[6] have introduced adjustable climbing walls. If necessary, these can be lowered to an approximate horizontal position. By use of such facilities, even persons with total lower body paralysis have been able to experience the joy of climbing.

There are also some examples of special adaptations of approaches to outdoor crags[7]. However, in such cases one will have to make thorough considerations regarding the ethics involved in intervening in natural areas[8].

The RettOpp Climbing Group

The RettOpp climbing group was established in the North Norwegian town Tromsø in 2007. The background was the integration project *Climbing for everybody*, initiated in 2005 by the Norwegian climbing pioneer Sjur Nesheim in collaboration with Tromsø Climbing Club. During this project, a number of persons with different kinds of physical impairments got the chance to get acquainted with sport climbing under the surveillance of instructors.

When the integration project came to an end a couple of years later, some of the participants wished to continue climbing on a regular basis. This was the start of the RettOpp climbing group. Since then, RettOpp - although also a climbing group on its own terms - has been an integrated part of the Tromsø Climbing Club, and the members have been climbing on a weekly basis in their common climbing hall.

There are seven core members who have been in the group more or less since the start in 2007. In addition, there are approximately three to five associated members joining in from time to time.

The core members are three women and four men. Five of them - three men and two women - are visually impaired, of whom one is totally blind, and the others have different kinds of reduced vision. The other two - one woman and one man - have experienced loss of motor and proprioceptive[9] skills due to accidents. These two have experienced great challenges when it comes to learning the most basic motor skills all over again, like moving hands or feet in the right direction.

Since the formation of the group in 2007 the members have developed skills regarding the integrating of their different capabilities - physical and psychological alike - into the collective entity RettOpp. They started out as strangers with an interest in climbing, and have eventually become a combination of climbing group and friends. How to communicate in different ways, and "reading" each other's movements during the climber/belayer relationship, is of fundamental importance in RettOpp. This communication is interconnected with a sense of mastery, solidarity, and identity - components which are often conceived as being central constituents of the concept of *empowerment*.

Climbing and Empowerment

The concept 'empowerment' has a vast number of applications within social work and the social sciences. Its core meaning is commonly understood as a sense of mastery, self-reliance, and autonomy. Empowerment is hence a phenomenon of central importance to all human beings; however, the concept is especially applied to understandings of persons or groups in life situations where some kind of physiological, psychological or economical support is needed[10]. The concept usually refers to individual situations, but is also adaptable to the understanding of collectives (Barnes et al, 2010). Comprehensively understood, empowerment may be grounded in rationality, feelings, will, and/or expression alike. Empowerment can influence the general life situation or certain aspects of it, in various combinations.

In sports and other kinds of physical activity, processes of empowerment might almost be viewed as self-given, at least to some extent. The using and exercising of one's body is very often connected to feelings of mastery and well-being. The psycho-social aspect is no less important: for example, exercising and doing sports may be an important arena for socializing with other people, hence contributing in developing friendships, identity building, and integration (Paterson and Hughes 1999, Grue 2004).

These general aspects of empowerment are also experienced by the RettOpp climbing group. In addition, the members also seem to acquire empowerment gains through the special concept that RettOpp is, in that all of the members have some kind of physical impairment and so they have had to develop different strategies of communicating and coping whilst doing climbing activities. There are some initial compensating techniques, for example the use of hearing to weigh up for lack of sight. When the belayer cannot actually see what the climber is doing, they are very dependent on oral messages between one another. A challenge in that respect, might be that while the climber is on a difficult route, the oral communication does not always flow very coherently. From the climber, more or less articulate messages might often be commingled with "moaning and grunting". There are also a complex set of sounds and noises stemming from the climbing itself, like kicking of feet or bumping of knees into the wall, clattering of belay carabiners hanging along the route, and so on. And the higher the climber is in the wall, the more difficult the communication is. Learning how to communicate effectively under such circumstances, for example the "reading" of the inarticulate utterances and noise from the individual climbers, takes time. Learning to know each other in this way in connection to the performing of a challenging sport activity, gives a sense of mastery which these climbers experience in RettOpp exclusively.

A Group within the Group: The Special Game

During climbing together on a regular basis for a long time, the members of RettOpp have learned to know each other in a complex set of ways within the framework of the activity. Their mutual "tuning in" on each other's special characteristics and capabilities make them feel like a well-integrated group on their own terms, and through this common experience and knowledge they have developed a certain collective identity.

Whilst climbing on their own premises, they have over time developed some unwritten, and also to some extent unconscious "strategies", or ways of doing climbing together[11]. It is about incorporating a certain set of skills which are to some extent different from what other climbers would need to learn.

This developing of the RettOpp activities into a game on its own terms started out as a result of the practical adaptations which the members needed due to their impairments. Organizationally, RettOpp is a "group within a group" when it comes to the relation to Tromsø Climbing Club. In the beginning, this was all about practical purposes, since RettOpp needed to pay attention to their own physiological presumptions. The reason why they needed to have the climbing gym for themselves a couple of hours a week, was - amongst other things - their need to hear each other better. If there are a lot of other climbers in the gym at the same time, it simply gets too noisy.

At the start, RettOpp was a group of persons with impairments exploring climbing, in the sense that they tried to do the sport as other climbers do it, with the necessary compensations regarding their impairments. Gradually, however, they went from "trying to do it like others do it", by compensating their impairments, to developing the RettOpp climbing into *a game in its own terms*. The members' impairments, in connection with the un-reflected and "tacit" understanding of each other based on movements and sounds, have become part of the principles of RettOpp's climbing activities; they have developed their own variety of the climbing sport, so to speak.

Impairment and the Game: Dimensions of Meaning

In this last part of the presentation some socio-philosophical analyses are made in relation to the above mentioned aspects. Based on empirical data about the RettOpp group and their climbing activities an alternative thinking about the concept of impairment will be attempted. The reason is to detect more subtle dimensions of meaning embedded in the activities of this climbing group. The reflections will be outlined quite briefly, with the main characteristics of the arguments being presented only. First, some central concepts are to be explained.

Within disability studies the term 'impairment' is used in close correspondence with 'disability'. Where the former denotes the physiological and individual condition commonly conceived as a medical fact, the latter (especially when used in contrast to the former) focuses on obstruction and/or oppression experienced by persons with impairments caused by established cultural and/or material structures in society. In many contexts where these phenomena are referred to simultaneously, however, the term disability is used in an overall sense, also including the interconnection and dynamics between them (as in "disability studies", and in referring to "persons with disabilities"). Thus, "being disabled" can - in an overall sense - be understood as the experience of obstruction and/or oppression resulting from the interrelation between one's physiological capabilities and established cultural and/or material structures in society (Thomas 2002, Hughes 2002).

Up to this point in the text, the term impairment has been used exclusively. The reason is that the focus has been more upon experiences of meaning resulting from the combination of doing sports and having "uncommon" physiological capabilities, than on feelings of obstruction or oppression in the encounter with cultural and material societal structures.

On the basis of the distinction between impairment and disability, it has been a common understanding within disability studies that the impairment does not imply any aspects of deprivation (hindrance, pain, loss, etcetera) *in itself*; the sense of deprivation is first experienced when an encounter between the specific physiological condition constituting the impairment and the surroundings makes it appear - that is, as an experience of *disability*.

As a response to and partly critique of this view, perspectives such as the 'sociology of impairment' has put focus upon "the carnal dimensions of everyday life". Here the body and corporal features such as impairment are perceived as "subjects of meaning" rather than mere formable objects which meaning can be imposed onto. In short, the incentive has been to highlight impairment as meaningful in its own right, both as concept and - not least - as phenomenon. The attempt to relativize the dicotomy between impairment and disability is also part of this agenda ("impairment is social and disability is embodied").

Some arguments have centred round chronic pain: e.g., how can a physiological condition (impairment) involving constant pain be viewed as *not* having the *potential in itself* to influence in a negative way aspects of one's life condition? Also, if one is not to use the argument about pain and takes a more general philosophical point of departure (as is often the case with perspectives applying phenomenology, for instance): If one's whole experience of the world is fundamentally connected to the body, in the sense that perception, proprioception, and tactile sensations are presuppositions for cognition, consciousness and feelings alike; how then can one strip the impairment of all of its own meaning content?

An assumption within the sociology of impairment is that our corporality is an existential presupposition and principle for all aspects of life, hence also constituting the epistemological framework within which our interactions with others take place. When we experience the world, e.g. engage in interaction with others, we do it "in, with, and through" our bodies. Our relations to the world and other people are *embodied*, in that experiences have established dynamic structures in our corporal being in the world. On this basis we express ourselves and understand the others as *carnal beings*, and we always take the physiological appearance and body language of the other into account – even if most of these mechanisms are taking place on a "tacit" and unconscious level (Crossley 2001, Hughes 2002).

The sociology of impairment also takes into account that the basic principles of corporality are given a culturally defined content. In interactions with non-impaired people, persons with impairments will constantly be reminded of their impairments due to the "normal" (non-impaired) corporal condition which is established as a defining structure within the culture, again structuring the norms of interaction which are internalized. In short: For the sociology of impairment, the reason for highlighting the concept of impairment opposite that of disability is the assumption that the bodily existence - the carnal dimension of daily life - has to be stressed more than has been the case within disability studies. If one is to understand the basic constituents of how it is to live with impairment, it is claimed, one cannot understand all of the important existential aspects related to living with impairment as inextricably linked with external cultural and material structures (Paterson and Hughes 1999).

Based on this brief theoretical backdrop, we can now return to the RettOpp group to make the point about impairment as discussed.

As mentioned, RettOpp has gradually established itself as a climbing group on its own terms. Organizationally, and as a matter of identity politics opposite Tromsø climbing club, it has developed into a "group within the group". The more important point here, however, is that their climbing activities are also taking form as a special collective *game* due to the members' impairments.

The following reflections are based on understandings put forth by the sociology of impairment, regarding the conceiving of impairment as "subject of meaning". However, the under-pinning thought will be the possibility of conceiving the meaningfulness[12] of impairment without the aspect of deprivation which the sociology of impairment seems to be consequently attaching to it. Here one could ask: How can one consider impairment (as opposed to disability) as having a meaning at all without any aspect of deprivation connected to it?[13]

Sometimes during the climbing activities of RettOpp, the members' impairments might seem to be experienced as *principles of the game itself*, rather than appearing as "handicaps" in a traditional sense[14]. The impairment as physiological phenomenon (as defined above, opposite disability) is clearly a constitutive element in how their climbing activities take form – and is thereby also a constitutive element in the "tacit knowledge" and un-reflected sense of the game at work during the climbing. However, the "aspect of deprivation" did not seem to be present in this particular realm of reality.

To mention an example: At a climbing session, the climber, who is blind, did not make the next move. He did not find it within reasonable time, and therefore became too tired in his arms and had to rest using the rope (strictly, a climber has not managed a route if he/she has been pausing using the rope during the ascent). For the observer, the reason appeared clear enough: he just could not see the hold. When asked about it afterwards, however - "why didn't you make that passage?" - the answer was "I couldn't remember the hold".

This is an important point. In this context, not seeing could be conceived as being part of the principles of the game itself, hence not being experienced as a "handicap"[15]. To make an analogical example: A soccer player would not say after a match, that "If I had been allowed to use my hands, I would have managed to score". Or "I am proud of how I did today, taken into account I couldn't use my hands". That would be nonsense. It is not about their experiencing an *obstruction* in the fact that they could not use their hands; it is simply about the hands being outside the *principles* (rules, terms) of the soccer game, or what could be called its area of relevance. And so with climbing and vision in the RettOpp sessions: The blindness, normally conceived as a physiological obstruction, is here amongst the defining features of the game, in the sense that it is embedded within the "constituting rules", or principles of the game (a little laconically put: You can not engage in "blind climbing" if you are not blind – at least not if you are going to do it "by the book"). In RettOpp's climbing the impairments can be perceived as presumptions and co-principles in the game, just in the way distance lines and the use of feet (and *not* the hands) are presumptions embedded in the rules of soccer - thereby regulating what is going on on the field, hence also making presumptions for senses of meaning, mastery, and empowerment being experienced on the field. During climbing (that is, while one is conducting and is "in the middle of" the activity, hence "embedded in and surrounded by it") the impairments of the members of RettOpp are not perceived as limitations *per se*; rather, they are constitutive features of the whole *relevance area* of the climbing (the game). Again a little laconically put, in order to make an epistemological point: This discipline of climbing could actually not have existed at all without the impairments.

The impairments are in part constitutive of RettOpp's game - and exactly therefore, in the playing of that game, there is no deprivation (obstruction, hindrance, loss) caused by the impairment. If it was to be so, "it would have been another game" (how can a rule in the game one is playing be conceived as an aspect of deprivation in the playing of the game?). Following this, one could also expect dimensions of meaning and empowerment resulting from the mastering of this game to be containing elements not being about *conquering* the impairment, experiencing mastery *in spite of* the impairment, *forgetting* the impairment for a while, or being *rehabilitated* from the impairment, and the like: rather, what we are dealing with could be mastery of an activity on its own terms, without a corporal difference being a point at all[16].

When RettOpp started climbing, the members had to adapt to the way non-impaired conducted the sport – that is, they were engaging into a game defined by non-impaired, so to speak. At this stage they had to develop compensating techniques because of their impairments, which then of course contributed in stressing the deprivation "embedded" in their physiological conditions. So when RettOpp started climbing, the impairments were also embedded in their climbing as *aspects of deprivation* which were to be compensated. But gradually, as the members were cultivating their own variety, or *discipline* of the sport and the impairments became embedded as *principles* of this "new" game, thereby leaving behind the aspects of deprivation, the meaning dimensions of their activities also changed[17].

This was an attempt to show that the phenomenon of impairment can also be seen in relation to dimensions of meaning (and further, to processes of empowerment) which the sociology of impairment can be said not to have accounted for. In the special case above impairment was taken seriously as a physiological phenomenon of difference imposing meaning onto a context, but without an aspect of deprivation connected to it. This understanding of impairment is hard to adapt to the usual impairment/disability dichotomy, as it to some extent transcends both (and also the word 'impairment' itself, as mentioned earlier). It also goes beyond the understanding promoted by the sociology of impairment, as this perspective (so far) seems to consequently connecting some dimension of deprivation to the phenomenon.

Conclusions

In this presentation attempts have been made to describe sport climbing as an activity suitable for persons with various kinds of impairments. In connection to this, the Norwegian climbing group RettOpp has been presented. As climbing is still considered by many as being off-limit to persons with impairments, we wish to express a hope that such assumptions may diminish somewhat in the future. As have been indicated, a variety of positive effects can be experienced from engaging in this sport, even if one has an impairment.

In the last part of the presentation, some more theoretical reflections were offered regarding dimensions of meaning in connection to impairment and physical activity. What could come out of these (to some extent abstract) reflections on impairment regarding the RettOpp group? Suffice it here to point to the theoretical awareness that there might be realms of meaning and empowerment connected to impairments that do not contain aspects of deprivation, even if they are in part relying on the same impairments to exist. And since these are realms of meaning hard to express (one is, one could say, in need of some kind of "non-impaired twin concept to impairment") they might be very easily "occupied" or "colonized" by already established meanings of impairment and disability. Revealing such mechanisms can thus have an emancipating function when it comes to understanding and taking seriously senses of meaning embedded in the combination of having an impairment and engaging into physical activity without at the same time adding to it "programmatic" aspects of deprivation having to be "compensated", "conquered", "forgotten", or "rehabilitated from".

Notes

[1] At Sogn og Fjordane University College, Faculty of Social Sciences, Norway.

[2] The intention is to reveal principles of and general features by the activity itself, more than providing information about existing climbing facilities, certain rehabilitation programs, or administrative issues.

[3] The revealing of information about RettOpp has been approved by the Norwegian Social Science Data Services (NSD).

[4] Such sports are also commonly referred to as *risk sports*. In our context, it is about doing a so-called risk sport in a non-risky way, hence the term challenging physical activity. Here, the term challenging also refers to psychological aspects, like the task of remembering a route, dealing with fear of losing the grip and falling, etcetera.

[5] Sport climbing under clear and controlled circumstances in an indoor wall differs greatly from traditional climbing on outdoor cliffs. Whatever type of climbing, the evaluation of risk is at all times the responsibility of the persons involved in the climbing.

[6] For instance, Valnesfjord Helsesportsenter (VHSS) and Beitostølen Helsesportsenter (BHSS) in Norway.

[7] I.e. at Hamarøy, Norway.

[8] At a crag for sport climbing, the level for accepting such interventions is normally lower than in "all-natural" areas, since the bolting of sport climbing routes will already have made a human impact on the local nature to some extent. Apart from this ethical aspect, there is also a practical, in that people engaging into traditional climbing (without any pre-placed equipment) normally do not have need for adaptations regarding the approach anyway.

[9] The innate sense of balance and position of the limbs (unreflected, corporal knowledge).

[10] Within institutional contexts in Western social systems, the meaning is often closely connected to client participation.

[11] A relevant social scientific concept regarding these mechanisms, is *tacit knowledge* (Polyani 1996). The concept refers to internalized and incorporated knowledge we are not necessarily aware that we have. The tacit knowledge is unconsciously activated under certain circumstances, and is also an active component in structuring the development of all other knowledge.

[12] Meaning in a cognitive and epistemological sense.

[13] It could also be mentioned that the word 'impairment' is itself (literally) imposing an aspect of deprivation to the phenomenon it denotes. As such, the word itself contains a resistance against attempts to investigate impairment as a physical condition constituting a bearing structure in an experience, without at the same time having a dimension of deprivation connected to it.

[14] That is, the impairment being experienced as an obstruction in a specific situation.

[15] This is used to examplify a tendency in the empirical material. It should be mentioned, however, that there *could* of course be other reasons as well for this particular answer. The climber could for instance be thinking about his impairment, but regard it as simply too obvious to mention.

[16] It is important to note that these are analytical descriptions of a limited area of reality, of heuristic purposes. Seen in a wider picture, power relations will of course have to be taken into account. Obviously, otherness and difference is also experienced by the members of RettOpp in different contexts, e.g. when one after the climbing session "transcends" the context of one's own discipline and makes some reflections about one's own personal capabilities in comparison to those of non-impaired climbers.

[17] These aspects of development are in part what distinguishes RettOpp's climbing from other disciplines of disability sports, and which may also provide their activities with some alternative meaning contents. In this presentation, we cannot go further on these issues, however.

References

Barnes, Colin and Geof Mercer. 2010. Exploring Disability. Polity Press, Cambridge.

Crossley, Nick. 2001. The Phenomenological Habitus and its Construction. Theory and Society 30, Kluwer Academic Publishers.

Engelstad, Gunn. 2010. Hva er kropp? Univeritstsforlaget, Oslo. (Perspectives on corporality in modern society)

Gangdal, Jon. 2008. Alt du bør vite om klatring - klatreteknikker, risiko, sikkerhet, klatreruter. Aschehoug, Oslo. (About climbing – tecniques, security, cultural understandings)

Grue, Lars. 2004. Funksjonshemmet er bare et ord. Forståelser, fremstillinger og erfaringer. Abstrakt forlag, Oslo. (On impairment and disability)

Hughes, Bill. 2002. "Disability and the Body". In C. Barnes, M. Oliver and L. Barton (eds.) Disability Studies Today. Polity Press, Cambridge.

Paterson, Kevin and Bill Hughes. 1999. "Disability Studies and Phenomenology: The Carnal Politics of Everyday Life". Disability & Society 14(5).

Polyani, Michael. 1966. The Tacit Dimension. New York; Doubleday & Company.

Thomas, Carol. 2002. "Disability Theory: Key Ideas, Issues and Thinkers". In C. Barnes, M. Oliver and L. Barton (eds.) Disability Studies Today. Cambridge; Polity Press.

Chapter 18: A Paralympian Alpine Skier in a Wind-Tunnel: A Case Study

N. A. C. Vinagre (Georg-August University, Germany & German Aerospace Center); A. Dillmann (German Aerospace Center); T. Russomano (Pontifical Catholic University of Rio Grande do Sul (PUCRS), Brazil); A. Niklas(Georg-August University, Germany)

Introduction

This is the second of a two-part wind-tunnel **(W-T)** investigation into the air loads that apply on a German Paralympic Alpine Skier, performed as part of an evaluation process focused on the next international competitions. The results obtained from this assessment should have applicability for increasing understanding of those variables that can improve the postural performance of the athlete when training and competing. The experiment aim was to collect data for aerodynamic drag from a Paralympic Alpine Skier, comparing this to data acquired from a previous test carried out in 2010, in order to understand its relevance in terms of athlete posture in relation to performance. The study protocol was approved by the German Federal Committee on Competitive Sports and the Federal Institute of Sports Science. Signed informed consent was obtained from the volunteer.

1. Volunteer (C1)

The analysed case is an athlete from the male alpine ski team from Germany, born on 13/06/84, and having a disability classification of LW11 in the sitting skiers (mono skiers) category (Pringle, 1987). He suffered a car accident at age 9, whereby he fractured the twelfth thoracic vertebra (T12) and this resulted in his becoming paraplegic. His impairment is considered to be moderate, preventing movement of his legs and part of his body trunk. He has practised mono skiing since 1995 and has trained for competitions with the *Deutsche Paralympic Ski team* (*DPS*) since 2004, where he has obtained satisfactory results in the sport and his performance has improved with each passing year.

Anthropometric measurements of the participant were collected for both campaigns, and it can be seen that C1 is 160cm tall and weighed 59.5kg at his last evaluation, giving him a Body Mass Index of 23.24 kg/m^2. Measurements of seated height and arm-span of the participant were also taken during the latter evaluative campaign, which allowed his Cormic Index and relative arm-span to be determined.

2. Material

Testing took place using a large low-speed W-T at the Technical University of Hamburg-Harburg to investigate the relationship between posture and relative wind speed on the seated skier.

2.1 Test Facilities

2.1.1 Test Section

The test section is 5.5m in length and features a central turntable capable of rotating 360° and this is connected to a 6-component balance. The open test section features manual and optical access from the top and the two lateral sides.

2.1.2 Test Equipment

2.1.2.1 Measurement Devices and Data Acquisition

The wind tunnel has a computerized control system equipped with modern 'state-of-the-art' data-processing software and computer hardware, all of which serve to maximise the use of the facility and equipment. A number of measurement devices are provided to facilitate the acquisition of computational fluid dynamics quantities.

2.1.2.2 Six-Component (External) Balance

The wind tunnel features an external subfloor integrated 6-component balance (SCHENCK Process *GmbH, Darmstadt,* Germany) that can measure forces of 200N to 400N and moments up to 200Nm. The balance is connected to a flush-mounted turntable which can be moved to allow for rotation and which supports operation in two different kinematic configurations (adjusting to different load levels).

2.1.2.3 Speed indicator

The instruments used for the measurement of wind speeds come from environmental and industrial measurement instruments (VAISALA Group – Vantaa, Finland). Two modalities of velocity measurements are available in the W-T namely, non-intrusive turbulence-resolving LDA and using hot-wire probes.

2.1.2.4 Barometer

The atmospheric pressure is measured in the settling chamber, the section that precedes the test area. Additionally this pressure (pressure by means of static/dynamic pressure probes) is also used to determine the wind velocity through the plenum method.

2.1.2.5 Thermometer
In addition to pressure, temperature and humidity are also measured in the settling chamber. The air density is calculated according to these parameters.

2.1.2.6 Photographic Cameras
The photographic equipment used for taking the lateral images was a Canon camera (model EOS 350D, Canon Zoom Lens EF-S 17-85mm 1:4-5.6 IS USM 67mm). Two different cameras were used over the two separate campaigns to record images from the frontal plane. These were a Nikon camera (model D5000, Nikkor 18-105mm VR 1:3.5-5.6 IS USM 67mm) for the first, and a Nikon (model D90 - Nikkor AF-S 18-200mm VR 1:3.5 - 5.6 G2 ED) for the second campaign.

3. Method
The test consisted of 4 body positions at 3 different speeds. The athlete held each position for 30s during which time 3 photographs were taken and the drag measurements collected. These images were used in conjunction with the aerodynamic values found (Watanabe & Ohtsuki, 1977).

3.1 Aerodynamic Test
This athlete was the first participant to complete the wind-tunnel test for the first campaign, even though no pre-determined order of participation had been arranged, which demonstrates the motivation on the part of the athlete. C1 followed the standard protocol in accordance with the pre-planned steps for the evaluations scheduled for test sessions. He was not familiar with this procedure involving the wind-tunnel test and had not taken part in such an evaluation before.

3.1.1 Preparations; Control; Immediately before, During, After the test; Recovery
C1 was the first athlete to take part in the W-T evaluation session and as such, he remained in the test section for a longer period of time and was exposed to more airflow than the other participants whilst calibration of the equipment to be used for the experiment took place, and all aspects related to the good performance of the evaluation section were verified. The volunteer was monitored closely during testing in relation to both his personal safety and to his performance of the test positions to be carried out. The support platform for the sit-ski was also checked to ensure that it did not come into contact with the W-T floor, and thus interfere with the action of the balance. C1 consistently performed and repeated every position requested of him,

showing no signs of fatigue during testing. The consistency of the force values, together with the respective photographic records for the evaluated settings was also ensured. The endpoint for both tests was carried out by the technical team who were responsible for control management of the W-T system and for the timing of photographic records for each position performed, as well as the interval between changes of velocity and position.

The athlete was asked about his experience of the nature and intensity of this new method of evaluation after completion of the test, and reported no discomfort or unhappiness with the procedure. Spontaneous comments made by the athlete in the course of Test 1 (T1) were recorded in field notes, while a questionnaire was applied both before and after the evaluation procedure for Test 2 (T2), bringing the session to an end.

3.1.2 Results of Aerodynamics Tests 1 and 2

C1 was able to complete the tests for both the W-T campaigns in accordance with the outlined protocol, as can be seen in Table 1. In terms of coordination, he was also able to accurately perform, maintain and repeat the requested positions. The biggest drag force (**D**) presented by him for each of the two tests was 200.83N for T1 and 189.13N for T2, both whilst adopting 1st position (P1) at 30 m/s. His lowest **D** value for T1 was 14.25N whilst in 4th position (P4) at 10 m/s, and in T2 the lowest value found was 14.27N whilst in 3rd position (P3) at 10 m/s. The biggest drag coefficient (**C_D**) presented by him in T1 was 0. 374 whilst adopting P1 at 30 m/s, and for T2 this value was 0.360 using the same position. His lowest **C_D** value for T1 was 0.248 whilst in P4 at both 10 and 20 m/s, and for T2 the lowest **C_D** value was 0.254 in P3 at 10 m/s.

It can be seen from the photographic records that follow that only the lateral photographs relating to the third stage of speed (30m/s) of each position performed are presented and not the whole photo sequence. Similarly, the values relating to these records were also used in the construction of the comparative graphs between each campaign and configuration performed.

Obs.: The values were obtained from the estimated frontal area of 0.5 m^2 of the athlete in 2010 and 1 m^2 in the 2011 test. The numbers highlighted in bold are the maximum and minimum values found in each session. The colours green and orange represent an improvement or deterioration in performance, respectively. The blue represents the values found for the CD from experiment 3 for the new values calculated of the frontal area based on the technique of counting pixels of digital photographs.

The sports equipment used by C1 was the same for both the campaigns (sit-ski, foot fairing and foot fairing cover, helmet, goggles, ski wear, ski outriggers and gloves), with the only difference being that he used his jacket to also cover the back part of the seat of the sit-ski for T2, this being the biggest difference between the two tests conducted by him. The recorded photos of the positions assumed for the experiments, can be found in the appendix. Figures 1 and 2 show the relationship between wind speed and drag force (**D**), while figures 3 and 4 present the relationship between wind speed and the drag coefficient (**C$_D$**) generated by the individual.

Table 1 – Wind Tunnel Test Data for C1

Pos.	Velocity [m/s]	C$_D$ [-] 2010	C$_D$ [-] 2011	Area [m²] 2011	C$_D$v2 [-] 2011	D Area [m²] 2011	Drag Force [N] 2010	Drag Force [N] 2011
Ref.								
1	10.0	(0.729) 0.364	0.353	1.2316	0.2869	0.434	21.70	19.94
	20.0	(0.721) 0.360	0.355	1.2316	0.2883	0.437	86.13	81.90
	30.0	(0.748) 0.374	0.360	1.2316	0.2926	0. 443	200.83	189.13
Ref.								
2	10.0	(0.687) 0.343	0.334	1.2145	0.2751	0.405	20.36	18.82
	20.0	(0.682) 0.341	0.343	1.2145	0.2824	0.416	81.22	79.00
	30.0	(0.689) 0.344	0.347	1.2145	0.2858	0.421	184.48	182.01
Ref.								
3	10.0	(0.571) 0.285	0.254	1.1082	0.2289	0.281	16.90	14.27
	20.0	(0.566) 0.283	0.278	1.1082	0.2512	0.308	67.29	64.03
	30.0	(0.601) 0.300	0.300	1.1082	0.2711	0.332	160.62	157.32
Ref.								
4	10.0	(0.496) 0.248	0.260				14.25	14.63
	20.0	(0.497) 0.248	0.272				58.63	62.45
	30.0	(0.553) 0.276	0.286				147.17	149.69

The general results of the anthropometric evaluation, the treatment of the photographic records, and the questionnaires and field notes completed by the athlete and trainer for both campaigns have now been presented. We would now like to put forward, in addition to the individual results presented in relation to test performed in the wind tunnel, a follow-up of the individual analysis by means of a discussion for the athlete in question.

4. Human Performance – Discussion

4.1 Objectives Assessment

The evaluation process was conducted with the intention of increasing the range of information and understanding of the performance structure that affects the world of the athletes from the *DPS* team. It also aimed to analyse (Hill, 1928; Schmitt, 1964) and compare individual results, contrasting them with other team members and to eventually relate these to other Paralympic athletes, for example, wheelchair sports (Vanlandewijck and Thompson, 2011).

This athlete, born in June 1984, has a training history of nearly 10 years with the DPS team. He participated in the Winter Paralympic Games in Vancouver, performing well but did not win any medals. He was exemplary in his performance of the experiments developed over the two evaluative campaigns of this study and presented interesting and respectable results for this competitive sport, as well as for the scientific community.

4.2 Anthropometric Assessment

From the anthropometric measurements taken, it was observed that the volunteer reduced his body weight from 62kg to 59.5kg during the period between the two evaluative campaigns. As a consequence, this altered his body mass index with it reducing to 23.24kg/m^2, however, remaining within the range considered as normal according to "The Practical Guide: Identification, Evaluation, and Treatment of Overweight and Obesity in Adults" (National Institutes of Health, 2000).

Data collected during the 2nd campaign included measurement and recording of the seated height (116cm) and arm-span (177.5cm) of C1. From this information it was possible to determine his trunk index (Cormic Index, the ratio between the seated height and total height; Relative Arm-span, arm-span in relation to height). C1 presented the highest Cormic Index (72.5) of all those athletes taking part in the 2nd campaign, and it can be said that C1 has an advantageous trunk height and larger relative arm-span (110.93) in terms of his total height. In relation to the sport of Alpine Skiing, this presents a disadvantage from an aerodynamics perspective (Brownlie *et al.*, 2010) given that his frontal area is subject to wind exposure whilst skiing, and an advantage from a motor point of view as his arms have greater reach, thus affecting his directional ability and maintenance of equilibrium (Fetz and Müller, 1991; Müller and Schwameder, 2003).

4.3 Aerodynamic Evaluation

The aerodynamics evaluation was intended to take account of the amount of drag produced by the athletes and generated innovative results without exposing C1 to risk. The performance of C1 over the two campaigns was very similar but he was still able to improve his results in the 2011 evaluation, conducting his test within the set parameters and recording lower values in almost all the positions carried out. As can be seen in Table 1 and in Figures 1, 2, 3 and 4, the values obtained in the test were quite consistent.

Figures 1 and 2 – Performance curves for **D** according to test stages performed in 2010 and 2011.

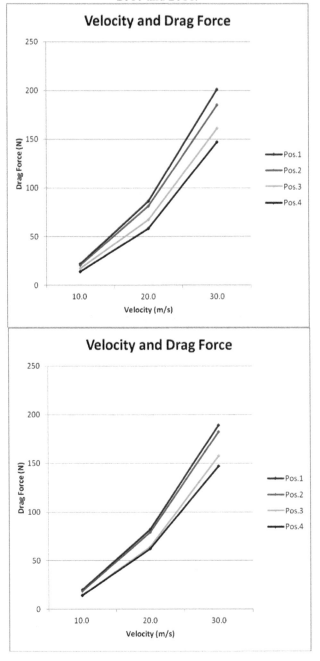

Figures 3 and 4 – Performance curves for C_D according to test stages performed in 2010 and 2011.

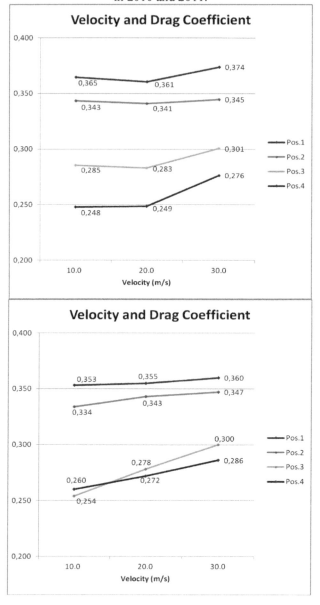

Figures 1, 2, 3 and 4: Aerodynamic Data recorded during the test 1 and 2.

In a comparison of the results for the **D** values in 2011 with those of 2010, it can be seen that C1 was able to reduce the **D** value generated by the posture P1, which creates the most resistance. Additionally, deterioration in the performance of P4 in 2011 can be seen, in relation to 2010. In the other previously performed positions, C1 was able to produce an improved performance for them all in 2011 in comparison to 2010, as can be seen in Table 1 and Figures 1 and 2.

However, when comparing the C_D values between the two years, a greater consistency in results was seen in 2011, reflected in there being an increase in C_D for all positions performed following an increase in wind velocity. This was not the case in experiment n.2 in 2010 for positions P1, P2 and P3 when a decrease in C_D was seen when passing to the second stage (20m/s). Incorporating calculation of the C_D according to the frontal area of the individual in the 2nd campaign in 2011 brought with it even more accurate values and refined data than was the case in 2010, or in other experiments from the 1970's (Bendig, 1975) conducted with the German Olympic alpine skiing team. The values of the **D Area** for C1 calculated from the frontal area at 30m/s represent $0.443m^2$ in P1, $0.421m^2$ in P2 and $0.332m^2$ in P3.

4.4 Postural Evaluation

4.4.1 Analysis of Lateral Photos

An analysis of the posture of C1 for both campaigns was conducted. A slight variation should be noted in that during testing for T2, C1 altered the manner in which his jacket was worn from the previous W-T test, with the bottom now being pulled over the top of the sit-ski. In P1 (See Fig.5), both in 2010 and 2011, the volunteer was able to carry out and repeat the posture with only small changes in trunk position. Comparing the postures adopted in this campaign with the previous, a fundamental change in head position can be seen (in 2011, C1 holds his head lower and more to the front) and in arm position (in 2011 they are positioned further back in relation to the longitudinal axis of his body).

Figure 5: Position 1 – Neutral Position

photo T1P1S3 – Drag Coeff. 0.374 **30 m/s** *photo T2P1S3 – Drag Coeff. 0.360*

In P2 (See Fig. 6), it can be seen that in 2010 C1 showed consistency in his performance, however in 2011 we can note that his trunk posture showed more variation. When comparing postures between the two campaigns, we can see that in 2011 C1 displayed greater trunk and elbow flexion.

Figure 6: Position 2 – Run Position

*photo T1P2S3 – Drag Coeff. 0.344   **30 m/s**   photo T2P2S3 – Drag Coeff. 0.347*

In P3 (See Fig. 7), both in 2010 and 2011, C1 showed a consistency in performance, indicating that this position is one that is easier to maintain and is well suited in terms of execution of the position. Comparing the postures from both campaigns, it can be seen that in 2010 C1 assumed a position having a more rounded back, whilst in 2011 he maintained a straighter back with greater flexion of the elbows.

Figure 7: Position 3 – "Aggressive" Position

*photo T1P3S3 – Drag Coeff. 0.300   **30 m/s**   photo T2P3S3 – Drag Coeff. 0.300*

In P4 (See Fig. 8), it can be seen that in both 2010 and 2011, despite the differing positions of holding the ski-outriggers, C1 could carry out and maintain the position easily, especially when compared to P2. When comparing the postures from one campaign to the other, it was in P4 that C1 was able to perform in the most similar way over the course of both tests.

Figure 8: Position 4 – Extra Position

*photo T1P4S3 – Drag Coeff. 0.276   **30 m/s**   photo T2P4S3 – Drag Coeff. 0.286*

4.4.2 Analysis of frontal photos

An analysis of the postures held by C1 in the frontal plane for the two campaigns (See Figs. 9-12) demonstrates that for both 2010 and 2011, the volunteer was able to carry out and repeat the posture for P1 with minimal alterations in head, trunk and ski poles position, with this also being the case for P2. In P3 a small difference was seen in the positioning of the ski outriggers with them being held further from the central axis. It is interesting to compare the additional diagrams created only in 2011 from the T3 photos for positions P1, P2 and P3, which give a clearer representation of the frontal area generated by the different postures assumed by C1.

Figure 9: Position 1 – Neutral Position

photo T1P1   photo T2P1   T2P1v2

Figure 10: Position 2 – Run Position

photo T1P2   photo T2P2   T2P2v2

Figure 11: Position 3 – "Agressive" Position

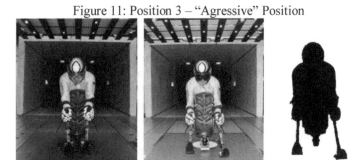

photo T1P3   photo T2P3   T2P3v2

Figure 12: Position 4 – Extra Position

photo T2P4

4.5 Questionnaires

Questionnaires applied in the 2nd campaign only, provided more important information regarding the details of the beginning of his training season (June) and of the overall progress of his training year. C1 trains on a daily basis during 3/4 of the year (June to March), and on some days carries out two different forms of training sessions. In the period from March to June after the competitive season has ended, the training schedule reduces with C1 completing only 2-3 workouts per week, with the emphasis being on aerobic endurance. In the months from Sept/Oct to December, the training developed to date is maintained, reducing the weekly frequency and increasing the technical work element to 3 times a week. It is the technical training that consumes the greatest amount of the athlete's time and can extend up to 4 hours in duration. The competition season takes place in the months from Dec/January until March, and C1 tries to divide his training schedule so that 50% of his time is dedicated to physical workouts and the remaining 50% to technical and tactical training.

His best results achieved in the world of Alpine Skiing (World Championship Sestriere/ Italy), took place between the two evaluative campaigns when he finished in 3rd place in the Slalom race. This is an activity that demands a greater degree of manoeuvrability than required for Downhill racing (speed), in which he finished in 7th place. It is important to point out that the season ended without him having suffered any accident or significant injury.

C1 indicated in the questionnaire that he feels comfortable in his wheelchair and that he is not generally in pain. In the replies related to the W-T evaluation, it can be seen that C1 was able to safely and comfortably conduct the test although he found its demands relatively difficult. He believes the test results to be important but does not know exactly how they can be incorporated into his performance and training routine. His completion of the post-test questionnaire confirmed what he had stated in the pre-test questionnaire, but added to the information that he feels the most enjoyable test position he performs to be P3.

Conclusions

During W-T testing the athlete must reproduce the same conditions for both experiment sessions in terms of posture, equipment used and manner of use. The result leads us to believe that there is a direct relationship between these three things and aerodynamic performance. The drag force generated by the body area and volume as a function of air resistance on the Paralympic Alpine Ski athlete may represent a significant difference to an event outcome.

Key words: Alpine skiing, aerodynamic forces, body posture, alternative evaluation environment.

References

Bendig HJ. 1975. Windkanalmessungen an Skispringern und Abfahrtsläufern Göttingen.

Brownlie L, Larose G, D'Auteuil A, Allinger T, Meinert F, Kristofic P, Dugas S, Boyd R, Stephens D. 2010. "Factors affecting the aerodynamic drag of alpine skiers 8th Conference of the International Sports Engineering Association (ISEA)". Procedia Engineering 2: 2375–2380.

Fetz F, Müller E. 1991. Biomechanik des alpinen Skilaufs. Stuttgart; Ferdinand Enke Verlag.

Hill, AV. 1928, "The Air-Resistance to a Runner". Proceedings of the Royal Society of London. Series B, Containing Papers of a Biological Character, 102(718): 380-385.

Müller E, Schwameder H. 2003. "Biomechanical aspects of new techniques in alpine skiing and ski-jumping". Journal of Sports Sciences, 21: 679–692.

National Institutes of Health (NHLBI). 2000. "The Practical Guide Identification, Evaluation, and Treatment of Overweight and Obesity in Adults". Obesity Education Initiative National Heart, Lung, and Blood Institute North American Association for the Study of Obesity.

Pringle D. 1987. "Winter Sports for the Amputee Athlete". The American Academy of Orthotists and Prosthetists. Clinical Prosthetics and Orthotics, 11(3):114-117.

Schmitt TJ. 1964. "Wind-Tunnel investigation of air loads on human beings". Navy Department – The David W. Taylor Model Basin - Aerodynamics Laboratory Aj WASHINGTON 7, DC.

Vanlandewijck Y, Thompson W, (eds). 2011. The Paralympic Athlete: handbook of sports medicine and science. Chichester,UK; Wiley-Blackwell.

Watanabe K, Ohtsuki T. 1977. Postural Changes and Aerodynamic Forces in Alpine Skiing, Ergonomics, 20(2): 121-131.

Lightning Source UK Ltd.
Milton Keynes UK
UKOW06f1811240814

237440UK00001B/1/P